How the West was Lost

DAMBISA MOYO

How the West was Lost

Fifty Years of Economic Folly –
And the Stark Choices Ahead

ALLEN LANE
an imprint of
PENGUIN BOOKS

ALLEN LANE

Published by the Penguin Group
Penguin Books Ltd, 80 Strand, London WC2R ORL, England
Penguin Group (USA) Inc., 375 Hudson Street, New York, New York 10014, USA
Penguin Group (Canada), 90 Eglinton Avenue East, Suite 700, Toronto, Ontario, Canada M4P 2Y3
(a division of Pearson Penguin Canada Inc.)
Penguin Ireland, 25 St Stephen's Green, Dublin 2, Ireland (a division of Penguin Books Ltd)
Penguin Group (Australia), 250 Camberwell Road,
Camberwell, Victoria 3124, Australia (a division of Pearson Australia Group Pty Ltd)
Penguin Books India Pvt Ltd, 11 Community Centre,
Panchsheel Park, New Delhi – 110 017, India
Penguin Group (NZ), 67 Apollo Drive, Rosedale, Auckland 0632, New Zealand
(a division of Pearson New Zealand Ltd)
Penguin Books (South Africa) (Pty) Ltd, 24 Sturdee Avenue,
Rosebank, Johannesburg 2196, South Africa

Penguin Books Ltd, Registered Offices: 80 Strand, London WC2R ORL, England

www.penguin.com

First published 2011

1

Set in 10.5/14 Sabon LT Std
Typeset by Jouve (UK), Milton Keynes
Printed in Great Britain by Clays Ltd, St Ives plc

ISBN: 978-1-846-14235-2

www.greenpenguin.co.uk

Penguin Books is committed to a sustainable future
for our business, our readers and our planet.
The book in your hands is made from paper
certified by the Forest Stewardship Council.

Contents

A senior business executive tells the story of a conference where the head of an established and leading Western telephone company boasted about all the things the company could do, and the innovations it had in the pipeline. He went on for quite a long time, as he demonstrated the company's range, and depth, and brilliance. His speech was met with enthusiastic applause. Then came the turn of the head of a similar Chinese company; undaunted, pointing to the Western executive, he said: 'We can do everything he can . . . for 40 per cent less.' He promptly sat down.

Preface

On 9 July 2008 the Chrysler Building, one of the best-loved icons of the New York skyline, was bought for US$800m by a foreign government. Thus one of America's most emblematic buildings, symbolizing its power, its industry, passed into the hands of outsiders. It was not just any foreign government; not Britain, not Germany, not France; indeed not any economic power from the West. The buyer came from the new power bloc of rapidly emerging countries, which are today threatening the more than 500-year-long economic reign of the West. It was the investment arm of the Abu Dhabi government. The Chrysler acquisition was a part of the estimated US$1.8bn spent on commercial property in the US by Middle Eastern investors in just the first six months of 2008. It was not the first such purchase; nor will it be the last. Indeed, after the 2008 financial debacle, and the collapse in asset prices that it brought with it, such purchases are only likely to accelerate.[1]

How the West was Lost is the story of how the world's most economically powerful nations have seen their wealth and dominant political position decline to the point where, today, they are about to forfeit all they have strived for – economic, military and political global supremacy.[2] There are three main reasons why the West has seen its substantial advantage erode; an erosion whose pace is accelerating with every passing year.

First, through blinkered political and military choices, the West (principally the US) has successfully managed to alienate the very emerging countries with whom it now competes. Although these countries continue to trade with their Western counterparts, it is often done through gritted teeth and with an underlying sense of mutual mistrust. Naturally, the net effect has been to encourage polarization, rather than foment credible alliances. Were it not for a profit motive, the real risk is that come the day when the emerging nations don't have to trade with the West, they won't.

Second is what Thomas Friedman describes as the 'flatness of the world' – the lowering of transport, communication and manufacturing costs, which has made the transfer of technology easier. Indeed, the technological and economic advantages of the West have made this possible, and as a natural consequence encouraged the worldwide adoption of best-practice technology and governance standards. However, these advantages once held in Western monopoly have, over time, dissipated, and will certainly continue to do so.

However, it is the third cause which is the prime focus of this book.

How the West was Lost charts how, over the last fifty years, the most advanced and advantaged countries of the world have squandered their once impregnable position through a sustained catalogue of fundamentally flawed economic policies.

It is these decisions that, along the way, have resulted in an economic and geopolitical see-saw, which is now poised to tip in favour of the emerging world.[3] Unless radical policy changes are made over the next decade the controlling hand of who owns what will quickly belong to China, India, Russia or the Middle East, and today's industrialized West is assured a savage economic decline.

Introduction

In September 2008, the world witnessed an unprecedented assault on the financial structure that the West had taken for granted for the previous fifty years. Shockwave after shockwave battered the system. Every day seemed to bring a new calamity. In just three weeks, Lehman Brothers, a stalwart of the US banking system, collapsed; the prime US mortgage lenders, Fannie Mae and Freddie Mac, had to be nationalized; AIG, the world's largest insurer, was brought to its knees and its very existence called into question (the company would receive a hefty US$85bn life-line from the American government to keep it afloat). And, in Britain, the bailout of banking giants Lloyds TSB and the Royal Bank of Scotland was running well above US$1.4tn (£850bn) in 2009. Through it all, trillions were wiped off stock exchanges from New York, to London, to Reykjavík, and most places in between, placing millions of people's pensions and savings in jeopardy.

But however extraordinary and cataclysmic these events were, *How the West was Lost* is *not* about the immediate whys and wherefores of this shattering and unexpected financial disaster. It is undeniable that the crash overwhelmed the world but just like a tsunami that appears seemingly out of nowhere and leaves death and destruction in its wake, the events of 2008 were the inevitable consequence of fault lines and shifts in economic tectonic plates that lay undetected under the seemingly calm financial waters upon which Western economies had sailed smoothly for the last half-century.[1]

However, unlike the plates beneath the sea, had these economic faults been detected and dealt with, the financial crisis of 2008 might never have happened; certainly not to the degree and with the ferocity with which it did occur. The collapse was the culmination of a catalogue of policy errors and mistakes that had been gathering momentum over the last fifty years, erupting into the worst financial crisis since the Great Depression. Extraordinarily now, as if blind to the real causes of the turmoil of 2008, many governments have kept these flawed policies in place.

But there is a bigger story to be told. It is a mistake to view what happened as an isolated and relatively contained episode. In fact, what happened in 2008 marked yet another step in a fundamental transition from one economic power to another; from the West, to the Rising Rest.[2]

For many a political scientist, this shift has troubling hegemonic consequences. To them, whether we live in a uni-polar world (for example, where the US dominates), a bi-polar world of, say, the Cold War era, or a multi-polar world governed by a multiplicity of states with differing political ideologies, is a matter of supreme importance.

But viewed through the narrow utilitarian prism of an economist, what matters most is economic prosperity (for the West, coupled with freedoms), rather than who ultimately rules the world. Economics and economists are guilty of viewing the world, economies and countries as if on a league table with only one winner, although it is undeniable that it is the global financier who decides who wields military and political might.

Should it really matter if some other country is richer and more militarily powerful? Who cares whether a country has economic supremacy, as long as your country is prosperous and can manage its own internal affairs? For example, the societies of Denmark, Sweden and Norway, each economically advanced, seem to have no qualms about who rules the world as long as they are left alone to be prosperous and peaceful, though their attitude might well change were whoever held the purse strings to start to curb their freedoms and encroach upon their way of life. But until that happens, whether the global financier is China, Russia or America seems, for them, largely irrelevant.

Obviously, the political–economic dichotomy is a false one. In reality, politics and economics are bound together, and even inextricably linked. That noted, however, in *How the West was Lost* I will focus on the economic shifts and how they are certain to transform the world in which we and future generations will live.

Time is running out. Unless the West adopts radical solutions, many of them offered in this book, and adopts them quickly, it will be too late. Not because China will necessarily become so much richer, but rather because of America's own folly in policymaking. How did the West give its undeniable lead away?

PART ONE

The Way It Was

I

Once Upon a Time in the West

Once upon a time, the West had it all: the money, the political nous, the military might; it knew where it wanted to go, and had the muscle to get there. Be it Portugal, Spain, the Netherlands or England, this held true for 500 years. However, the story of the West's dominance in the second half of the twentieth century is the story of America.[1]

Whether it was the US troops pouring on to the shores of Normandy with the Allied forces or the *Enola Gay* dropping the bomb on Hiroshima, by the end of the Second World War the baton of global power (economic, political or military) passed from Great Britain to the United States. While it took almost fifty years for the Cold War to play itself out, for the most part the US firmly maintained its paramount position for the next five decades and into the twenty-first century.

Of course, in the prelude to the Second World War, the United States had suffered the consequences of the 1929 Great Depression (by 1933 the value of stocks on the New York Stock Exchange was less than 20 per cent of what it had been at its peak in 1929, and US unemployment soared to around 25 per cent) and the trauma and casualties of the First World War. Although it did not end the economic crisis of the 1930s, President Franklin Roosevelt's New Deal was an attempt to reconstruct American capitalism, and give the not so invisible hand of the government a new and more dynamic role. At its core America would remain a supporter of free enterprise, but the plan was for government to play a key role in orchestrating, supervising and directing the faltering economy, leading, not following, private enterprise and administering large-scale endeavours. All this would prepare America for and enable it to capitalize on the war that would break the back of Western Europe.[2]

Thus, despite any remaining weaknesses, with the advent of the Second World War America was in a unique position to direct the industrial, military and manufacturing sectors to its best economic advantage. In this sense, the Second World War was not seen simply as a political and military necessity, but as an economic opportunity to which it was ready to respond.

For example, in 1941, President Roosevelt signed into law the Lend-Lease Act which would sell, exchange, lease or lend to America's allies any military equipment deemed necessary. From 1941 to 1945, under this programme, matériel worth US$50bn (equivalent to US$700bn at 2007 prices) – battleships, machine guns, torpedo boats, submarines and even army boots – were shipped across the waters to its beleaguered allies. Europe took on a heavy burden of future debt repayments to the US through the Lend-Lease programme (Britain made the final payment of its Lend-Lease loan of US$83.83m on the last day of 2006 – fifty years later), and America peaked economically after the war, in the 1950s, as a result. Because of Lend-Lease (the Marshall Plan was, of course, a wholly different proposition) the US had become the best-in-class manufacturer.[3]

America's actions were a marriage of political imperative and economic savvy. The manufacture of goods to be shipped abroad was not just a political act to help the Allies; it also helped boost the US economy. Indeed, the results of this 'great American intervention' were staggering on almost every level. Thanks to the global need for US production, America's sluggish economy was transformed into a manufacturing powerhouse.

By the end of 1944, US unemployment had shrunk to just 1.2 per cent of the civilian labour force – a record low in its economic history which has never been bettered (at the worst point of the Depression more than 15 million Americans – one quarter of the nation's workforce – were unemployed). The US GNP grew from US$88.6bn in 1939 to US$135bn in 1944 – an 8.8 per cent compounded annual increase in half a decade. All this meant that everything was geared to manufacturing – and scientific and technological changes intensified. By the end of the war, the rest of the world was broke: Japan destitute,

Europe bankrupt and United Kingdom penniless, leaving the United States as unquestionably *the* economic force.[4]

In its crudest form, the only thing that America lost in the Second World War was men. And even then, their losses compared to those of other warring countries were small. Out of the more than 72 million people who lost their lives in the war, the United States lost 416,800 – 0.32 per cent of its population. But, politically, militarily and economically America won hands down. The war was, in the most perverse sense, a resounding success.

America came out of the Second World War hugely rich. As the economic historian Alan Milward notes: 'the United States emerged in 1945 in an incomparably stronger position economically than in 1941 ... By 1945 the foundations of the United States' economic domination over the next quarter of a century had been secured ... [This] may have been the most influential consequence of the Second World War for the post-war world.'

By the middle of the 1950s America was financing the rebuilding of post-war Europe and beyond, while at the same time establishing itself as the foremost exporter of cultural norms and technological know-how. It was going to be America's century, and indeed it was.

Not only had the USA avoided direct collateral damage on its own soil (saving the outlay of potentially billions of dollars to rebuild its own infrastructure), the very fact that America could win the war, bankroll its allies during the war and institute the Marshall Plan (aid to Europe worth US$100bn in today's terms, which was around 5 per cent of the 1948 US GDP) demonstrates just how enormously wealthy the country had become.

Christopher Tassava wrote: 'economically strengthened by wartime industrial expansion ... possessed of an economy that was larger and richer than any other in the world, American leaders determined to make the United States the centre of the post-war world economy.' The Cold War would continue for the next fifty years, but it was this strategy that ultimately prevailed. Barely scathed, fantastically rich, no country could come close to the United States. The world was hers.

Rising America infused all aspects of society. Such was its strength, its confidence, its energy, that it permeated and infiltrated every sphere of Western-influenced human activity. The ensuing decades, the 1950s and 1960s, seemed to bear this theme out. Politically this was the era of social conscience and the civil rights movement, culturally there was a revolution in music, literature and art, and American innovation dominated in science and technology, putting a man on the moon and further developing the atomic bomb.

The success of the Manhattan Project and advances in the nuclear arms race heralded an age when America's scientific and technological mastery seemed unassailable in the West. United States exports increased from US$9,993m in 1950 to US$19,626m in 1960. This expansion in exports in just one decade was supported by the increase in US gross fixed capital formation, which grew from US$58bn in 1950 to US$104bn in 1960.

The three decades from the 1950s saw America wield its influence in every quarter. From the great industrial complexes such as General Motors, Ford Motor Company, Mobil Oil, International Business Machines, United Fruit Company and Dow Chemicals, to the Hollywood film industry and the music business exemplified by Motown, all came to symbolize the power of Americana, at home and abroad. It did not just stop at business.

Through the Peace Corps, established in 1961, America stamped its moral authority as it exported its values via its youth to everywhere Americans believed was not like them; with a remit to 'promote world peace and friendship through a Peace Corps, which shall make available to interested countries and areas men and women of the United States qualified for service abroad and willing to serve, under conditions of hardship if necessary, to help the peoples of such countries and areas in meeting their needs for trained manpower'. And, of course, American values were not just exported through the Peace Corps. Militarily, the US invaded Korea, and Vietnam to this day remains the great blot on America's conscience. The fact that America was growing bolder, and wielded unparalleled power outside its borders, was unquestionable.

All in all, this was the era that belonged to what the American journalist Tom Brokaw calls the 'Greatest Generation': the generation of Americans who fought in the Second World War and returned to build America into the greatest country in the world. For the next five decades they appeared to have succeeded – America was the epitome of wealth, power and cultural dominance, its tentacles reaching to every part of the globe. The rest of the West was firmly held in America's orbit – how could you not be in its grip, mesmerized by its power and brilliance? It was the sun around which other countries all revolved.

Good times, bad times, America was undeterred. From the oil spikes of the 1970s, the debt burdens and the Wall Street crash of the 1980s, and even the fall of communism in the 1990s, which would spawn its fiercest economic competitors, America seemed unassailable. Through its military might, its industrial capability, helped by free-market capitalism, and its cultural monopoly, America had planned it that way – *Made in America* was the logo of the times.

But fast-forward to today. See how much has changed. Western states are facing untold financial calamity, their populations ageing with few resources to sustain them, much of the necessary political reform remaining politically unpopular, and their economic supremacy susceptible to challenges from around the globe in a way never envisaged before. And while there have been setbacks before, such as America's savings and loans crisis of the 1980s and 1990s, the recent financial crisis and the policies the USA continues to pursue are proof positive that America is fast losing the hold it once had over the rest of the world. It has become a region of financial weakness and economic vulnerability in this, the first decade of the twenty-first century, to such an extent that, like bad blood, it has infected the rest of the Western body politic, making the story of economic decline necessarily one of the West versus a number of emerging upstarts. However, among the countries of the West, there remain good reasons to bet on the US being economically stronger than European countries in years to come.

But what exactly, in economic terms, drives growth?

THE PILLARS OF GROWTH

Much ado has been made of the seemingly inevitable economic decline of the industrialized West – the United States, in particular – and the 'rise of the rest', led by China. While most of this debate has tended to centre on historical patterns of imperialism and strategic and military considerations, canonical models of economic growth also offer a framework that highlights just how the West continues to misallocate the key ingredients necessary for long-term sustainable economic success and growth, to its detriment.

The evolution of growth theory has been a fascinating one, and one that cannot adequately be expounded in the short space that this book allows. An earlier incarnation in the economics literature began with the Harrod–Domar idea, which identified growth as solely a function of one input – capital.

In 1956, Robert Solow, an American professor at the Massachusetts Institute of Technology, built on this one-input model by demonstrating that labour too played a crucial and determinate role in delivering growth. For 'his contributions to the theory of economic growth', Solow was awarded the Nobel Prize for Economics in 1987, and for a time the Solow model, which saw growth as determined by capital and labour, remained the backbone of the macroeconomic growth literature for many years.

However, it must have come as something of a surprise that when these seemingly logical explanations for growth were subjected to empirical scrutiny, they accounted for only 40 per cent of a country's economic prosperity. There was a missing component; and a large one at that. This hitherto unidentified factor – the 60 per cent – has come to be known as total factor productivity, a catch-all phrase which encompasses technological development as well as anything not captured by the capital and labour inputs, such as culture and institutions. Thus canonical economic models point to three essential ingredients which determine economic growth: capital, labour, and total factor productivity.[5] These are the pistons which drive the cylinders of economic growth. Finely tuned and working in unison, they motor an engine of near limitless power.

Perhaps nothing illustrates the might, the sheer potency, of these three components coming together better than the American moon landing in July 1969. The gauntlet thrown down by President Kennedy in 1961, to land a man on the moon by the end of the decade, could not have been more ambitious. Goaded by the seemingly more adept Russian space programme, which was first with an object – Sputnik-1

(1957) – first with a living creature – Laika the dog (1957) – and, of course, first with a man – Yuri Gagarin (1961) – Kennedy captured the spirit of the times in his famous words: 'We choose to go to the moon in this decade and do the other things not because they are easy, but because they are hard.'

The history of the Apollo programme, its personalities, its spirit of adventure, remains one of the most celebrated moments in American (and world) history, and rightly so.[6] But it is also the supreme example of the confluence of capital, labour and technology, each at the height of its powers and all of them working as one. America had the capital, it had the labour, and, ultimately, it had the technology. The facts and figures speak volumes.

In terms of capital, the costs of the Apollo project were astronomical. The annual budget of the National Aeronautics and Space Administration (NASA) increased from US$500m in 1960 to a high point of US$5.2bn in 1965 – representing 5.3 per cent of that year's federal budget (5 per cent of today's US budget would be around US$125bn). As a reference point, the Vietnamese war is thought to have cost around US$111bn (US$686bn in 2008 dollars). All told, the final cost of the Apollo project was between US$20bn and US$25bn in 1969 dollars (or approximately US$135bn in 2005 dollars).

Cash was only one component of the Apollo challenge. To realize its goal America had to draw upon the two other essentials: labour and technology. Luckily for America, it could.

To this end, a huge army of personnel were enlisted. By 1966, NASA's civil service list had grown to 36,000 people from the 10,000 the agency employed in 1960. NASA's space programme would also require that the agency call upon thousands upon thousands of outside technicians and scientists. From 1960 to 1965 individuals working on the programme increased by a factor of 10, from 36,000 to an astonishing 376,000. The more critical point here was not that NASA needed to find such a vast amount of talent, but rather that it could. And where the talent did not exist, NASA created it. Private industries, research institutions and universities provided the majority of these personnel. It was this labour force that would invent and build the technology which would catapult America to the forefront of the space race and put Neil Armstrong and Buzz Aldrin on the moon – an accomplishment often cited to this day as the greatest technological achievement in history.

The technological feats of the Apollo programme were truly awe-inspiring. While marvelling at the wonder, the approximately one fifth of the world's population that watched the live transmission of the first Apollo moon landing would have struggled to appreciate the phenomenal behind-the-scenes technological brilliance that had made this possible.

The idea of a lunar landing had been through ten years of trials, prototypes and numerous setbacks in order to make it a reality. From the huge Saturn rockets that had the power to lift a US destroyer into space, to the lunar module that landed two 150-pound men on the moon, and to each of the hundreds of thousands of components and parts that had to be researched, designed, built and tested, the apparatus of the Apollo was breathtaking in its vastness and complexity.

It did not stop there: the programme spurred advances in many areas of technology peripheral to rocketry and manned spaceflight, including avionics, telecommunications and computing, as well as in the fields of engineering, statistical methods, and civil, mechanical and electrical engineering. This is the power of ideas. Beyond the immediate machine or contraption the spill-over effects are the real gains of technology. And because once an idea is out it can be used and improved upon by anyone, anywhere, an idea has a marginal cost of zero.

Even if it had wished to, no country other than America had the capability – the capital, the labour, the technology – to plan, to develop and to execute the moon landing. Russia was not so far behind in space investment, hence the emergence of the Space Race, but over time it became clear that it would not be able to compete.

The absence of any one of these elements would have meant that America couldn't have achieved its lunar ambitions. The point is, with these three factors in place the implausible becomes possible; economies, and therefore countries, become forces to be reckoned with. Yet if they are misused, misallocated, a country's economic decline is not just on the cards but accelerated.

What is clear, and what this book will demonstrate, is that deliberate (American) public policies are making things worse, exacerbating this economic step down by weakening these three components. America's economic growth is not only less than it would otherwise have been, but its overall economic decline is undoubtedly faster and more acute than it would be with better policymaking.

What follows is an exposition of how these three factors are individually and collectively contributing to the decline of the West. Further, two aspects are fundamental: their respective quantity and quality. To hammer home the point, it is not only the quantity of capital, the quantity of labour, the quantity of technology that is of concern; what has equal bearing in determining economic success or failure is their quality. That is to say, the manner in which the capital is allocated, the aptitude of the workforce and the nature of the technology.

From the early days of the growth debate, capital has always been regarded as the prime mover in defining a country's failure or success. So it seems right and proper that the book should first turn its attention to this all-important subject.

2

A Capital Story

'Capital is money, capital is commodities. By virtue of it being value, it has acquired the occult ability to add value to itself. It brings forth living offspring, or at the least, lays golden eggs.'

Even capitalism's most vigorous detractor, Karl Marx, recognized the overwhelming power that capital impresses on us all; it is, after all, the lifeblood of every economy. It should come as no surprise, therefore, that early economists identified capital as the prime ingredient for growth.

Capital encompasses everything from the physical treasures of the earth that man regards as valuable – gold, silver, land – to houses, turnpikes, factories and even livestock. Indeed one can go back at least as far as 1086, when William the Conqueror commissioned the Domesday Book to put a value on England to such an extent that an observer of the survey noted that 'there was no single hide nor a yard of land, nor indeed one ox nor one cow nor one pig which was left out.'[1] At the time of the publication of the Domesday Book, the total value of land recorded in the survey was valued at approximately £73,000.[2]

The bulk of the survey was devoted to the assessment and valuation of rural estates that were then the only important source of national wealth, and, very much as capital is valued today, the tally included arable land, the number of plough teams, river meadows, woodland, watermills and fisheries. Ultimately the purpose of it came down to providing a guide to the King for where he should look when he needed to raise money.

In the United States, analogous data that offer a snapshot of the state of the economy are presented in the National Income and Product Accounts (NIPA). According to the Bureau of Economic Analysis, which produces the NIPA tables, the estimation of national income and the national balance sheet was initiated during the early 1930s, when the lack of comprehensive economic data frustrated the efforts of presidents Hoover and Roosevelt to design policies to combat the Great Depression. The Department of Commerce commissioned the Russian-American economist Simon Kuznets, who later became a Nobel laureate, to develop estimates of national income. These estimates were presented in a report to the Senate in 1934, *National Income, 1929–32.*

However capital is defined, governments have tended to view it all in terms of that man-made stuff – cold, hard cash (itself, of course, originally partially made of the precious minerals). So much so that in today's parlance capital has become synonymous with money. Rightly or wrongly, money has become the yardstick by which individuals, governments and societies as a whole are judged. The worth of something is exactly that. The amount of money produced by an economy has become its most revealing indicator. Which is why, in modern times, economists tend to focus on what a country produces – the Gross Domestic Product (GDP).

STOCK OR FLOW?

An important technical point is the difference between stock and flow. Whereas the Domesday Book offers a snapshot value of the economy (i.e. what is known as a stock number), GDP is calculated as a flow, and therefore represents the total production a country generates over a specified period – call it a year. For example, a country with an annual GDP of roughly US$14tn, such as the United States, has produced that value of goods and services in that year, but this does not represent the value of America's total stock. In fact, it is best to think of the modern-day version of the Domesday Book as a nation's stock of assets, not its GDP (flow).

To further elucidate this point: consider the fact that if one were to bulldoze a country, raze it to the ground and rebuild it within the same year, this would be reflected as a high GDP flow, but low GDP stock (many emerging and poor countries fall into this category).

Conversely, a country could have a zero, negative or low GDP growth rate (its flow), but have a GDP stock that is very high. Think of old Europe and the US (particularly after the 2008 financial crisis) as possible examples. Furthermore, GDP estimates should not be equated to the amount of capital. For, it is quite clear that while the United States has the largest GDP today, the country is also short on cash.

We digress, slightly. Why then focus on GDP? Well, the point here is that the economic decline across the West and primarily the United States is driven by two factors: these economies are increasingly capital-constrained, and their GDP estimates are on a precarious path of forecast decline. The point of mentioning GDP at all is that it gives one the ability to look at and measure a country's economic performance individually and vis-à-vis other countries. In what follows, we do just that.

HOW MUCH HAVE YOU GOT?

The story of the West's rise and fall is primarily a tale of how it has viewed, stored and wasted its capital. The West's behaviour over the last fifty years has been like that of a profligate son, squandering the family wealth garnered over the centuries – frittering it away on heady indulgences and bad investments. Left unchecked, the last half-century will also mark the start of the decline of the 500-year interlude in what previously had been 2,000 years of Asian economic pre-eminence. It is after all useful to remember that as far back as the first century BC, the Chinese developed the decimal system that underpins global finance and virtually all measurement today.

Historians and macroeconomists owe an inordinate debt of gratitude to Angus Maddison, who published his inimitable economic database which stretches as far back as 1500 and includes estimates of growth, populations and breadth of infrastructure from old world Europe, to China, to India and latterly the US.[3] The uniqueness of the Maddison log is that, by going as far back as it does, it provides a picture of not only how the world's economies have fared individually, but also how they expand or shrink in relation to each other over time.

One of the most fascinating sets of figures is the snapshot of the share of world GDP in 1820. At the time China's world share of GDP stood at 32.4 per cent – larger than any other region of the world, and greater than those of Europe (26.6 per cent), the United States (1.8 per cent) and Japan (3 per cent) combined. China's dominance was largely driven by a seemingly insatiable Western demand for porcelain, silk nankeen (a coarse cotton) and, principally, tea, which rose from 36 per cent of America's imports from China in 1822 to an unquenchable 65 per cent of US imports in 1860.

As an economy India too was surprisingly buoyant during the early 1800s. Although the Indian economy had declined from its position in 1700, when its share of world GDP matched both China's and Europe's (at around 23 per cent), by 1820 it still had a dominant position with a share of 16 per cent thanks to a healthy export base of tea, cotton and spices and to the rapidly expanding opium trade. And, indeed, from 1870 to 1913 nearly 50,000 kilometres (31,250 miles) of new railway lines were laid down – roughly ten times the distance between New York and the coast of California.

In the seventy years from 1820 to 1890, China's share of world GDP drops by almost 40 per cent, whereas America's share rises almost fourteen times to 13.8 per cent. By 1890 the pattern of Western economic dominance that has been the norm for the past hundred years begins to assert itself. With the surge powered by the industrial revolution, Europe (but perhaps principally Britain) leaps forward to take a lead position in the world share of GDP (at 40 per cent). At this time, China and America are each at around 13 per cent – the difference of course being that China is experiencing a rapid decline, whereas America is firmly on the ascendant.

Come 1950 it all seems over, and we are living in the post-Second World War world we know. Now America and Europe are booming, standing at the economic helm, together representing a massive 60 per cent of world GDP – America at close to 30 per cent. Meanwhile, unable to stem its decline, China has nearly reached rock bottom at 5.2 per cent of world GDP (indeed, it spends the following twenty-five years floundering in the 5 per cent share of GDP doldrums), while India stands at a paltry 3.8 per cent (only nuclear-bombed Japan is lower, at 3.4 per cent).

Indeed, with the collapse of Chiang Kai-shek's government army in 1949 the US Secretary of State, Dean Acheson, told Congress, not to be alarmed; he said that China is 'not a modern centralized state and that the communists will face almost as much difficulty in governing it as had the previous regimes'.

By 1978 this world-view appeared confirmed, with America and Europe firmly in the economic driving seat. India, like China, had suffered a catastrophic collapse, slumping to her lowest ever share of world GDP at a mere 3.4 per cent. Upon closer examination, however, while Europe was holding steady at 27.9 per cent, America had already dropped a significant 7 percentage points in favour of a rebounding Japan, which was capitalizing on its own industrialization boom, driven by technological innovation. For America, the consumer age was just beginning, and Japanese innovation was there to meet this demand. Even at this time, it was still predominantly a Western story. China, India and others had yet to make their move.

THE RISE OF THE REST

In the south-east corner of China, in Guangdong Province, lies Dongguan, one of the world's fastest-growing cities, with a population in 2007 of nearly 7 million (up from 1 million in 1979). It was now home to some 15,000 international companies, one of the leading centres for the manufacturing of PC components. In addition, with China being the world's largest producer and exporter of toys, Dongguan (with more than 4,000 factories at its peak) is the leading toy manufacturer in a province which contributes 70 per cent of China's overall toy output. In 2002, with nearly US$3bn of goods exported worldwide – the majority to the US – Dongguan ranked third among Chinese cities (behind Shanghai and Shenzen).

No country has come to symbolize the profound economic transformation witnessed in the past half-century better than China. From a country whose outlook has for centuries been inherently internal and introspective, China has emerged as one of the most potent economic forces on the planet. At the time of writing, China was the largest exporter in the world, and surpassed Japan to rank second in terms of GDP.

It is not happening in just one town – this story is being replicated to a greater or lesser extent all over China, and all over the emerging world: Brazil, India, Russia, the Middle East, South Africa, parts of Eastern Europe and South America, the list goes on. Such is their power and their influence that this new force has been given a collective noun in recognition of their position on the global economic stage, taking the West on at their own game – 'the Rest'. Were it just one country, the West might have been able to tame it, to absorb it. But faced with the combined might of the Rest, the West is forced to grapple with a relentless onslaught of challengers from all corners of the globe. And all these countries are growing in confidence, gaining in competence, and jockeying for a frontline position in the world's economic race.

The key question here is how damaging is this for the West? Is it bad for America if millions more people in the emerging world have better-quality lives and higher economic living standards? Given cross-border trade and the tendency for progress to move across a broad front, perhaps not; however, where there is a resources squeeze – commodities, water and energy, and an environment with a population still on the rise (some forecasts put the number of people on the planet at over 9 billion by 2050) – this becomes a pertinent question. As the world becomes a true global village through convergence – the sustained rise in incomes and reduction in poverty towards Western living standards across the emerging world – something has to give. All else being equal, convergence will necessarily entail economic upward peaks (on the part of emerging economies) and downward dips (for the richer countries). In other words, even while globalization could contribute to a rising tide for all boats, it is clear that the relative quality of life will almost certainly have to decline in the West to accommodate a rise in the Rest. Of course, the West has, thanks to the emerging economies, benefited from cheap products, cheap labour and cheap funding costs. However, greater global demand on the back of rising incomes across the new economies must mean that real cost rises are inevitable, resulting in a reduction of relative Western living standards. Put differently, as the world flattens out it will always be inevitable that the West will lose on a relative basis, but it is not predetermined that it has to lose on an absolute basis – although that is where the West's policies are leading it.

Look at China again. By 1952 China's world GDP share had bottomed out at 5 per cent – a 158-year decline since its zenith of 1820. But this inexorable and disastrous fall pales when compared with its subsequent rise. China turned the situation around to such an extent that between 1978, when it abandoned Maoist economic theocracy in favour of market-led pragmatism (more on this later), and 2000, China's share of world GDP had more than doubled from 5 per cent in 1952 to 12 per cent in 2000, a meteoric rise in just twenty-two years; while, according to Maddison, the US share of world GDP has been steadily trending downwards from a 1952 high of 28.4 per cent to 22 per cent in 2000.

Although Asian countries, like China, had already been dominant economic powers as far back as the 1400s and 1500s, emerging economies have done the unfathomable – moving from virtual economic obscurity fifty years ago to consistently, systematically posting the largest year-on-year growth gains in the last several decades. Their economic revolution has been so dramatic and so pervasive that to summarize the huge importance of the implications for the human condition and human experience – education, knowledge – is very nearly impossible.

Of course varying statistics abound; the rosy picture painted by Angus Maddison differs from data estimates on the GDP share breakdown as postulated by the International Monetary Fund and Goldman Sachs. The latter put China's 2000 and 2006 respective shares at 3.8 per cent and 5.4 per cent, and those of the United States at 30.8 per cent and 27.7 per cent, respectively – neither set of figures as dramatic as those suggested by Maddison.

Nevertheless, to dwell on diverging data points is to miss the broader trend, that the US share is falling, while that of China, and of other economic upstarts (Brazil, Russia and India), is rising. In a world where there are winners and losers this trend matters. Indeed, 2006 marked a watershed moment when, for the first time in post-Second World War history, the emerging market economies combined overtook the United States as holding proportionally the larger share of world GDP (27.4 per cent versus 26 per cent).

It's not just China's rising *share* of world GDP that underscores its mounting economic influence. So too do its notional stock of wealth (i.e. how much money the country has) and its population's per capita income (i.e. the average income per person), which have risen spectacularly thanks to the country's extraordinary growth rates – since 1989 China's growth rate has never dipped below 6 per cent, and sometimes has reached 10 per cent.

If one were to put a GDP value on the world in 2009, it would be worth US$60tn. That is the sum total ascribed dollar value of the annual output all the world's countries – rich and poor. For the current global population of roughly 6.5 billion people, this averages out as just over US$9,000 for every man, woman and child on the planet. (Of course the realities of income inequality mean this is not the actual case.) At US$14tn, the largest share of this capital resides in the world's wealthiest country, the USA; very nearly one third of the world's GDP. At a rough calculation, this means that, as of 2008, the average American took home about US$45,000.

Back in 1978 (when the US was also the richest country), its GDP stood at around US$5tn and a per capita income of US$22,300. World Bank estimates, which enable comparisons to be made across countries over time, put American GDP in 2008 at US$12tn, and per capita GDP at US$38,200. Compare this performance with China's. In 1978 its US dollar value GDP stood at US$150bn. By 2008 it had surged to US$4tn; an unprecedented rise in per capita income from US$155 (in 1978) to nearly US$3,000 in 2008. Had China's population been static at this time, this would have been an impressive enough figure, but when one realizes that its population increased by 100 million people at the same time, the per capita income figures are truly stupendous. For those who have so far participated in China's economic boom, the numbers are even better still, and although there are hundreds of millions of Chinese (many of whom are farming peasants) for whom economically things are more or less unchanged, the trend is in the right direction.

The Chinese economy has exploded. And like its legendary firework displays, the explosion has been dazzling. In just thirty years China has shifted some 300 million of its people from abject poverty and wretched indigence to economic standards that rival the West's – a feat unprecedented in the history of the world. In the past two decades China has been the world's fastest-growing economy, overtaking Germany (the world's third) in 1982, Japan (the world's second) in 1992, and by 2003 vying to match the USA, representing 73 per cent of America's GDP. Before the first decade of the new millennium is over, China is already first in mobile phones, cars and internet users, first in exports, second in electricity consumption[4] and first in terms of reserves. In the first seven months of 2009, the US bank Morgan Stanley reported that vehicles sold in China reached 12.3 million on an annualized basis, exceeding the United States for the first time ever. At the end of 2008, China recorded more dollar millionaires than the UK (364,000 versus 362,000, respectively).

China has not been alone in this relentless economic march, but has been followed by India. Like China, the last fifty years have not been the first time that India has flirted with being a player on the world economic stage. Its turnaround might have been slower than China's (the Indian subcontinent's growth rate averaged nearly 5 per cent a year, which is markedly lower than China's at 7.5 per cent over the last several decades), but all the while it has been as consistent.

According to Asymmetric Threats Contingency Alliance (ATCA), India – still regarded in many Western eyes as a poor country – has an estimated US$1.5tn residing in Swiss banks (more unaccounted-for monies than the rest of the world put together), and an amount ten times larger than its foreign debt. It is also home to fifty Indian billionaires. Every year around 80,000 Indians travel to Switzerland, of whom 25,000 are frequent visitors.

In the interests of full disclosure, Russia lies second (US$470bn) in the league tables of Swiss bank depositors, with Ukraine and China fourth and fifth at US$100bn and US$96bn, respectively. Surprisingly, the only Western country in the top five is Britain, with US$390bn.

CASH IS KING

On 24 June 2008, the *Financial Times* published its list of the top 500 global companies by market capitalization (after all, what is relevant is the market capitalization, not simply the existence of a big conglomerate flagship). Nearly half of the top ten companies were non-Western; two from China (with PetroChina muscling in at number two and the Industrial and Commercial Bank of China straddling the opposition at number six), one from Russia[5] and another from Hong Kong. Five in the top ten were American, but for how much longer? As Western companies grow weaker, the cash-rich companies of the emerging world grow stronger.

It's not just the companies. Across the emerging world, government-owned pools of money are playing hugely significant roles and are poised to shape the global economic landscape in years to come. China may be hogging the media limelight, but the stash of money comes from a much broader cast.

In purely cash terms neither China nor India controls the top five largest government-owned investment pools of cash, or sovereign wealth funds as they are more commonly termed, although at the time of writing China's funds alone are growing at over US$1bn a day. Unsurprisingly, thanks in large part to oil (the Middle East region accounts for around 40 per cent of the world's proven oil and 23 per cent of natural gas reserves), three of the top five funds are from the Middle East, making the region an economic bloc every bit as testing and intimidating as its Far Eastern rivals. And at the last count, eight of the top ten global sovereign wealth funds were owned by the Rest; the largest such US fund crawls in at number sixteen (the Alaska Permanent Reserve Fund, with US$37bn).[6]

Yes, the United States is home to vast pots of capital, but unlike in the emerging world where cash piles are 'owned' by the government, most of the large pools of money in the US are held privately (in pension funds, insurance companies, mutual funds, etc.). These structural differences, in who owns and oversees the money, have already proven to be critically important in the flexibility and speed with which the 2008 financial crisis could be addressed. It will be even more critical in terms of economic strategy and accomplishment going forward. Ultimately, however, selling commodities and having a large cash pile do not make a nation a big economic force; rather it's what the owners do with them that matters.[7]

Not long ago the world would have baulked at the notion of China and the Middle East riding to the rescue of a financially weakened

United States. But now a survey of 600 senior business executives by the law firm Eversheds concludes that Shanghai will probably over-take London in the next decade, just behind New York, as a global financial centre, thus becoming a leading contender in the competi-tion to be the world's capital of finance. Meanwhile, these emerging regions have already been propping up failing Western financial insti-tutions (and potentially the broader economy) on the brink of collapse.

Abu Dhabi ploughed US$7.5bn into Citibank, the Chinese CIC invested US$5bn in Morgan Stanley and another US$3bn in the US private equity house Blackstone. At the last count, in early 2008, the total amount invested by the emerging world in Western financial institutions had topped US$30bn. And yes, although many of these investments were all left underwater in the wake of the financial crisis, the point is that the emerging countries had the money to do this. While the US government (and other Western governments) did engineer bailouts on the heels of the financial crisis, much of the cash raised will have to be covered by the ordinary taxpayer rather than government-held reserves.

The uncomfortable truth is that the West is desperately strapped for cash. Like the rules of engagement that have governed the market economies of the industrialized West for more than 200 years, it all boils down to cash; who has it and who doesn't.

In the global bidding war – for property, for companies, for com-modities, for anything of value – the West will rarely be seen: it's fast running out of money. But it wasn't always this way. It once had plenty, and even surplus. The reason the West finds itself in this predicament is because of what it did with the money when it had it – it misallocated it.

At the close of 2008 America's banking sector looked much the same as Detroit's car industry – battered and bruised. With roughly 20 per cent of America's GDP (including real-money investors and insurers), and many hundreds of thousands of employees, the banking sector and its 2008 crisis placed America at the precipice of disaster.

Although the 2008 crisis will most certainly not knock Western economies (and America specifically) off their perch, viewed in a broader context this economic wobble, trip and stumble is the latest step in the steady decline of the West's capital dominance and a har-binger of things to come.

The recurring theme of this book is how Western governments and private institutions – the think tanks, academic faculties, university research programmes – all burrowing away feverishly to design the best economic policies, yielded unintended and detrimental consequences. At the heart of the American financial system were layers of agency risk, i.e. the possibility that company managers would not act in the best interests of its stakeholders.

Perhaps it was folly, perhaps wilful blindness, or perhaps capricious political myopia – regardless of the motivation, in the last fifty years Western policymaking has placed an unbearable burden of unsustainable mounting costs on future generations, the full extent of which the Western world has just begun to experience. Time and time again, it will become clear how this has come about. As we will see, many policies propelled by good intentions produced short-term benefits, but also long-term detrimental costs.

In the specific case of capital, for example, the unintended consequences of Western (American) policies to broaden access to capital for its citizens (i.e. to fulfil the American dream) have left the United States and indeed the Western world at large teetering on the verge of bankruptcy. So carried away were policymakers that they failed to appreciate the collateral damage that would invariably, inevitably, follow in the wake of these policies, eventually sweeping aside everything in its path.

DEBT IS CHEAPER THAN EQUITY

In July 2009 Barney Frank, a senior US policymaker and crucially the Chairman of the House Financial Services Committee – responsible for overseeing the financial services industry, i.e. the securities, insurance, banking and housing industries – made the following statement: 'Management owes a duty of care to its shareholders to reduce the company's risk.'[8]

This seemingly innocuous statement demonstrates a fundamental lack of understanding of the capital structure, the important differences between the role of the debt holder and the role of the equity holder, which has not only led to the 2008 financial crisis but also underscores how through faulty policymaking the West continues to misallocate its capital and why this will lead to its continual economic decline.

What follows is a brief explanation of how a company finances itself. The reason why understanding a company capital structure is important is that once explained it will be easier for the reader to appreciate three things: (1) how a company's capital structure is widely misunderstood, especially by policymakers; (2) the implications of this misunderstanding on the housing market; and (3) how deliberate homeownership policies on the part of Western governments (and the United States, in particular) have led to a misallocation of capital, which has in turn placed industrialized countries on a path to economic demise.

A good way to investigate key aspects of corporate capital structure is something called contingent claims analysis. This framework shows how a company finances itself – largely via what are called equity claims (e.g. ownership through stocks) and debt claims (e.g. lending to the company). As will become clear, the attitude of these different claimants to (1) earning volatility and (2) debt levels (also known as leverage) drive the manner in which companies finance themselves.

Let's suppose you own a company, which costs you US$10,000 to set up (e.g. you pay a licence fee to the government). For simplicity let's assume these are sunk costs and are therefore non-recoverable – you don't get them back. The moment the company has a value over zero (i.e. it has an income), your equity claim has a non-zero value. Put another way, as soon as the enterprise has some value, the equity holder is making money.

In financial lingo, you, as the sole shareholder, are 'long' the company, but this also can be viewed as you being 'long a call option' struck at zero (i.e. you make money anywhere after zero). Because you have an option, if the company were ever to be worth zero or worth a negative value, you as the equity holder make no money and crucially can walk away without any further loss (as there is no recourse to you as an owner, and in this sense it is like a limited liability enterprise). What this means is that the more money the company makes, the more money you as the sole shareholder make.

To gauge the value of the company, you have to watch and understand what is known as the enterprise value. The enterprise value

(EV) is a measure of a company's worth, and is computed as the sum of the expected value of the equity (EQ) and the expected value of the debt (ED), so that EV = EQ + ED.

Assume a friend lends you US$50,000 to develop the company. The equity claim still behaves as a call option; the only difference is the strike (the point after which you start to make money) has moved. That is to say, you the shareholder make money as the company makes money (i.e. the company or enterprise value goes up). However, now you have to consider the fact that you have to pay back the US$50,000 loan before you garner any benefit.[9] Specifically, the strike is now US$50,000 (i.e. the level of debt) so that when the enterprise value is greater than that, your equity claim is equal to the difference between the enterprise value and US$50,000. You're making money. If the enterprise value is ever below US$50,000, the sensible thing for you to do, as the equity claimant, is to exercise your right to walk away.[10]

As a debt claimant, although your friend wishes the company to be a success, he is only concerned about one thing – getting his US$50,000 back (plus interest). However, his upside is capped in that regardless of how successful the company is, the maximum he can ever make is his US$50,000 plus interest back. In the lingo, he is 'short a put option'[11] – he makes money up until the US$50,000 is paid back and then earns nothing more. In other words, the equity claimant is long an option, and the debt claimant is short an option, and the value of the option is correlated to company earnings volatility.[12] The debt claimant gives the equity claimant the option to either pay back the US$50,000 or 'put' the company back to him if the company is less than US$50,000, so the debt claimant always gets whatever is left.

In contrasting these two claims, it should not be missed that there is a natural tension between these two parties.

For the owner of the company (the equity claimant), the greater the risk he takes, the higher the expected potential profit. The thing is, there is a direct and positive correlation between risk (as measured by the asset volatility or debt level) and expected profit, so that the equity claimant likes higher volatility and higher levels of debt, and therefore is prone to taking a higher risk.[13] Usually, standard practice is that the owner of the equity claim is responsible for the day-to-day management of the business and makes key business decisions about the future of the company. Of course, the equity claimant and debt claimant both want a higher enterprise value.

More to the point, for a given expected enterprise value of the company, the equity claimant would like to increase the volatility or variance around that expected enterprise value more than the debt claimant.[14] What follows demonstrates this point.

The greater the risk the equity claimant takes the higher the expected return. The greater risks taken by operating the business increase the expected value of the equity claim. For the equity claimant the volatility (or variance) in the value of the company is a good thing. Given the choice the equity holder will always want to take more volatility. What follows is a simple numerical example to show that an equity holder will prefer more variance (volatility) in the enterprise value, rather than less.

With the information we have, at Day 1 of the company's life, the business has an enterprise value of US$50,000, a debt value of US$50,000, and as we are financing the business completely by debt, the equity value is equal to zero. (The cross-check is simply, as before, EV = EQ + ED.)

If the equity holder is faced with a choice of (a) 50 per cent chance of an enterprise value of US$75,000 and a 50 per cent chance of an enterprise value of US$25,000, or (b) a 50 per cent chance of an enterprise value of US$100,000 versus a 50 per cent chance of an enterprise value of zero (US$0), which gamble will the equity holder pick?

Remember that in either case the expected enterprise value of the company is US$50,000, so he will choose the scenario that will give him the better odds for making money. The answer to the question is that the equity claimant will pick option (b), where the expected value of the equity claim is US$25,000, as opposed to option (a), where the expected value of the equity claim is only US$12,500.

How do we get these figures?

The value of the company can go up or down. In a year's time, according to the first scenario, the company's value could be either US$75,000 (with a 50 per cent chance) or US$25,000 (also with a 50 per cent probability). If the company ends up worth US$75,000, with the debt standing at US$50,000, the equity value has to be US$25,000. Similarly, if the company ends up valued at only US$25,000, with the debt still standing at the same US$50,000, the company is effectively bust, as it cannot even cover the debt. This means the equity value must be worth zero. Remember that these two scenarios each have a 50–50 chance of happening; therefore, the overall expected equity value must factor in these probabilities and is calculated as (50 per cent multiplied by US$25,000) plus (50 per cent multiplied by US$0), which equals an expected equity value of US$12,500.

However, there is another possible choice, which changes the equity holder's outlook. Recall that in this scenario there is a 50 per cent chance that the value of the company ends up at US$100,000 and an equal 50 per cent chance the company ends up worth nothing. Using the same formulas as before, and with the proviso that the debt claim is still US$50,000 and must be paid first (i.e. ahead of the equity claimant), if the company does end up worth US$100,000, his equity rises from zero in Day 1 to US$50,000. On the other hand, if the company (enterprise) value plummets to zero, the outstanding US$50,000 debt means the equity holder walks away with nothing. But using the overall formula to calculate the odds as before (factoring in the probabilities of each scenario), the overall expected equity value must be equal to US$25,000 (i.e. (US$50,000 multiplied by 50 per cent) plus (US$0 multiplied by 50 per cent)).

What this tells us is that the equity holder will prefer to bet on the scenario with more variance around the enterprise value (i.e. more upside for him), whereas it's not in the interest of the debt holder (note in the case of wider variance option (b), the debt holder risks not getting paid back).

Obviously the equity and debt holders want the enterprise value to go up, so they are in sync directionally. However, the equity claimant is much more willing to accept a wider variance in the enterprise value, i.e. take a wilder punt. Given an expected gain or return for an asset value, the equity claimant has a higher expected value if the variance in the enterprise value goes up. And, as demonstrated before, the expected value of the debt claimant is the expected enterprise value minus the expected equity claim. Of course, because, as before, the equity claimant is long an option, while the debt holder is short an option, the debt claimant's appetite for volatility is the flipside of the equity claimant's stance.

From this, it should be easy to see that if variance is good for the equity holder it must be bad for the debt claim. In our case the debt holder will prefer the first scenario; i.e. the US$12,500 enterprise value. The debt holder, anxious to get his principal US$50,000 back, is in essence indifferent to how much the company makes, as long as it can pay him back. Of course, he's happy if the company does well, but he would prefer less volatility around the company enterprise value and would also prefer that the equity holder take on less, rather than more, risk. All told, he is wary of the company taking an unnecessary risk.

The first example demonstrates that, for a given expected enterprise value, the higher variance benefits/favours the equity claim at the expense of the debt claim. In that sense, the equity claim is long volatility and the debt claim is short volatility.

The example that now follows will show how the equity claimant also loves leverage and is prone to taking on more debt, and not less. Again the opposite is true for the debt holder. Remember that the fundamental point of all this is to show how, unlike Barney Frank's proclamation, equity holders – and by extension the management that work on their behalf – love risk, and deliberately seek it out. This is exactly how they make their money.

Let's again begin with the simple case where on Day 1 our fictitious company has an enterprise value (EV) of US$50,000. As before, the enterprise value is a measure of a company's value, and is computed as the sum of the expected value of the equity (EQ) and the expected value of the debt (ED), so that EV = EQ + ED. In this case let us assume that this US$50,000 enterprise value is made up of US$20,000 in equity and US$30,000 in debt. Let us also assume that in a year there is a 50 per cent chance that the business (the enterprise value) will be worth US$40,000, and a 50 per cent probability that the company will be worth US$100,000.

If the case where the company ends up being valued (i.e. its enterprise value) at US$40,000 were to materialize, say, a year later, then with a debt still at US$30,000 the expected equity value is reduced to US$10,000. This is simply EV = EQ + ED (i.e. US$40,000 = US$10,000 + US$30,000 (remembering that the debt holder always gets paid first – ahead of the equity holder)). If, however, by Day 2 (a year later), the company's enterprise value has risen to US$100,000, then with the expected debt of US$30,000 the expected equity must have increased to US$70,000. Of course, again we must factor in the probabilities of each of these scenarios occurring (i.e. 50 per cent each) so that the overall expected equity value ends up being US$40,000, i.e. (50 per cent multiplied by US$10,000) plus (50 per cent multiplied by US$70,000).

The return on equity (ROE) is calculated as (equity value on Day 2 minus the equity value on Day 1) divided by (equity value on Day 1 times 100), recalling that the equity value on Day 1 was assumed as US$20,000. Therefore when the EV was US$40,000, the ROE is calculated as –50 per cent, i.e. ((10,000 – 20,000)/20,000) times 100. Not a great figure.

However, using the same computation on the scenario where the EV ends up at US$100,000, the ROE stands at a respectable 250 per cent ((70,000 – 20,000)/20,000) multiplied by 100). Once again, adjusting for probabilities of outcome occurring, the probability-adjusted overall ROE here is 100 per cent, i.e. (50 per cent multiplied by –50 per cent) plus (50 per cent multiplied by 250 per cent). Keep this 100 per cent return on equity figure in mind.

LOVING LEVERAGE

Now consider another scenario when, on Day 1, the company decides to finance itself by more leverage (debt). Here we have a company with the same US$50,000 enterprise value as before, but with a debt value of US$40,000 and an equity value of only US$10,000.

As before, assume that there are two possible states of the world on Day 2. Once again, the company's enterprise value can end up at US$40,000 (with 50 per cent likelihood) or US$100,000 (also with a 50 per cent chance).

Using the same mathematical formulas as before, it is plain to see that if the company ends up with an EV of US$40,000, the expected equity value must be equal to 0 (zero) since the value of the debt is also US$40,000. Put another way, the total value of the business will be used to cover the debt.

However, if the business flourishes and ends up with an EV of US$100,000, then again by using the equation EV = EQ + ED (and paying off the debt), the expected equity will be a much improved US$60,000. Again factoring in the 50 per cent chance of ending up with an expected equity value of either US$40,000 or US$100,000 leaves us with an overall expected equity value of US$30,000 (i.e. (50 per cent times US$0) plus (50 per cent times US$60,000)).

Now look at what happens to the return on equity under this scenario of more debt. When the EV ends up at US$40,000, the ROE is a miserable –100 per cent (again ((0 – 10)/10) multiplied by 100). But if the company value surges to US$100,000, the ROE is 500 per cent (i.e. ((60 – 10)/10) multiplied by 100). The overall ROE (factoring in the 50 per cent probabilities of each of these scenarios) is +200 per cent ((50 per cent multiplied by –100 per cent) plus (50 per cent multiplied by 500 per cent)).

Compare this debt-financed 200 per cent ROE to the 100 per cent ROE where the equity holder had to put up more of his own money. For the equity claimant, debt financing wins hands down.

A lot of figures to go through to illustrate the simple point that the greater the debt, the greater the reward for the equity claimant. All in all, the equity holder will always favour more debt and will be keen to pile on the debt and leverage up.

In summary, vis-à-vis volatility, risk and levels of debt, what becomes clear is that the two claimants (equity holder and debt holder) have widely different and competing appetites for each. So whereas the equity holder welcomes volatility and prefers to stack on debt, making him risk-loving, the opposite is true for his debt holder counterpart – he abhors volatility and stands shy of piling on layers of debt, i.e. he is risk-averse.

Perhaps crucially, in the normal workings of a company, the debt claimant acts as a break or automatic trigger to the freewheeling ambitions of the equity claimant. The debt claimant's motivation is to get his money back by stringently overseeing the over-reaching ambitions of the equity claimant. In baseball or cricketing terms, the debt claimant prefers to hit singles, rather than home runs or boundaries.

So when government officials like Barney Frank say: 'Management owes a duty of care to its shareholders to reduce the company's risk' he misses the fundamental point that risk-taking is *precisely* what equity holders expect management to do. In fact, risk-taking is what management is paid for, and the reason why bonuses are paid to those who take on more risk. Risk is the *raison d'être*.

SAFE AS HOUSES

The lack of understanding of equity claims and debt claims inferred from Barney Frank's comments (and unfortunately displayed by many other government officials) does not end with corporate finance.

In the most damaging way possible, this muddled thinking has permeated the policies directed towards the housing market; the trouble being that, in pursuing homeownership policies, policymakers clearly don't fully understand the results of what they are doing. This blind spot in their knowledge is so pernicious that governments are actively involved in parlaying policies that misallocate capital and which in the long term will seal the economic fate of the West, and perhaps provides the most potent example of good intentions leading to unintended consequences. How can this be?

COLLATERAL DAMAGE IN THE HOUSING MARKET

Given that housing and food are things that every person needs, we should expect that good government policy would aim to keep the prices of these goods as low as possible. Yet, as will be demonstrated, US government policy around housing has encouraged the exact opposite, by specifically, though inadvertently, creating a regime that lives and thrives on house prices being high . . . and rising.

Indeed, over many decades the US government has very successfully convinced the majority of Americans to save individually (the move from defined benefit to defined contribution pension schemes in the 1980s is just one example of this), and has also managed to convince

Americans that the best way to save is by owning a house. As a natural consequence, Americans have tended to over-invest and over-allocate their savings into housing stock (as down payments initially), very often at the expense of other investments, such as stocks and bonds. Despite the well-known benefits of homeownership (painting the fence, watering the lawn), establishing a policy of 'homeownership for all' through a government-sponsored subsidy programme was a colossal mistake.

Housing stock is a unique asset because once one lives in a house it does not generate an income or a cashflow yield. In that sense, the benefit of owner-occupied housing should be viewed as a convenience (non-cash generative) yield. Because there is no cashflow, in order to generate a positive return on housing investment, the government needs to engineer price increases. Naturally this creates a treadmill effect, where prices have to keep going up and up and up in order to keep the positive returns going. These price rises mean ultimately that what the economy ends up with is a bubble that invariably blows: making property less for occupation and more for speculation. More on this later.

THE CASE OF THE SCHIZOPHRENIC HOUSEHOLDER

Previous discussion highlighted how a debt claimant and an equity claimant interact and how each of their actions is guided by their attitudes to risk – leaving the equity claimant loving more variance around the enterprise value, prone to higher levels of debt, and the debt claimant not.

The mirror image is true when looking at the housing market.

Take the case of the rented housing market, i.e. a house owned solely as an investment property. Here there is a landlord who depends on a steady stream of rental income, much as an equity claimant relies on company cashflows. Of course, in both cases (the landlord and the company shareholder) they are also looking for a capital appreciation in their underlying assets. They are also similar in that if the rented property is foreclosed on (the analogy of the company going bust), the landlord can just walk away, losing only the initial amount he put down on the rented property. In this case, the landlord plays the role of the equity claimant.

And, as before, the debt claimant, a mortgage lender – usually in the form of a bank – is left holding whatever is left (worst-case scenario: the lender gets back the home which was itself the collateral).

Like the company shareholder before, the renting landlord loves volatility in the housing market (loves the variance in the enterprise value of the house), as the expected value of his return rises, the larger the variance (volatility) is around the house price; he has a large appetite for leveraging up as much debt as available, and a seemingly insatiable penchant for taking risk. Meanwhile, in the vein of the company debt claimant, the mortgage debt holder (i.e. the bank) does not like a lot of volatility around house prices, and prefers to curb the amount of debt the landlord piles on. And because he wants the certainty that he will get his money back, he keeps the risk-loving landlord's aspirations in check. So far, so good.

The problem emerges when one lives in one's own mortgaged property. Think of this person as the schizophrenic homeowner.

Part of him is in exactly the same position as the company equity holder; in that he loves the house price volatility. For sure, like the company shareholder, he wants the value of his holding (i.e. the house) to rise – the quicker the better. And while there is a very real risk that the house prices could fall, leaving him with negative equity, on the whole most homeowners tend to discount this risk, favouring the notion that (as most people harbour the ambition of owning their own home) the only direction for house prices is up. Implicitly, like the company and like the rented house, this homeowner's house is being viewed as an investment.

The owner-occupier (i.e. the inner landlord), like the equity claimant, prefers more variance in the expected value of the house, i.e. he clearly wants prices to go up, but also prefers the increased variance in the value of house prices. However, there is another part of the homeowner that makes him very different to the company equity shareholder or indeed the rental income landlord.

This is the unique fact that in the case of the company, the most the shareholder could ever lose is the company itself (or in the case of the rental income landlord, his properties) – so what? Life goes on.

But in the case of the homeowner living in his primary residence, if he loses the house he is out on the street. He has no home. In other words, he has a natural 'short' – he is born without owning a roof over his head. And it is because of this short that he will always have the fear of losing his house hanging over him like the sword of Damocles. He *can't* just walk away. Or put differently, if he were to walk away, there is a replacement cost to that. This gives him a very different perspective on his property indeed. In particular, his feelings about volatility, levels of debt risk and risk are diametrically opposed.

What living in a mortgaged home does is to change the contingent claim analysis from simply one of a debt versus an equity holder, to a situation where there are ostensibly three actors: a debt holder (in the form of the mortgage lender or bank), an equity homeowner (much as discussed before) and a newcomer, in the form of a 'satiator' who inhabits the same body as the homeowner. The bugbear is that these three claimants each have their own, and different, profiles for volatility and the level of debt.

In this scenario, the owner of the debt claim (the mortgage lender/bank) and the equity claimant homeowner are no different from what was discussed previously. Specifically, as before, the equity homeowner loves volatility, is drawn to risk and embraces debt, whereas the bank/mortgage lender prefers low volatility, is risk-averse and disapproves of and keeps a watchful eye on the homeowner taking on too much debt.

The schizophrenia of the homeowner takes hold because of his desire to take care of his natural short; i.e. the fear of being homeless. The natural short is illustrated as follows: think of the company equity holder as moving from a position of *flat* (i.e. no company, but no loss to his well-being) to a position where he is *long* a company (i.e. +1, where he owns the company; this is the identical position as the renting landlord). Contrast this with the house owner living in his mortgaged primary residence. Here the move is from a position of being *short* (i.e. −1, nowhere to live; think of it as being someone leaving home at eighteen years old) to a *flat* position of 0 (zero), i.e. with somewhere where you own the home. If the bank were to foreclose he moves to the uncomfortable position of being short housing (−1) all over again.

The wish to satiate the natural short has far-reaching (yet

conflicting) implications for the homeowner's appetite for volatility, debt levels and risk.

In terms of volatility, whereas the equity claimant loves more volatility in house prices (which is why people talk up house prices at cocktail parties and homeownership is a staple at dinner conversation), the satiator is worried that too much house price volatility could lead to negative equity or outright foreclosure (say, if the housing market were to collapse), leaving him homeless. (Of course, he is also fearful in his role as a mortgage payer that volatility around his income could leave him in a worst-case scenario where he would not be able to meet his dues.)

There is a subtle yet important point here. The satiator does not care if house prices go down – in fact he does not care about the volatility of house prices whatsoever, nor about negative equity. He does, however, care about income volatility, in that a fall in his income could lead to his inability to meet his mortgage payments, which could put him on the street. Even as an equity claimant, his willingness to give the house back to the bank is reduced, because he needs to satiate his short – he needs somewhere to live. Furthermore, the value of the option is radically reduced when you are the equity claimant as well as the satiator, rather than just the equity claimant alone. With respect to levels of debt, the satiator will undoubtedly prefer less debt, thereby minimizing the risk of homelessness, but this, as discussed earlier, contradicts his equity-holding, debt-loving side.

The fundamental problem that has arisen is the fact that, over time, government policy in industrialized countries like the US (and, indeed, the decisions of the individual households themselves) has all but completely ignored the risk-averse satiator, catering instead to the risk, volatility and debt-loving equity holder. The result of this blindness has been catastrophic, the full extent of which is yet to be realized.

A DELIBERATE POLICY OF DEMISE

When, as early as the 1930s, the United States government embarked on an aggressive homeownership strategy designed to get millions of Americans on the housing ladder, it did not foresee what it was letting itself in for. Distracted by the siren call of home ownership for all, policymakers inadvertently launched a fifty-year culture of debt and spawned a generation that set their economies firmly down a path of economic destruction. US Census data put the percentage of Americans who owned homes at 47.8 per cent in 1930, 61.9 per cent in 1960, and 66.2 per cent in 2000.

By ignoring the 'satiator' in us all and, instead, feeding the equity homeowner governments have supported an insidious culture of leverage – to the extent that most people in the West now live way beyond their means. Western nations, their governments and households alike, are buried under seemingly insurmountable mounds of debt (the only way out seems to inflate their way out of these obligations). By promoting a strategy of broad homeownership sweetened by subsidy, Western governments have done more harm than good and are actually contributing to the demise of Western economies as a whole.

This strategy has been assiduously accomplished by a dual-pronged strategy of (1) providing incentives for individuals to borrow, through subsidized debt mortgages and tax relief on mortgage interest payments, and (2) the wholly negative gift of providing guarantees to the mortgage-lending institutions. On the latter point, the issue here is that Fannie Mae and Freddie Mac were (implicitly) government-guaranteed but were simultaneously for-profit companies.[15]

It is clearly not the case that *all* subsidy is bad. There are arguably benefits to helping the satiator get a roof over his head, and compelling arguments that homeownership (rather than renting) incentivizes the occupant to take care of the property. And while there is a case for subsidy so that it is easier for more people to buy a house, there is a clear case for limiting its extent. For it is one thing to get someone into a house, but it need not be a mansion that burdens them with too much debt. Which is precisely why lower, subsidized mortgage loans may have been made available in good faith, but not to the correct extent. The motivation for granting subsidized mortgages was well understood to start with, but the interaction between the quasi-private sector (in the form of Fannie Mae, Freddie Mac, etc.) and the government allowed good intentions to spin out of control.

The direct consequence of the subsidized homeownership culture was the emergence of a society of leverage, one where citizen and country were mortgaged up to the hilt; promoting a way of life where people grew comfortable with the idea of living beyond one's means. So deeply engrained has this ideology become that even though it was ruinous debt that led to the 2008 financial crisis, it is debt itself that governments have, in the post-crisis era, offered as the panacea to getting out of the quagmire.

Now, it's true that adding on debt when an economy is vulnerable is not so crazy in the short term. Indeed, such a stance is a classic transition effect. Even if a less leveraged (indebted) society is desirable, if de-leveraging occurs too fast (as in a crisis without intervention) then the risk is that an economy will spiral into depression. This is why governments have to offer more leverage in order to ensure a smooth and orderly transition. But what actually happens in practice is that private borrowing is replaced with public borrowing – of course with the unfortunate outcome that the eventual de-leveraging process can end up being a gift to bondholders and equity holders.

In Britain, America and elsewhere in the developed world, the public policy response to the 2008 financial crisis was almost consistently some combination of slashing interest rates (with the expectation that banks would restore lending levels to individuals so that they could keep themselves afloat by getting further into debt) and national governments themselves taking on more debt.

The other policy option (the one which is profoundly more sustainable and restorative), of tightening belts, cutting consumption and encouraging living within one's means, was not politically palatable, and remains so. When, in June 2009, some of the UK's banks audaciously started marketing 125 per cent mortgages, it served as a reminder of just how little we've learnt and how spellbound society has become on the idea of debt cure-all. Equally astonishing, first-time home buyers in Britain are being told to live on their credit cards; this is the only way to secure a mortgage. A mortgage adviser is quoted as saying: 'My best advice to someone hoping to buy with a small deposit is to live on a credit card. Buy your groceries on it, go out to dinner on it, spend on it what you'd normally spend on a debit card.'

But it's not just in subsidized loans where policy has encouraged an over-leveraged and indebted ethos. In America, homeowners receive an extra enticement to borrow through a government-led tax break on the interest rate they have to pay on their mortgages. The culture of homeownership was not just supported by the surfeit of cheap loans and tax breaks; it was also buttressed by the fact that governments have systematically over time provided debt guarantees for those lending the money.

The perverse effect of these guarantees meant that the loan providers, no longer worried about whether they got their money back or not, felt free to embark on unrestrained and reckless risk-taking, providing a licence to engage in sub-prime lending.

As noted previously, theoretically speaking, a case can be made that sub-prime lending itself is not a bad thing, rather the mispricing of it (making it too cheap and easily accessible) and the risk of over-leverage – when people load up on too much debt. The pertinent question is how much regulatory interference does a society want? There is an argument that if institutions and individuals can go bust – and they are aware of this risk – then it should be left to them individually to make the best decisions for themselves.

Of course for society as a whole the problem is systematic risk with institutions and lots of people going bust at the same time – in a correlated way, leaving a situation where whole economies are negatively impacted. Leverage limits can fix the latter, while better capitalization of institutions, and the risk of individual downside risk (not just institutional risk) for people working in financial institutions down to the level of mortgage broker, could arguably help. One fixes systemic risk, the other fixes agency risk.

It is perhaps no surprise that the industry which over time has shown the greatest appetite for risk is *precisely* the industry that has had the most government guarantees on its debts: the banking sector. In the US, debt guarantees can take the form of FDIC (Federal Deposit Insurance Corporation) insurance[16] on retail deposits or SIPC (Securities Investor Protection Corporation) insurance,[17] which kicks in when a brokerage is closed owing to bankruptcy or other financial difficulties and customer assets are missing. Here SIPC steps in to return customers' cash, stock and other securities. MBIA (Municipal Bond Insurance Association),[18] primarily an insurer of municipal bonds on asset-backed and mortgage-backed securities, has enabled some financial institutions to take punts they most certainly would not have taken had the guarantees not existed, or at least if the guarantees had been correctly priced. The fact that the MBIA was insufficiently capitalized to meet its potential insurance liability was ludicrous – a castle built on sand, if ever there was one! Remember, these banking activities are not illegal. Banks and bankers are simply operating under the policies stipulated by the governments. These are the rules of the game.

As banks have moved from partnership business structure (where the debt obligations are borne by the owners) to publicly owned commercial banks with government guarantees on their debts and deposits if things go awry, there has been a lock-step increase in risk-taking – very often in instruments that were unfamiliar and highly complex. The Bank of International Settlements data indicate that there were around US$100,000bn of outstanding derivatives contracts in the early 2000s, a fivefold growth over the previous decade.

After all, what well-run partnership would risk its shirt investing in the alphabet soup of the derivatives market in the form of CDOs, MBOs or ABSs that are so inherently risky and inadequately understood? They wouldn't. Whereas a bank whose downside is covered by debt guarantees could (and did) indulge itself in an orgy of risk-taking. Remember it is because the management of the banks was now hedged (on the debt side – governments had provided guarantees), and because management was driven by shareholder returns, that the unfettered risk led to the 2008 financial collapse. True, plenty of investors made the mistake – it's not only agency risk that caused the fall; there are many others who fell for the allure of the market.

The fact that the mortgage institutions of Fannie Mae and Freddie Mac had their debts guaranteed by the US government (remember, their debts are everyone's mortgages) meant that the bondholders were lax in policing who they lent to, and therefore they had little incentive to vet people's ability to absorb the mortgage payments, i.e. how risky each individual was. No surprise that the Chinese (one of the biggest holders of Fannie Mae and Freddie Mac debt) called the US government – and not Fannie and Freddie's management – to ensure they'd get their money back when things started to go awry. Had the government-guaranteed safety nets not been there in the first place, Freddie Mac and Fannie Mae bondholders would have been much more vigilant in forcing management to be more diligent in vetting the willingness and ability of their subscribers to repay.

The guarantees – a good idea in the very narrow sense – have proven to be at the root of the financial disaster; a disaster exacerbated by another act of US government 'generosity'. In the UK and Canada if you lose your mortgaged house through foreclosure, you still owe the value of the debt you assumed from the mortgage company. You are still on the hook. But, in many states in America, there is no such recourse. Once you mail in the keys, you owe the mortgage company nothing. The government guarantees will kick in. There is no further consequence – not to the mortgage payer, not to the banks, only to the government (although, of course, many face homelessness). Or so it would seem – after all, when faced with ruin itself, the government will turn around and tax its citizens just so that it can stay afloat.

THE DEATH KNELL OF CAPITAL

Why is all of this relevant? The answer is simple: governments want to drive economic growth, and capital is necessary to drive growth. Yet, capital is being misallocated.

The US government, through interest rate tax breaks and loan subsidies in the form of guarantees, spurs over-investment in its housing stock. This excess demand for housing invariably leads to price appreciation, which itself is made worse because investment in housing assets does not itself yield a stream of cashflow. In fact, the only way to generate a positive return on such an investment is for house prices to rise. This distortion in price signals, in turn, does three things:

First, it ensures that valuable capital is redirected from productive cashflow-generating investments (such as much-needed infrastructure) towards other assets such as non-cash-generative, low-yielding, 'convenience assets' like housing.

Second, the current US housing policies have the paradoxical outcome of making certain that one of the fundamental needs of Americans is, over time, being priced beyond their reach. Because shelter and food are goods that all individuals must consume, sound government policies should aim to keep these prices low. But under the auspices of its 'homeownership for all' policy, the US government encourages many people to over-allocate their life savings into their home asset, which leads to higher average home prices.

Finally, to further compound the problem, the policy approach to housing promotes over-leveraged, debt-financed control of housing assets (as opposed to equity-financed purchase), and this ultimately leads to higher house prices and economic instability. Continuous price appreciation attracts more attention from the general public, which leads to over-allocation of money to the sector, which causes price appreciation, which inevitably, due to the psychology of markets, leads to overshooting of pricing fundamentals over fair value (so that actual prices exceed and no longer reflect true values), and this creates explosive housing price bubbles.

Many argue that there is a case for subsidy, that government guarantees make it easier for more people to buy a house. Once again, the trick is not to stop subsidies altogether, but to instead limit their extent or at least correctly price the additional risk they represent. In practice this would translate into lowering the overall subsidized mortgage capitalization by limiting the notional size of the Fannie Mae and Freddie Mac loans.

But from recent experience what the 'homeownership for all' strategy does is to raise debt levels for countries and individual citizens, and the very houses that are already highly leveraged are further used as collateral to borrow against even more for credit card consumption and non-productive ventures.

Moreover, because society can't unload one big lumpy investment on any one person, everyone, society as a whole, suffers. Which is why 2008 was the first time in the history of the United States that home prices fell nationwide. Although diversification is a fundamental tenet of investment, government guarantees have encouraged millions of people to pile into one asset – housing; and when the housing market goes down a large proportion of society is negatively impacted.

How then should people be evaluating the housing market? Notwithstanding any social impact, in the absence of government subsidies it is not *ex ante* obvious that it is better for someone to own their house than to rent a home and invest the down payment and monthly principal components into a diversified portfolio of stocks and bonds.

As an efficient economic agent, right away I should rent a place so as to keep a roof over my head (i.e. cover the needs of the satiator). With the cash I have left over, I should then evaluate all the potential investment opportunities, be they in stocks, bonds, cash or indeed housing, and if I do decide to invest in housing my options need not be limited to housing investment in my own home market. In other words, it should be perfectly legitimate for me to rent a place in London and chose to buy a place in Florida as an investment.

Governments should be indifferent to whether their citizens rent a place or buy. Instead in the US they drive housing purchases (for example through the Housing for All policies), thereby making property seem at first glance to be the most favourable investment, but actually, via leverage, they are encouraging their citizens to pile into one asset class even when it may not be the best investment decision.

There is another, more subtle point. Under the government guarantee system which propels the rapid appreciation of house prices, the only winners are those who can downsize (downgrade) their housing, or move to a different area, and buy a smaller (cheaper) place. Everyone else loses. Think of a young man who leaves a university dormitory, saves to get his foot on the property ladder (his first purchase a flat or condominium apartment), then graduates to a bigger, more expensive home to accommodate a wife and kids. At each stage he has to pay more to play. Yes, his flat or condo's value may appreciate from the time he buys it (call it T_1) to the time he sells it to upgrade to a larger place (time period T_2), but, remember, he has to pay more in T_2 as the price of the four-bedroom house has also appreciated. This 'escalator' effect continues until the time that the kids go to college. It's a wealth transfer from the younger generation to the older generation as house prices become more expensive.

Only in retirement can the homeowner 'win' as he/she can sell the large house, capture a cash windfall, and downgrade to cheaper accommodation. The only way to get ahead and win in the property game, it seems, is at death or retirement. No wonder that Robert Shiller finds that over the long term the real return on housing is zero – exactly what it should be, given that house prices are essentially tracking demographics.

Demographics being what they are across much of the West – steadily moving to a time when there are more older people than there are younger – there could soon be a time when there will be fewer and fewer people to buy the housing stock as more people reach retirement. More housing stock to be sold, with fewer buyers; a recipe for a collapse in house prices.

THE PROBLEM AT ITS ROTTEN CORE

Across the industrialized West vast amounts of capital are being misallocated. At the core of this misallocation is the breakdown of the relationship between debt and equity holders – a relationship whose fundamental workings are at the centre of a functioning capitalist system and indeed an economy. Despite good intentions, government policies and a broader misunderstanding of the manner in which the financial markets work have contributed to this erosion. Ultimately, this chapter is about the confluence of three key factors, which together have contributed to the misallocation and squandering of capital in the US.

First was the tension in, and then the fundamental breakdown of, the relationship between debt and equity claimants, courtesy of government-sponsored policy in the form of subsidies and guarantees. As detailed earlier, management (as representatives of the equity claimants) does not (primarily) work for debt claimants, which is why it is the core duty of the debt claimants to keep equity claimants (and management) in line. Indeed, it is these checks and balances that make capitalism work. However, US policy has, in particular through guarantees to bondholders, banks and other lenders, eroded the checks and balances, leading to the misallocation and the erosion of capital. As recent experience has now shown, the debt guys who were supposed to play chaperone at the party, supposed to criticize CEO excesses, monitor unshackled risk-taking and police lavish bonuses, instead sat out the dance. In a sentence, debt claimants failed in their fiduciary duty to police the equity holders because they were hedged by public policy.

The debt holders' fiduciary duty is to the people whose cash they are lending to various companies and investments and not to the company shareholders. In a similar fashion, the fiduciary duty of Fannie Mae and Freddie Mac is really to the US taxpayers, with whose money they have been entrusted, and not the people who got the sub-prime mortgaged houses (of course, many of the people who took out mortgages are also taxpayers). The government guarantees have meant that debt holders have increasingly failed to effectively execute their role as minders over the risk-loving equity holders, to detrimental effect.

Second, the misguided belief that asset prices could only, and would only, go up permeated the financial markets as well as the thinking of the average citizen. Even the most sophisticated market participants appear to have suspended decades of knowledge about the vagaries of the market and replaced it with an iron-clad belief that market prices could only appreciate. They were wrong. This erroneous assumption, by borrowers and lenders alike, meant that investors all but discounted a scenario where prices would decline. Worse still, for the same amount of assets they held, borrowers were viewed as over-collateralized.

Third, and as a direct consequence of the last two points, no lenders really knew who they were lending to. A culture that fostered a complete and utter breakdown of the lender–lendee relationship emerged. The zeitgeist manifested itself in the increasing level of complacency regarding debt agreements, which became more and more 'covenant-lite', with lenders imposing fewer and fewer conditions on borrowers. Debt investors increasingly abdicated their responsibilities to vet debt products. As these grew more complex and complicated over time, debt holders increasingly relied on rating agencies and Wall Street financial firms to do their vetting job for them. Of course, the trouble was that rating agencies and, even more so, the banks had every reason to see debt investors invest and get involved – they were themselves incentivized to sell the complex products. The net result was that lenders had virtually no clue who they were lending to; a further erosion in the core lender–lendee relationship.

The housing story is the perfect example of the convergence of these three factors (government subsidies and guarantees; the staunch belief that the asset prices would go up; and a culture of debt (often via securitization) where the lenders had little clue who they were lending to). However, the housing market is by no means the only sector where they collided in a heady mix.

The October 2009 *New York Times* article 'Profits for buyout firms as company debt soared' tells the story of Simmons, one of America's best-known mattress companies.

Over five years the company was bought and sold five times, with virtually every subsequent buyer of the 133-year-old business loading on debt (partly to reinvest in the company and partly to pay itself dividends). As debt got cheaper, and stock prices soared, owners were able to leverage the business even more and take cash out to reward themselves with sizeable payouts. Meanwhile, in a short period of time, the company's debt had grown from around US$164m in 1991 to US$1.3bn in 2009. A fantastic example of a corroded system and the trinity of flawed policies if ever there was one.

True, in this case there were no explicit government guarantees to speak of (although one could credibly argue that the banks that did much of the lending did have government guarantees in place). However, with debt levels spiralling out of control while the equity holders cashed in, it's pretty clear the company debt holders were not doing their duty. It is evident that this trade relied crucially on the asset prices going up (so the private equity businesses that owned Simmons were able to cash in and subsequent owners raise even more debt), and that the true owners of the debt were obfuscated. Perhaps worst of all, many people got paid lots of money while the long-term veracity of the company should have been questioned; not just for companies like Simmons, but for the broader housing market and the economy as a whole. Smart policy should absolutely respond to America's housing crisis. The question is, how should this be achieved?

WHAT'S A GOVERNMENT TO DO?

In a public speech in London in 2009, General Stanley McChrystal, the Commander of the US Forces in Afghanistan, proclaimed: 'You have to start where you are, not where you wish you were.'

By the time this book goes to print, there will have been no short-age of suggestions, debates and, perhaps, even implemented policies on how to get America and much of the developed world out of its housing quagmire.[19] It seems of questionable value, if not quite pointless, to ponder here what the central US housing policy should be; and, in particular, whether or not the US government should intervene in the housing sector in the first place.[20] The reality is, after all, that the US government is already engaged – and heavily so – in the housing sec-tor, supporting it through its subsidy programmes and contributing to many of the market dislocations seen today.[21]

This reality makes General McChrystal's comments seem espe-cially appropriate – US policy now should focus on what to do next *given* that the government is involved in the housing market. What therefore should the government be doing in regards to the housing sector?

Rather than focus on stealth subsidization as it has done, the gov-ernment should now encourage people to assume less debt and put more equity down upfront in the form of down payments which could be matched. This would be the smart thing to do. Ultimately, policy should be focused around weaning the financial system off guarantees for mortgage loans and removing tax benefits on mortgage debt, instead providing a subsidy for equity (cash) down payments. Mean-while, whether it's through the creation of a government-sponsored real estate trust so that the average person could participate in the housing market as an investment without having to 'own' a house, or through encouraging a housing forward market, these are better alter-natives worthy of consideration in lieu of the current system, which is simply another example of good government intentions gone awry.[22]

3

The House of Cards

The previous chapter showed that the biggest failure in the West's long-term financial and economic policies has its roots in the inability and failure of debt holders to fulfil their core fiduciary duty of managing the freewheeling and risk-loving exploits of equity holders. The amount of debt accrued over the last twenty years is fundamental in the story of the structural decline of America's economy. America – individuals, companies and the government – is so indebted, its economic future is fraught with challenge and danger.

The systematic failures outlined previously were undoubtedly magnified by the sheer extent and magnitude of the debt that was outstanding. All this invites questions: how and why did the US get so leveraged? How and why did so much debt build up in the system? The answer to these questions is in two parts: the insatiable demand for debt on the one hand, and the easy supply of debt on the other.

This chapter is about how debt demand was fuelled by people's lack of appreciation of what they actually 'owned' as against what they merely 'controlled'; and, relatedly, how debt demand soared because people did not understand their rights and, more importantly, the rights they were giving up as they piled on the debt.

This chapter is also about the supply of debt. While debt demand rocketed, so too did debt supply; spurred by a range of factors. First was the fact that someone (mainly China) was willing to finance the debt gorge. The Chinese strategy, from very early on, was to adopt a mercantilist approach in relation to the West – acting as volumizers (selling as much as possible, with relatively less regard for the price) rather than profit-maximizers (where profit and pricing are sacrosanct). Indeed, the Chinese were willing to make losses as long as, much like the US Lend-Lease programme construct before it, they could lend into the American market so that, in return, Americans bought Chinese products.

History was repeating itself, this time just with different actors. In much the same way that during the Second World War years the US sold ammunition and guns, providing Europe with what it needed, China sold to the world all that it wanted. The parallel is not simply that the post-Second World War US and China today both made their vast economic fortunes by being manufacturers and the foremost sellers of goods; the similarities run deeper than that. Both China and the US made sure that the buyers of their products also became their debtors. China has very masterfully provided the world (and, ironically, America in particular) with consumer goods while plying it with debt, and keeping it in hock to itself.

Debt also soared on the back of encouragement from policymakers in the richer, industrialized West; the low-interest-rate regime overseen by America's longest-serving Chairman of the US Federal Reserve (or Fed, the US central bank), Alan Greenspan, is just one example of the generous public policy that led to the debt binge. Of course, rapid innovations in how financial products were sold and growth in securitization helped democratize credit, making debt easily available, in one form or another, to very nearly everyone. Finally, more macroeconomic factors such as the sequential decline in volatility around GDP and the similar decline in the variance around personal incomes meant people became erroneously convinced that they could take on more borrowing – and borrow they did.

As the world witnessed, the very costly outcome was the creation of asset bubbles – most memorably, the housing market bubble.

A BRIEF HISTORY OF THE 2008 FINANCIAL CRISIS

It would seem unreasonable to publish a book on capital erosion in the West without spending a bit of time on the calamity of the 2008 financial crisis. It is after all the most recent and glaring example of capital misallocation. Media coverage, be it TV, newspapers, books or other print journalism, have examined in grave detail the minutiae of virtually every aspect of what happened. Nevertheless, there are more philosophical questions which are fundamental to how the events unfolded that still remain under-appreciated.

Lying at the heart of capital misallocation is the issue of debt – its excess, its consumption, its perverse hold on the way Westerners today conduct their lives and manage their economies. Most crucially, leverage has distorted our understanding of ownership versus merely control, and has helped fuel our craving to keep up with the Joneses. But least forgivable is that our ability to gorge on debt – as governments, corporations and individuals – has persuaded us to waste valuable cash resources on objects of little worth. Debt, as a way of Western life, has become an addiction.

KEEPING UP WITH THE JONESES

Not long ago it was pretty easy to decipher who was financially rich and who was poor, the haves versus the have-nots. The family who had a new car, the latest toys and the most advanced gadgets were unreservedly rich. And those that didn't weren't. For the most part, the rich financed their lifestyles through hard-earned income or inheritance. Either way they had money. And even if the rich took out loans, it was only they who had access to them.

Now the picture is much more blurred. Nearly everyone can go on fancy holidays, buy a new car and live in an enviable home; but the mountains of debt they need to do these things show the true state of their finances. And like the US economy itself, millions of families become more adroit at maintaining the façade of being much wealthier than they really are. What they don't understand, in actual fact, is that when it comes down to it, they don't own anything.

POSSESSION IS 9/10THS OF THE LAW

Ask most people who live in a home and have a mortgage on it whether they own their own home and the answer is almost guaranteed to be a resounding 'yes'. Yet it's the wrong answer. Technically speaking, until they have paid the mortgage off, they don't own it. Herein lies the difference between reality and illusion, between ownership and control. This confusion lies not only at the individual level, but also at the heart of government thinking. Here is another manifestation of the misallocation of capital.

A securities lawyer (someone trained to the highest levels of finance, and well versed in the business of debt and equity) was asked how much he would lose on his mortgaged property were the price of the house he lived in to decline by 10 per cent. He remarked condescendingly that, of course, he'd lose 10 per cent, his answer displaying an astonishing degree of ignorance. For clearly, because he has a lien on the property (in the form of mortgage debt) the correct answer should have been 'it depends', for the true figure depends on the amount of leverage he has.[1]

Assuming he lives in a house valued at US$500,000, where he has put down US$100,000 (i.e. his equity, leaving a mortgage debt of US$400,000), should the house price fall by 10 per cent, he will not have lost US$10,000 as he thought; rather he will have lost 10 per cent of the *full* value of the house, i.e. US$50,000. Put another way, the remaining value of his stake is not US$90,000 as he erroneously believes. It now stands at US$50,000.[2]

One suspects that his lack of comprehension is by no means confined to his world alone. If anything, it's likely that if *he* doesn't understand the implications, few will, and actually few, it seems, do. Like most other mortgage-holders, he is under the mistaken impression that he owns the house, whereas all he has is 'control'. Until he has paid the mortgage off completely, he is nothing more than a sitting tenant.

Why is this misunderstanding important? It is important not least because virtually all of Western society, certainly many millions of people, are leveraged in one form or another – be it mortgage debt, auto loans, credit cards, etc., etc. And in much the same way they too are sitting tenants, and they too 'own' nothing. Unfortunately, governments are no more astute.

Consider a simple balance sheet where, like a company, an individual's assets are equal to his liabilities plus his equity. Comparing an individual who has US$1m in assets, no liabilities and US$1m in equity, against one who has US$1.5m in assets, US$500,000 in liabilities and US$1m in equity, most people in the West will say that the latter trumps the former.

To them, it doesn't matter how you finance your asset position; as long as it looks bigger, it is bigger. The trouble is no one focuses on the wider picture; by focusing only on the left-hand side of the balance sheet (the asset side) and conveniently ignoring the right-hand side (the liabilities and the equity), one comes away with a distorted picture of wealth. In exactly the same way that the mortgage-holder acts as if he owns the house, individuals in general have acted as if they truly own their assets, whereas in fact they don't.

True ownership comes only when you own 100 per cent of an asset. And true (complete) ownership is the most stringent form of control. Partial control, which is the case when one has a mortgage on a property, simply grants you access, but you don't own it in the purest sense, precisely because there are states of the world where the asset (or house in the case of a mortgage) can and will be taken away from you.

A CASHLESS KINGDOM

The arrival of credit card culture across the West meant that people made little distinction between what they owned and what they just controlled. The surfeit of credit cards and credit lines deluded people into thinking they had more than they actually did.[3]

The story of the credit crisis is also reflected in the story of how cash, the cold, hard currency of it, has taken a back seat in most people's lives. In Britain, up to the seventies and early eighties, well over half the population was paid in cash, every week, in hand – to buy their food, to pay their bills, and to put what was left aside. The Wages Act of 1986 changed all that. Now employers could (and did) pay into their employees' bank accounts. There were chequebooks before, to be sure, but the boom of the credit card was about to start.

From 1980 to 1990 credit card usage in Britain tripled. According to the British Bankers' Association,[4] as of August 2009, there were 62.8 million (Visa and MasterCard) cards in circulation with credit card debt outstanding equivalent to £63.6bn – i.e. over one card and one pound for every Briton in the country. The US Bureau of Census, 'Statistical Abstract of the U.S., 2008' puts 2005 American credit card usage at 164 million cardholders, with almost 1.5 billion cards in circulation and a whopping US$832bn credit card debt outstanding.

Credit cards were (and are) wonderful inventions. They are easy to use, you don't need to carry money around (thus they are safer) *and* (and this is a big *and*) you can get credit on them. You can spend more than you earn. Of course there were always ways of spending more than you earned before (hire purchase or instalment payments, loans, etc.) but hire purchases were for specifics. You went into a shop, signed the form and came back with a television or a car. Now you could go into any shop, any time and (within limits) buy whatever you wanted to. Suddenly money, what you had, wasn't cash any more. It was the psychology behind the use of chips, rather than money, in casinos. It was desire made corporeal. The population's relationship with its money had undergone a fundamental change. Money seemed no longer a concrete, tangible thing. It had somehow transferred itself into the imagination, into make-believe, the world of wish fulfilment. Live the dream, wasn't that the motto of the nineties?

Similarly, such prosaic transactions as the buying and selling of shares have changed for ever. A British government minister, Lord Myners, a former investment banker, commented that 'We've lost sight of the fact that a share certificate – in fact we don't have them now, it's all recorded electronically – but a share certificate is a right, an entitlement of ownership which carries certain responsibilities.'[5] A share certificate, in other words, represents something solid, something real, something that makes employees people, that has a purpose beyond and more important than varying its electronic life.

The feeling of financial detachment – where we are no longer in touch with our money – has been the precursor to the electronic age, where personal interactions exist not in the home, or on the street, or in your purse, but on the screen. Dreams have become reality. This illusion of ownership, fostered by the debt culture, doesn't end there. So common has debt become that it spawned a society hooked on buying anything whether it has inherent value or not. There was no longer a need to think before you bought.

Like the British lottery winner Viv Nicholson (five husbands, luxury sports cars, fur coats, jewellery, a battle with alcohol, and finally bankruptcy), all people wanted to do was 'spend, spend, spend!'. And spending unleashed on such a massive scale could only lead to one thing – bubbles. The result of all this is that capital in the West has been and is still being eroded. It all boils down to ownership versus control.

In order to truly understand the evolution of capital in the US, and the West in general, and why bubbles matter, one needs to be armed with a few basic tools.

WE NEED TO TALK ABOUT LEVERAGE

Leverage lies at the heart of the credit crisis. At its crudest level, leverage is the same as borrowing, but it raises ordinary borrowing to a different level.

Let's say you want to buy asset A. It costs US$100. Using your money (i.e. equity), you buy it for US$100, and it goes up in value to US$110. You sell it and make US$10, so a return on equity (ROE) of 10 per cent. Now, let's say someone had lent you US$100, and you bought two units of asset A. The two assets that you hold (i.e. your portfolio) go up from US$200 to US$220. You sell the assets at US$220, and pay back the US$100 that you owe. With leverage you have made US$20, whereas without leverage you only made US$10. Apart from the interest charge, which we assume away in this example, you haven't had to use any more of your own money to make more money. And, indeed, the person who lent you the US$100 only gets his US$100 back; he doesn't participate in the windfall gain. In essence you have made US$20 on an equity investment (i.e. cash from your pocket) of US$100, which is a respectable 20 per cent ROE.

So the ability to get more leverage, or, to put it another way, the ability to put a lesser amount of your equity into an investment, increases the potential returns on equity (in the example from 10 to 20 per cent) – an enormously attractive proposition. Not surprisingly, financial institutions were enthralled at the prospect of making returns this way. Many banks were hyper-focused on reducing their regulatory capital requirements, which in other words means these financial institutions were very keen on increasing their leverage – which many saw as the path to greater financial gains.

For financial institutions this was a golden era. They had spent the previous ten years, along with households and corporations in general, borrowing rapaciously. Leveraging up was the catchphrase. But come the credit crunch, and the freeze on lending, the banks had to reduce their leverage, de-leverage, and fast. De-leveraging was essential to open up the credit channel and restore the flow of borrowing and lending. The fastest form of de-leveraging is bankruptcy, whereby the amount of debt available to individuals, corporations, etc. falls sharply towards zero. Although it did not occur in all cases, a number of financial institutions did find themselves bankrupted, e.g. Lehman in the US and the Kaupthing Bank in Iceland. This is how it all went awry, and why. There are two equations that really matter here:

First, leverage (i.e. borrowing) equals assets divided by equity (cash) (L = A/E). Simply put, the leverage of a bank with US$100 of assets, and US$10 of equity is 10:1. The important thing about leverage is that regulators use this measure as one gauge of the amount of risk a bank is taking on. The second key equation, as seen before, concerns the bank's assets, which at all times must equal the sum total of a bank's liabilities and its equity (A = L + E).

Together these equations tell the whole story of the catastrophe that overwhelmed the banks. A simple exposition illustrates what went wrong: consider five episodes in a bank's life over the last decade. Not every bank went through this scenario, but in some form or another many of them did.

Initially, in the first period, the bank has assets worth US$100, liabilities worth US$90, and it has US$10 in equity – noting, as mentioned before, that the bank's assets equal the sum of its liabilities and equity. On this basis, its leverage (assets/equity) is US$100 divided by US$10, i.e. 10:1 (or leveraged ten times over). In other words the bank's owners have US$1 of their own money to every US$9 that customers/debt holders have put in. As detailed in the leverage example earlier, the danger is that the banks can use the additional cash from the leverage to invest and support investments in ever-riskier propositions, with little or no increased return to the bank customer – in other words many banks use 'leveraged' money to raise their returns. Really bank customers and bondholders should charge more to more leveraged banks, but they don't, and they didn't, because of the implicit hedge: the guarantees from the government, e.g. the FDIC.

In a world where credit is cheap, debt readily available, asset prices (such as houses) are rising, and defaults are low, the changes are reflected on the bank's balance sheet in the following (second) period. Say, for example, the value of the bank's assets rise from US$100 to US$200. Assuming in this period the bank's liabilities are still the same (i.e. US$90), the equity must adjust to keep the balance sheet financial equation shown earlier in equilibrium. So with liabilities at US$90, it follows that the equity must rise from US$10 to US$110 so that A = L + E, i.e. US$200. And by extension the bank's leverage – defined, as before, as the assets/equity – is 1.8:1, a solid balance sheet position: less leverage and an improvement on the initial period. (As an aside, for accounting purposes gains (and indeed losses) in assets are not only reflected on the balance sheet, but must also flow through the bank's income statements, so that the change (increase or decrease) in asset value – in our example an increase of US$100 – must be reflected on the balance sheet as a rise in equity of US$100.)

But consider what happens in the third period (the re-leveraging period) when the bank has the opportunity to re-leverage itself. Because the bank is no longer leveraged 10:1, it has more capacity to acquire assets at the current price level and hence re-leverage its balance sheet to a 10:1 ratio. The bank borrows US$900 from the market and purchases US$900 more in assets.

This rise in borrowing is reflected in a sharp increase in the liabilities on the bank's balance sheet from US$90 to US$990 assuming that the bank's equity remains fixed at US$110, so that again A = L + E. Also note, however, that leverage (A/E, i.e. US$1,100/US$110) has gone back up to 10:1.

Now look what happens in the fourth period, when asset prices start to decline (think about the drop in house prices precipitated by the rise in US interest rates in the summer of 2006). In this example, the bank's assets decline from US$1,100 in the third period to

US$1,000 in the fourth – a US$100 decline. On paper this US$100 fall in assets looks relatively innocuous, but see what happens to the bank's leverage. Assuming that liabilities remain constant at US$990, the bank's equity must fall from US$110 to US$10 (mirroring the US$100 decline in assets). Now the bank's leverage has ballooned from a manageable 10:1 ratio to a risky and arguably unsustainable 100:1.

As house prices (and other bank assets) continue to fall, the crisis gathers rapid momentum, leaving the bank only two options: raise more equity (it needs a US$100 equity capital injection to bring leverage back down to a sustainable level, i.e. a 10:1 leverage level) or sell off the bank's assets – which, of course, shrinks the bank's balance sheet, making the banking institution smaller. Clearly if the bank does nothing, leverage is the least of its problems, as it won't be long before its assets are depleted, its equity dissipated, and the bank itself ceases to exist.

As the world discovered in late 2008, the ability to raise new and additional equity finance for banks (and indeed companies and individuals alike) in the climate of the credit crunch became well nigh impossible, leaving banks with basically one option: to sell their assets. But in a world where asset prices are plummeting, consider what this meant.

At the end of the fourth period, the bank has US$1,000 of assets. Desperate to lower its leverage, and save itself from its demise, the bank is forced to sell its assets (for this example, assume the bank decides to sell half of its assets – i.e. US$500). But this decision is happening in a world of ever-falling prices, meaning that the pain is dealt in two places.

First, although the bank attempts to sell assets worth US$500, they are no longer worth that in the market and the bank can only get, say, US$250 for them. Second, the assets the bank sought to keep (i.e. the remainder, worth US$500) are now also only worth US$250, and dropping; a decline that, according to a regulation known as marking-to-market (which aims to reflect as closely as possible the true market value of an asset), must be reflected on the bank's balance sheet.

The net position of the bank, therefore, is that it has US$500 of assets – i.e. US$250 in cash it received from selling half the assets –

and an additional US$250, the value of the remaining assets. The tragedy is that the balance sheet reflects a bank that is now insolvent – it has negative equity (this implies a infinite leverage ratio). Indeed, even if the bank were to use the US$250 garnered from the sale of its assets to reduce its liabilities (i.e. from US$990 to US$740), the fundamental balance sheet equation that A = L + E no longer holds, leaving the bank with negative equity. The bank's assets are US$250, its liabilities US$740; therefore, its equity is *minus* US$490.

This in essence is what happened on an unimaginably grand scale: across different financial institutions, different countries, all around the world. The better part of 2008 was spent de-leveraging highly leveraged positions as banks sold their assets and tried desperately to raise more equity; in many cases, to no avail.

This stylized example shows that when banks manage to a fixed leverage ratio, they exhibit procyclical behaviour such that they are willing to buy more assets when asset prices are high, and they are forced to sell when asset prices are low; they do the exact opposite of the old adage: buy low, sell high.

NOT ALL BUBBLES ARE
CREATED EQUAL

The Domesday Book placed a value on Britain's capital by aggregating the individual and collective assets in the country. In this sense, assets, what they are worth, are at the core of estimating a country's or an individual's capital. But a rapid and indiscriminate rise in the price of assets can lead to a bubble, and virtually without exception bubbles lead to losses. It's just that some are worse than others.

Asset bubbles arise when the volumes of the asset traded and the price quoted for it are so high that they are at complete odds with the actual intrinsic value of the asset itself.

This dry and matter-of-fact explanation of what an asset bubble is does not adequately describe the lunacy, the uncontrollable feeding frenzy that takes place – the sense of compulsion in the air that, at any cost, the asset must be bought.

A good illustration of this would be the tulip mania that occurred in the late 1630s, in which, at its height, the rarest bulbs traded for as much as six times the average person's salary. Tulip contracts were sold for more than ten times the annual income of a skilled craftsman. (In 1635, forty bulbs were sold for 100,000 florins; according to the International Institute of Social History, approximately €1,028,000 in 2002 prices.)[6]

Bubbles are notable for the ferocity (and, *ipso facto*, the insanity) of their growth, and the devastation that they leave in their wake. Effectively functioning economies hone the skill of allocating resources to the most productive uses. What bubbles do is to cause resources (capital, labour, etc.) to be redirected to less optimal and even non-productive investments. Rather than invest in the tangible real economy (say, directly investing in home building), those with cash are persuaded to make quick returns by putting their money into the financial sector (say, by buying home builder stocks), where the chunky yields are made in a fraction of the time and with relatively little effort.

Everything looks fine until the inevitable happens, and the bubble bursts. In the panic that ensues wealth is destroyed as stock prices crash. In fact wealth is destroyed at the point that money is spent on useless, sub-optimal activity – but this is only recognized when the asset prices come down as holders of the assets rush to sell. Moreover, as experience from past bubbles has shown, the economic malaise that takes hold in the form of a recession (or downright depression) is often protracted and always devastating.

But the nature of a bubble, its extent, its severity, the damage it will cause, is determined by (a) the type of asset, and (b) whether the bubble has been financed by leverage in the banking sector or un-leveraged claims (equity or debt) from the capital markets. (While it is possible that some capital market claims are leveraged (such as hedge funds and repo) the majority of investors take un-leveraged positions in equity and debt claims.)

Assets can be classified in two ways: there are productive, cash-producing assets, which generate a constant flow of cash, such as equipment, a railway track, livestock or a company; and then there are other, call them unproductive or convenience, assets (tantamount to consumption), which, though providing a status or aesthetic benefit, do not produce a steady cashflow – think of a painting or a rare stamp. Clearly, an asset that produces a stream of cashflows over time is more beneficial to society as a whole than one which can only derive a rarity or 'eye of the beholder' value and cannot deliver a broad-based reward, and an easily assessed return on capital.

Over time in the US, households, companies and individuals have transformed their financial positions – balance sheets in particular – from positive carry balance sheets (with assets that produce sustained and positive cashflows) to negative carry balance sheets (i.e. with non-cashflow-producing or more intangible convenience-yielding assets such as services or housing, which have no interim cashflows).

More specifically, across America balance sheets have systematically been altered: from positive carry balance sheets, where the cashflows spun off by assets could more than offset the monies needed to service liabilities, and where any incremental windfall would trickle through and go towards building the equity position on the balance sheet on a consistent basis over time, to a negative carry balance sheet, where in order to generate the cash needed to cover any liabilities we need to harvest capital gains by selling assets (preferably at higher prices than when they were initially bought), and the proceeds are then used to cover the interest costs and interim cashflows due on the liabilities. Of course, the obvious problem arises when the asset prices which one can sell at are falling (and are lower than when they were initially acquired).

If you're going to have a bubble, the 'best' type of bubble is a productive asset bubble financed by capital markets. The technology boom of 1995 to 2000 is an example of this. After a time the bubble bursts, the equity values are wiped out, but there is no vicious de-leveraging process that gums up the banking system and causes a credit contraction. The losses can be contained. In addition, when the dust settles, the productive asset eventually returns to its proper valuation and ends up being owned again and put to productive use.

The 'worst' type of bubble is one in unproductive assets financed by banks. Japan's real estate bubble between 1986 and 1990 is one such example. The Nikkei 225, Japan's stock market index, peaked at around 38,915 in December 1989. When the bubble burst, the banking system broke down and good companies (through no fault of their own) were dragged down in its wake, unable to gain access to capital. Land prices and equity prices shed some 60 per cent of their value in the mêlée, leaving a cost of over US$250bn (6.5 per cent of Japan's GDP) for bank recapitalization.

In addition, although the speculation in land made people fortunes, like a true convenience asset bubble it did not add to the productive assets of the country. To this day, most economists agree that this was a bubble from which Japan has never fully recovered.

The 2008 housing crisis is the West's worst bubble since the Great Depression, not simply in its impact on the financial sector but because of its reach into the real economy – people's jobs, companies and the governments themselves.[7] The true scale of the fallout is yet to be felt. What the world is less willing to acknowledge is how the US government has presided over and continues to create and foment the worst kind of bubble: a bubble in an unproductive asset financed by bank debt (the housing bubble).

Here's what Congressman Barney Frank remarked on 27 June 2005 on the floor of the US House of Representatives:

> Those who argue that housing prices are now at a point of a bubble seem to me to be missing a very important point. Unlike previous examples we have had when substantial excessive inflation of prices later caused problems we are talking here about an entity, home ownership, homes where there is not the degree of leverage where we have seen elsewhere. This is not the dot-com situation. We had problems with people having invested in business plans of which there was no reality; people building fibre optic cables for which there was no need. Homes that are occupied may see an ebb and flow in the price at a certain percentage level. But you're not going to see the collapse that you see when people talk about a bubble and so those of us on our committee in particular will continue to push for home ownership.

He is, of course, right. There is always a need for housing. The problem is that bubbles can create and have created 'too much' house demand. He is also right that bubbles are different. However, he is wrong in thinking that the housing bubble is 'better' than the fibre optic bubble. It's worse, much worse, particularly as it is financed by the banking sector rather than by the capital markets, as was the case with fibre optics.

Why should this be so? It's in large part because the traditional banking sector, where financial institutions lent money to companies and individuals, has undergone a transformation which substantially increased the banks' ability to hand out more cash and pile on the debt.

How did this happen? Where did all the money come from?

LIVING IN A DEFLATIONARY WORLD

The tale of how Western individuals, companies and countries became awash with cash is a relatively straightforward one.

Think of it this way: assume there is a company based in the West that produces trenchcoats. It manufactures at home a high-quality trenchcoat at a cost of US$100 and sells it retail for US$150 – making a profit of US$50. Over time, the lowering of communication and transportation costs, technology advances that contribute to 'just in time' inventory management, globalization (greater trade linkages and business networks with countries around the world), and the ability to access cheaper labour, particularly in emerging countries, result in the same coat, of the same quality, being manufactured for just US$10 abroad (while still being sold for US$150 at home), making the company a tidy profit of US$140.

Although some of this profit is reinvested, and a portion may go towards higher wages for Western staff, a proportion of this new-found wealth is placed for safe keeping in a local bank. The bank coffers have now expanded, meaning it has more money to lend – which is what banks are there to do. Mr X, looking to purchase the trenchcoat, decides to borrow the money from the bank, and the bank, flush with extra money, is only too happy to lend. But it's not just Mr X who wants a new coat; it's Mr Y and Mr Z and many others.

Meanwhile, across the water, and thousands of miles away, as demand for the coats rises, more potential coat-makers are attracted to coat-making, which drives wages down and lowers the cost of production. Now the coat can be made for much less – say US$5. Back home, the manufacturer's profit is now U$145. Of course, the relatively cheap labour is one reason why foreign markets tend to be more competitive than the domestic (US) one.

Increased demand, and increased profit, means the company can put more money into the bank, pay its home staff more and pay dividends to its shareholders – everyone has more money. Of course, people are not just buying coats; they are buying flat-screen TVs, cars, toys, watches, on and on and on and on. In other words, the ramifications for manufacturing are huge.

But it does not end here. The staff with extra wages and the shareholders with increased income can now head to the bank and get bigger loans – as debt becomes more democratic. Naturally this leads to a bull run (a rise in value) in assets (equities, bonds, houses, etc.) and the proliferation of household debt.

Early on, the amount of cheap money that flooded the US financial system meant that the US could import non-inflationary growth, where prices did not rise in a detrimental way (hence the failure of America's monetary policy in not better anticipating and addressing this eventuality). The price appreciation across most assets, which cheap financing helped fuel, encouraged the misallocation of capital and labour, as people erroneously over-invested in housing assets and labour talent was sucked away from productive sectors, such as the sciences, and into the financial service sector on Wall Street.

What are other governments doing while all this is going on?

Across the world, governments saw deflation, i.e. the price of goods and services going down. Wages, transport costs, telecommunications fees and the prices of production were all falling. As their natural response in a deflationary environment is to cut interest rates and to keep them low, they help ensure that liquidity – the amount of money sloshing around the system – remains high. And as interest rates remain low, people choose to spend rather than park their money in low-interest-bearing bank accounts and this, of course, means more cash is pumped into the economy.

What some tend to forget is the central role of a commercial bank. It is not there to hoard money and keep it safe in a bank account – its purpose is to lend money, and all the while to turn a profit. However, the more money the banks have, the greater the pressure for them to lend, and the further they must look for borrowers (this would later come back to haunt them).

It sounds good, having a lot of cash floating around; the trouble is, all this newly created money needed to find a home. And find a home it did.

To begin with consumption went up (for example, people took more holidays and bought more consumer goods – in the US alone, consumption rose from around 65 per cent of GDP to 72 per cent of GDP in the past decade) and demand for assets (cars, houses and other items one can borrow against) also went up. As the value of assets rose (thanks to demand), so too did the amount of collateral one could borrow against them.

Yet with more money flooding the system, and ever more pressure to find places for the money to go, people's demand was outstripping asset supply. There are, after all, only so many houses in New York at any given time, and most tangible assets (such as cars) take a while to come off the production line. Money had to find a new home. This is where true financial engineering was born.

By 2000, financial institutions found themselves at the crossroads. People and investment funds, with a surfeit of cash, were desperate to find new places to invest. Such had been the excess and the availability of cash over the last decade that traditional assets were pretty much all taken. Fund managers were begging banks to innovate and create new avenues for investment.

The banks, desperate not to lose custom, had to come up with a solution – fast. Money managers – those who run pension funds, hedge funds, private equity funds and banks – live or die by the returns that they generate. End-of-year bonuses are simply calculated as a function of how much one brings in. So, banks pondered, what was it that these money managers could be persuaded to invest in that they had not invested in before?

The answer lay in areas that investors and banks had shunned for decades – most notably a section of the (American) housing market known as sub-prime.

Traditionally, the last way that investors would look to garner returns was by lending to those either whose credit rating was low or who had none at all, i.e. those people most likely to default on their loans. But as the novelty of repackaging standard financial instruments such as stocks and bonds took hold, the banking industry magically transformed bad debtors into viable investments. Everyone was happy – the pension funds had new, reconstituted assets to invest in, through innovation the banks satisfied their clients' demands and earned their bonuses, and more people got a foot on the housing ladder (as those who once would have been refused mortgages were granted them for the first time). Money was gathering momentum. And this fell right in line with the US government's policy of targeting housing.

THE CONTAMINATION OF THE BANKING SYSTEM

Virtually every country today, whether rich or poor, whether independent or subject to a foreign government's control, has a central bank charged with overseeing and regulating its financial health.

It is that bank's responsibility to maintain the stability of the national currency and the supply of money. In this sense, central banks control the source and speed of money. The amount of money in the system is the product of two concepts: the stock of money and the velocity of money. The stock of money is decided by the central bank. It controls the stock of money by raising and lowering interest rates. In the US, like other places, the way it works is via open market transactions: the Fed buys, or sells, securities in the market to reduce, or increase, the amount of money in the system.

Historically, the velocity of money was controlled by the commercial banks, trusts, thrifts (also known as savings and loans associations, these institutions take in savings deposits, on the back of which they make mortgage loans), etc. In a fractional banking system, because a bank is obliged to hold only a fraction of the deposit (via the reserve requirement), and can loan out the rest, this causes total loans made to be multiples of the initial deposit. For example, if you put US$100 into your current or checking account, your bank can then make US$1,000 in loans to businesses or individuals. Those businesses will deposit some of the cash in their corporate account, so then that bank now gets to make loans in multiples of that infusion. The quicker the money moves around the system, dictated by how easily the banks make loans, the more money is available in aggregate.

Furthermore, it is (or was) the responsibility of the central bank to supervise financial institutions to ensure that they do not behave recklessly or fraudulently, and it has sufficient statutory power to act swiftly if and when they do. Together with the Securities Exchange Commission (and other such regulatory bodies), central banks are the financial policemen.

Central banks have control over the banking system in three ways:

First, through rate-setting, they directly set the (short-term) interest rate, which itself influences the market determination of long-term deposit and lending rates. Second, they use open market operations (buying and selling bonds in the marketplace) to regulate the amount of money circulating in the national economy. By buying bonds they are able to increase the money supply, by selling bonds they are able to reduce it. Third, they set the reserve requirement – i.e. the amount of money that banks are required to set aside at the central bank.

By raising or lowering rates, buying or selling bonds, and increasing or decreasing the reserve requirement, central banks are able to influence the amount of money on-lent by the banks into the wider economy. Ultimately each of these tools (alone or in unison) is designed to aid central bankers in what has become their central role, which is to manage, control, and combat inflationary or deflationary pressures. Inflation-watching became the policymakers' and central bankers' obsession, to what seemed to be the near exclusion of all other responsibilities. Across the world, inflation-targeting (i.e. keeping inflation measures bound between strict constraints) became the fad, and academics, advisers and researchers spent an inordinate amount of time trying to devise the optimum inflation measure.

Indeed, over his eleven-year tenure as Chancellor of the UK's Exchequer, for Gordon Brown keeping inflation low became the yardstick by which he judged his (and Britain's) economic success, with the promise that 'we will never return to the old boom and bust'. Such was the fixation with inflation, that should the targets ever be breached, the Bank of England was required to write an open letter to explain in grave detail why and how it had failed. Meanwhile, across the Atlantic, just as Fukuyama had predicted the End of History, the Federal Reserve's Chairman, Alan Greenspan, was predicting a world without inflation and warning of the risks of deflation. As he saw it, in the new globalized era, characterized by an ever-expanding labour force (as hundreds of millions of Chinese and Indian workers came on stream), the fear was that as both wages and the price of goods were driven downwards, deflationary pressure would take the place of inflation as being the key destabilizing factor.

Whether this fear was well founded or not, the point is that policy-makers saw the inflation–deflation tradeoff as being the key metric by which economic success and their own career success would be judged. The unfortunate (and costly) consequence of this was that their essential supervisory and regulatory duties were jettisoned, leaving a regulation-lite world governed by toothless outsourced supervision, and/or supine self-regulation. This was a stark example of the corruption of the relationship between the private sector and the government, piled on to the misunderstanding of the importance (and innate workings) of asset values. Gordon Brown's decision to split the Bank of England's traditional role into two separate and independent bodies – one there to set interest rates, the other (the Financial Services Authority) to regulate and supervise the financial marketplace – was a classic example of this.

There is clearly a strong case for central banks to look out for market mispricings and hubris in asset markets and to react. This is the same observation that should be made on the regulation side, which is why the two entities should reside together. Yet what was created was one organization, a rate-setting entity (the Bank of England) that monitored daily every twist and turn of the British macroeconomy, and another organization (the Financial Services Authority) almost completely de-linked from the realities of the economic workings that would threaten to destroy the economy. What they couldn't see, they couldn't know, and therefore couldn't act upon. In this vacuum, another player was bound to step in.

In the US, Chairman Greenspan, as a convert to and proselytizer for self-regulation, oversaw the rise of what came to be termed the shadow banking system. This was the network of hedge funds, private equity firms and off-balance-sheet entities that were outside the purview of the Fed. There is nothing inherently wrong with this, except that what eventually happened was that the velocity of money (such a key component of a functioning economy) was no longer wholly set or controlled by the Fed, but increasingly by the private sector.

As hedge funds grew in power and wealth, so too did the amounts of money sloshing around the system. Through a complex web of new-fangled financial instruments known as derivatives, which arguably no one really understood (Warren Buffett, one of the most respected and savvy investors of our time, described them as 'time-bombs'), the shadow banking system was able to leverage at an astounding rate. The US$100, which could in the past be leveraged up to US$1,000 (i.e. leveraged ten times), could now be leveraged to astronomical figures – your US$100 could now be leveraged sixty times (i.e. to US$6,000). This was turning water into wine; lead into gold, alchemy of the most potent kind.

What is more, such was the Byzantine nature of the derivatives complex that no one actually appreciated the size and indeed the whereabouts of this labyrinth of debt.

Perhaps the most spectacular unmasking of this ruse occurred on 2 December 2001, when Enron (run by the 'smartest guys in the room'), seen as the epitome of modern-day American industrial might, was forced to file for bankruptcy.[8] What killed the golden goose was not the US$13.15bn of debt detailed in its financial statements and accounts, but rather the US$13.85bn of off-balance-sheet and contingent liabilities, debts that were craftily hidden in the (very legitimate) off-balance-sheet entities known as special-purpose vehicles; making the total company debt closer to US$27bn!

What these special-purpose vehicles allowed them to do was tantamount to the ordinary man on the street being able to borrow without it appearing on his credit report. It must be said that this imaginative interpretation of financial reality is not confined to the wild and woolly world of the shadow banking system.[9]

Governments, too, use off-balance-sheet wizardry to make their accounts look better. For instance, the official records outlining the financial position of governments tend to place some of the major debt obligations of a government in off-balance-sheet entities, thereby masking the true position of the government debt burden. This means the debt-to-GDP numbers can and very often do look much better than they truly are. Headline numbers for the UK, for example, do not adequately reflect the multibillion-dollar long-term debt obligations in the form of pension payouts that the government knows it owes, and this closely guarded secret is even worse in Europe.

As the financial success of the shadow banking system grew, so did its muscle. Alongside seasoned global policymakers – such as the Indonesian Minister of Finance, Sri Mulyani Indrawati, and the Bank of Mexico's Governor, Guillermo Ortíz – Mohamed El-Erian, the CEO and CIO of Pacific Investment Management (the largest bond investor in the world), and Robert Rubin, a former stalwart of Goldman Sachs and a Citigroup Senior Counsellor, were recruited to a select International Monetary Fund committee.[10] The committee's mandate was to assess the adequacy of the Fund's existing framework for decision-making and advise on any modifications that might enable the institution to fulfil its global mandate more effectively. It is this shadow banking community which eventually nudged the Fed out of its pole position and (ostensibly) took charge of the velocity of money. [11] Nor is it active just in the policymaking sphere; the shadow banking leveraged system has also infiltrated the banking system (previously the non-leveraged lending business) and virtually all areas in which it could make money.

All in all, the housing sectors in the United States and also in Europe have been stealthily financed by the leverage of the banking system, which would carry severe costs when it came to de-leveraging. So if a pension fund invested US$1m (un-leveraged) in a company and then the company failed, all that would be lost is US$1m; whereas if the banks invested the same US$1m, such was the multiplicative factor that the actual value lent to the market was more like US$10m. The crux of the problem in this case was who it was who lost the US$10m. With the government bailouts it was clearly the whole economy that suffered – taxpayers included.

More broadly, what this all means is that de-leveraging and withdrawing the money from the battered system would prove much more painful and damaging, as witnessed in 2008/2009. So what triggered the crisis?

HOUSES BUILT ON SAND

Even as late as spring 2007 (just months before the financial storm hit in earnest), no one could have predicted the severity of the crisis that was about to ensue. Sub-prime lending had been the key factor in the rise of homeownership and the demand for housing in the US. In the ten years between 1994 and 2004, overall US homeownership rose from 64 per cent to an all-time high of 69.2 per cent. But as the old adage states, all good things must come to an end. The days of the financial and housing boom were numbered.

In 2007 the sub-prime market, so favoured up to this point, collapsed. This would be the catalyst that would herald the beginning of the end of the post-war capitalist financial model as we know it. What began as mortgage defaults swept like a raging wildfire throughout the financial landscape, leaving utter destruction in its wake. By the end of 2007, nearly 1.3 million US housing properties were subject to foreclosure proceedings, a rise of nearly 80 per cent from 2006.

Try as governments might to tame it, towards the end of 2008 the returns on the S&P equity index equalled the single lowest-ever recorded figure (matched only by the performance in 1931, at the depth of the Great Depression) for 182 years (i.e. from 1825 to 2007). The jig was up. But what exactly happened?

The sub-prime debacle is very often portrayed in the media as a comparatively recent aberration from the norm, but in fact its antecedents (i.e. lending money to those who ostensibly cannot afford it) stretch back into the 1950s, with the government-backed construction of Levittown, USA.[12]

Built initially for returning Second World War veterans and their families, through government-financed loan programmes, prospective homeowners could buy a Levittown home with little or no down payment. Best of all, the mortgages were often cheaper than renting an apartment in the city. The ideal of Levittown marked the spread of suburbia throughout good-life America, as well as being a shining example of encouraging people to own a house whether they could afford it or not – a belief which reached its apotheosis in the 2008 sub-prime saga. True, in theory, if it had been done right it might have helped people afford their own home, a roof over their head; the trouble was that it wasn't done right at all.

Despite the opprobrium heaped upon the bankers for their enthusiastic role in the financial wizardry around the sub-prime industry, the responsibility must also lie with well-intentioned policymakers stretching as far back as the post-Second World War period. Well-intentioned policies also created vested interests, which then ran out of control. Once the financial sector was able to benefit from the subsidies meant for homeowners, the process of lobbying for and maintaining these policies was set in motion – and, not long after, it became the norm.

In the run-up to 2006, lax lending standards, easy terms on loans – even for first-time borrowers – and climbing house prices enticed borrowers to take on ever larger debt burdens, deluding them into thinking that they would be able to refinance their mortgages at favourable terms, without much ado. In the midst of the boom-times, everyone came to the party. The banks posted record profits, investors locked in substantial gains, and the average man boasted of exotic holidays, summer homes and second family cars. Remember, from the earlier example, the procyclical nature of bank management of its leverage: as asset prices went up, banks were enabled.

Well before the sub-prime fiasco, the US government had established Fannie Mae and Freddie Mac, which were precisely mandated to provide easy access to subsidized home loans and mortgages for hard-working Americans. Keen to win votes, governments ensured that no one was left out; wanting to be seen to help spread the wealth. If anything they implicitly backed the culture of risky lending.

The mandate came from on high, with an increase in homeownership a stated goal of both the Bush and the Clinton administrations (and even that of Jimmy Carter). In 1996, for example, the Housing and Urban Development Agency[13] instructed Fannie Mae and Freddie Mac to provide at least 42 per cent of their mortgages to borrowers with incomes below the average in their respective areas. In 2005, this target was increased to 52 per cent.

An additional proviso was that Fannie and Freddie were to provide 12 per cent of mortgages to borrowers with less than 60 per cent of their respective geographical area's median income. What this meant was that by November 2007 Fannie Mae was holding sub-prime mortgages worth almost US$56bn.

While laudable in its intent, the 'housing for all' approach had met with vigorous protests even from the early days. On 10 September 2003, for example, in an address to Congress, the US Congressman Ron Paul[14] noted that government policies which encouraged lending to people who couldn't afford to repay loans would inevitably lead to a financial bailout. Prescient he might have been (going as far as to introduce a bill to abolish these policies), but it is unlikely that even he could have foreseen the scale of the coming destruction.[15]

By the time the series of interest rate hikes kicked in in 2006, the cracks of the crisis had begun to show. The US housing bubble, which had been inflating over the preceding five years, was about to burst. As interest rates marched higher and house prices started their decline, mortgage refinancing became near impossible, leading to the inevitable consequence – house by house, street by street, in a thousand towns all across America, people began to default on their mortgages. Sub-prime and adjustable-rate mortgages were the first to go as interest rates reset higher. The lowly rated households that had been transformed into higher-rated must-haves (i.e. the BBBs that had become single-A-rated) could no longer pay their monthly dues.

It's fair to say that at the outset no one seemed particularly perturbed. Indeed, many shared the opinion of the US Federal Reserve Chairman, Ben Bernanke, when on 28 March 2007, in a speech on the economic outlook before the Joint Economic Committee of the US Congress, he was quoted as saying:

> Although the turmoil in the subprime mortgage market has created severe financial problems for many individuals and families ... [a]t this juncture ... the impact on the broader economy and financial markets of the problems in the subprime market seems likely to be contained ... We will continue to monitor this situation closely.[16]

Yet the ensuing effect was to be shattering. In the same month, the value of sub-prime mortgages in the US was estimated at US$1.3tn, with over 7.5 million first-lien sub-prime mortgages outstanding.[17] By July 2007 (just four months later), although the sub-prime-type mortgages represented only 6.8 per cent of the outstanding loans, they represented 43 per cent of foreclosures. By October, around 16 per cent of sub-prime adjustable-rate mortgage loans (known as ARMs) were either ninety-days delinquent or in foreclosure proceedings – roughly triple the rate of 2005. And things would only get worse.

Indeed, the following year the picture was even bleaker. In January 2008 the delinquency rate had risen to 21 per cent and by May 2008 it was 25 per cent. By August 2008 the US mortgage market, estimated at US$12tn, had approximately 9.2 per cent of loans either delinquent or in foreclosure. Invariably the banks suffered as well.

By the middle of July 2008 major banks and other financial institutions around the world reported losses of almost US$500bn. And in just the ten months between January and October 2008 shareholders in US companies lost a seismic US$8tn, as their holdings declined in value from US$20tn to US$12tn.

With the crisis in full swing, Fannie Mae held US$324.7bn of Alt-A type mortgages (mortgages that required little or no documentation of a borrower's finances), and Freddie Mac held around US$190bn of the same class of mortgages. Combined they held more than 50 per cent of the US$1tn of Alt-A mortgages. In March 2008 an estimated 8.8 million homeowners – i.e. roughly 10.8 per cent of total US homeowners – had zero or negative equity (implying that their homes were worth less than their mortgage). Congressman Paul's bailout prediction was about to come horribly true.

Easy credit and a consumption boom led to over-building, and like a classic bubble prices went well beyond valuations and eventually exhausted all sources of demand – there were no buyers left. It was this mismatch between demand and supply, the surplus inventory of homes, and the tightening of credit in the summer of 2006 that caused home prices to decline.

The myopic, if not foolhardy, belief that interest rates would forever stay low, and that house prices would continue to rise, encouraged millions of borrowers to buy into loan schemes they ultimately could never really afford. Naturally, increasing foreclosure rates increased the supply of housing inventory available.

The sub-prime crisis has affected the American psyche as much as the American purse – and indeed that of the world. It shattered the illusion of prosperity and left people dumbfounded. The poorest pockets of America had been led to believe that they could own their own homes, and thus share in the American dream, only for those hopes to be dashed, and the reality to sink in that it was just a pipedream.

4

Labour Lost

The editor of one of the world's leading newspapers tells the story of how a few years ago, in one of its daily editions, it carried a feature on China's President Hu Jintao. It was acknowledged to be a fair and accurate (if innocuous) summary of his career. Each new edition is printed in China overnight and shipped across the country in the early hours of the morning.

This particular edition was duly printed, but when it landed on people's doormats or on the shelves of the shops, the page containing the article on Hu Jintao was missing. As the story goes, in a matter of hours an army of workers had been corralled to remove the offending page. Assuming that it took five seconds (top speed) to tear out the page in each of 2 million papers, this exercise would have required around 3,000 man hours (1,000 people working three hours each), at short notice. Not to mention the fact that the newspaper had to be read and vetted, the decision made, and instructions sent out before all this happened.

Only in China.

LABOUR IS BEING MISALLOCATED

Thus far, the discussion has focused on the West's misallocation of capital. However, its labour too has been misallocated, again to the West's detriment. Across the industrialized West, labour – a key ingredient in economic growth – is being misallocated in at least three ways.

First, the rapid introduction of pension plans in the period after the Second World War inadvertently led to a widespread mispricing of labour contracts that, in turn, has made the cost of labour look cheaper than it actually is. The postponement of these hidden pension costs to the future – essentially delaying the cost of labour – is coming to haunt the West now.

Second, the broad societal shift to favour the service sector over the productive industry has created a society where exorbitant salaries and rewards are stacked in favour of those whose societal benefits seem relatively narrow (sportsmen, CEOs, hedge fund managers), and less towards sectors with arguably broader societal gains (e.g. doctors, nurses, teachers); an exodus driven by bad labour-pricing signals.

Third, laws governing the global migration of labour are becoming ever more stringent, and more restrictive. America was always known to be the destination of the best and the brightest, but today government policies are making it much more difficult to draw on the global pool of talent. All to the USA's detriment.

QUANTITATIVE EASING

There are two aspects of labour that affect a country's ability to excel as an economic market: one is quantity and the other quality – and on both counts the West is holding a losing hand. In the first instance, it is a matter of simple demographics.

Based on the sheer size of their populations the West's most obvious challenges come from China and India. With their inherently overwhelming numbers, China and India were always going to give the West a run for its money, particularly once they figured out the key policy ingredients for economic success. The West faced, and continues to face, demographic threats on at least two major fronts.

First, in the West, the post-war baby boomers born between 1946 and 1964 failed to produce anywhere near as many children as their parents. In the 1980s demographers began to highlight the very real prospect that by the mid-2000s there would not be enough young people to take their parents' place in the labour market – the baby boomers who drove America forward in their furiously productive years would now be past their prime. That the population of the West was ageing and declining was bound to have knock-on effects on its ability to compete economically.

Second, a characteristic of emerging economies was (and still is) the fact that a large proportion of their populations is young. For many countries, and for many years, as much as 50 per cent of their populations have been under the age of fifteen, as compared to around 18 per cent in the West – a well-stocked pool of labour, ready and willing to learn new skills and man new industries. With estimates forecasting that emerging economies could add as many as 2 billion additional people to the global middle class by 2030, the inordinate demand they will generate will provide opportunities for this enormous labour supply. It is worth noting that policies such as China's long-running one-child edict will ostensibly alter dependency ratios, but for now the West faces a sea of rising talent.

Ultimately, owing to healthcare innovation and dietary improvements, people are living longer. But simultaneously the young are having fewer children, so that together the work pool is shrinking and this inevitably will lead to a contracting GDP pie. While it's true that healthier people can work longer, an ageing population adds a burden on social services, and will have enormous implications for health services and private and public pension schemes.

To make matters worse, despite their good intentions, many governments again are guilty of pushing policies (this time in the form of pension plans) that have helped misallocate resources and once again have left industrialized nations poised for a great economic freefall.

DEMOGRAPHIC TRENDS

In 1997 a ninety-year-old Alec Holden placed a bet with the book-makers William Hill that he would reach the age of 100. William Hill gave him odds of 250-1. In April 2007 he won the bet. As he picked up the cheque William Hill announced that they would no longer offer such generous odds – raising the target for such wagers to 105. Said a spokesman: 'If you're prepared to bet you'll live to 105, you'll probably be offered odds of 150-1 – to get the full 250-1 offered to Mr Holden, you've now got to get to 110 – and you can only wager up to £100.'

Mortality tables – a schedule worked out by actuaries which estimates the probability that a person will die before their next birthday at each age – confirm William Hill's thinking. In October 2009, for example, Danish researchers on ageing argued that more than half of the babies born today in developed, industrialized nations will live to see 100. In a report in the journal *Lancet* they noted that life expectancy has been increasing since 1840 and that since 1950 the probability of living past eighty years of age has doubled for men and women across developed countries. The United Nations central forecast for rich countries is that by 2050 one in three persons will be a pensioner, and nearly one in ten will be over eighty years old. Centenarians (those a hundred years or older) are the fastest-growing segment of the American population, increasing from around 3,700 in 1940 to now around 100,000 on record.

All this is saying is that the West is getting older. The less productive and more expensive to maintain this growing ageing population becomes, the greater the burden on already stretched fiscal balances, and of course on an economy overall, raising the prospects of labour shortages, lower productivity and invariably slower economic growth. Of course, the challenge of ageing populations is not just the bailiwick of the rich, industrialized world. The UN's latest biennial population forecast estimates that the median age for all countries is due to rise from today's twenty-nine to thirty-eight by 2050. And the fact that women everywhere are having fewer children (the current global average is 2.6 children per woman, down from 4.3 in the 1970s, and expected by the UN to further decline to just 2 by 2050) means the balance will, before too long, certainly tip in favour of the aged.

Nevertheless, despite the bleak global population dynamics, the immediate challenge is strikingly in the domain of the industrialized nations. The trouble is that although there is some tacit acknowledgment that the costs of a large pensioner population are huge, few are facing up to the reality of just how monumental these hidden costs truly are. They are bound to overwhelm the economies of the West.

WELCOME TO DETROIT

In the summer of 2008, in New York, a business journalist asked the harassed CEO of a large international bank what he thought about the global financial meltdown. His telling response: 'Welcome to Detroit.'

In its heyday in the 1950s Detroit, Michigan, was the automobile capital of the world, home to the big three – Ford Motor Company, General Motors and Chrysler – and with a population of 2 million people ranked as the fifth-largest city in the United States. Such was the reach of the car industry that one in every six working Americans was employed directly or indirectly by it. This behemoth that once straddled the American economy now lies in virtual ruins, as witnessed by the bankruptcy of Chrysler and the purchase of the once indestructible General Motors (global sales leader for seventy-seven consecutive calendar years from 1931 to 2007, manufacturer in thirty-four countries, employer of 250,000 people, and maker of 8.5 million cars in 2008) by the Italian motor company Fiat, an event unimaginable just a couple years earlier.

Today Detroit's population has fallen to just 800,000 residents, and many of the glistening buildings that once adorned the city's skyline have been reduced to rubble.[2] Whether it was the advent of automation that replaced the car industry's large workforce, or the increase in competition from car manufacturers in Japan and Germany, one thing is for sure: Detroit, and the car industry that sustained it, will never be the same again. These reasons aside, a major factor in the decline of America's motor car industry was the growing and unsustainable burden of its pension obligations.

THE PONZI SCHEMES THAT ARE THE GOVERNMENT-SPONSORED PENSION PLANS

There is nothing inherently wrong with people putting cash aside for their old age. Everybody needs a pension. After a lifetime of work, and contributing however small an amount to the wealth of the nation, it is only fair that in their later and non-productive years their basic needs are somehow met. The difficulty arises when the government builds an elaborate matrix that is predicated on a system with little intrinsic value.

Forget Bernie Madoff, forget Allen Stanford, the biggest Ponzi scheme has got to be the looming car crash that is Western pension funds. And like any well-run Ponzi game, its results will be devastating. It will all end in tears.

Ponzi schemes are named for the notorious 1920s conman Charles Ponzi, who engineered a scam that paid early investors returns from the investments of later investors. A plausible Ponzi scheme can run 'profitably' for a number of years, but in the end the new monies flowing in can never meet the growing spread of the old demands. In the end a Ponzi scheme will always come unstuck.

Governments across the Western industrialized world have, through pension funds, very successfully sold their citizens something that they can never possibly finance. In the erroneous belief that pensions would be on offer later in life, individuals chose to increase their consumption, and this contributed to a depression in savings. While it is true that pension schemes have evolved structurally – gradually shifting the onus of saving for the future from the government on to the individual – the fact remains that the state still bears a crippling amount of the cost. In the US, for example, the 2008 retirement bill (the public pension liability calculated at pension schemes' own discount rates) was a rapacious US$2.1tn – eating up around 15 per cent of GDP. An ever worse situation looms in Britain, where the 2008 annual pension charge is around US$1.3tn (64 per cent of GDP), and across much of continental Europe – in Germany, for example – the government's pension expenditure trumps even the country's wage bill.

The new monies flowing in from the incomes of the young workforce of today will never be able to meet the financial demands of the ever-growing army of pensioners. They are increasingly faced with the grim reality of having to pass on less cash to many more people. Across the industrialized world, the young are now facing the unsavoury prospect of 'double taxation', having to put money aside to pay for current retirees and also having to save for their own retirement. The net result is lower consumption and higher savings (or at least in theory it should be – we now know that in the early 2000s figures for household savings in America became negative).

In its most simplistic form the value of a pension fund is equal to the pension assets (i.e. the cash that's flowing in plus the value of the

investments the pension fund holds) minus the future pension obligations that have to be paid out. Although they are *future* liabilities,
they are assessed in today's money by a discounting formula that trans-
lates the future obligations into current monetary terms. This formula
sets today's value of the liabilities as equal to the future value of the
pension requirements divided by an interest rate which captures the
difference between today's money and tomorrow's; because US$100
tomorrow is worth less than US$100 in the pocket today.

Clearly, overall pension fund losses can occur when the assets decline
or the liabilities grow so much that they are no longer covered by
what is in the pot.[3] The double-whammy is when both happen simultaneously.

There have already been harbingers of the dire things to come. For
instance, the British pension fund collapse (2000–2002); the German life
insurance fiasco in 2000 after the equity bubble, with Guaranteed Annuity Obligations (GAOs); the failure of the North American life insurers
in 2008 to properly hedge variable-rate annuities; and, of course, the
swathe of bankruptcy filings from steel, cars and airline corporations
that rippled across American industry, brought to their knees by pension
deficits over the last several decades. The common theme was mispriced
optionality, intergenerationally and between employer and employee;
one group promised a payment to another without giving due consideration to how it would make that future payment.

The most recent example has been the 2008 sub-prime crisis. The
collapse in house prices (and of course other investment assets as
well) substantially reduced pension assets. This fall in pension assets
was exacerbated by historically low interest rates as this virtually
eliminated any expected income on bond holdings. Moreover, because
of the discounting formula, the lower interest rate environment (set to
aid the faltering economy) also caused pension liabilities to balloon.
All in all, pension funds have been left underwater. The situation is
made worse by concentrated flows, as baby boomers, who had piled
into stock investments helping make the equity markets soar, retire, at
which point money flows out of the riskier stock markets into 'safer'
bonds. As demand for bonds rises, so do bond prices, while conversely bond yields (interest rates) decline. This causes future pension

liabilities (calculated on a present-value basis, so that future debt is discounted by lower yields) to climb, and pension deficits to widen. The net effect, of course, is that the future stream of pension payments (the annuity) is not much of anything when the time comes.

According to an August 2009 report by the actuaries Lane, Clark & Peacock, Britain's biggest company pension funds face their largest shortfall ever as a result of the financial crisis. They estimate a pension fund deficit of more than US$160bn – more than double the US$65bn estimated for these companies a mere twelve months previously.[4]

If there is one lesson to be learnt from past experiences, it is that the damage inflicted by mispricing optionality – the government selling pension funds that it will not be able to fund – has severe implications not just for the financial markets but also for the fabric of the real economy, by putting people out of work and deploying trillions of dollars away from productive investment and into propping up pension funds and other financial institutions.

The frightening thing is that all the hallmarks of the 2008 financial crisis, the elements that brought the global economy to the brink – faulty financial engineering, mispriced options and misallocated resources – can be seen in the unfunded pension benefits problem. Furthermore, looking at the fallout from mispriced options, in the selling of variable annuities, the selling of derivative products and sub-prime mortgages for example, there is no rational reason not to believe that the selling of government-engineered pension schemes will not be next. Indeed, government has added a layer of capital misallocation and mispricing to companies because of government pension funds.

THE GOLDEN YEARS

Today, virtually all Western countries have government-sponsored defined benefit plans in place, and virtually all of them are significantly underfunded and therefore unsustainable.

In the US, public pension schemes under the auspices of social security (including Medicare and Medicaid) gobble up 40 per cent of the US government's annual budget. The pension saga permeates government at all levels – federal, state and even local. In their 2008/2009 financial results, the California Public Employees' Retirement System and the California State Teachers' Retirement System's losses between them were nearly US$100bn, equivalent to about one quarter of their pension assets.[5] While this book is being written, there is an ongoing dispute because California has forced state workers to take days off, known as furloughs, in order to reduce their salary and pension costs.

A HIDDEN AGENDA

If these staggering pension shortfalls sound bad enough, remember that Western governments have masked the true size of the pension deficits by deliberate obfuscation – known as off-balance-sheet accounting. This form of accounting trickery, by which the true value of the future pension obligations is set aside, usually as a mere footnote to the core balance sheet, enables governments to distort the figures they publish and conceal the true value of the debt burden that the public are carrying. Of course, burying the pension in the fine print also allows them to turn a blind eye and not fess up to the elephant in the room, even to themselves.

Companies are guilty of the same sin. For years they have been legitimately allowed to sweep the inconvenient truth of horrendous pension liabilities under the carpet. Deferred benefits (in the form of pensions and, for that matter, healthcare) have meant that the true cost of labour remains hidden, and this causes market distortion on at least two fronts.

First, without knowledge of the true costs of the pension benefits, business planning strategy across America has been compromised. The result is that wrong strategic choices have been made to the expensive detriment of companies, whole industries and the country. Companies and industries such as car-making, steel and airlines have been able to continuously roll forward the true cost of labour, with little concern about what will happen when the bill eventually comes due – let alone knowing what the true cost will be. As has become clear, many companies have, with sleight of hand, made it look like they have been running in profit, whereas they were and are, in fact, facing substantial losses. Businesses which should have been closed years ago and their productive resources redistributed to better opportunities have been kept alive as managers and investors were unable to assess the true economic situation.

Second, deferred benefits have also led to mispricings that have negatively influenced labour supply decisions, encouraging people to favour jobs with a fixed and back-loaded pension compensation schedule over careers that may require more initial training and have less (pension) compensation certainty. The classic example would be how people have chosen to forgo a university education and the unpredictability of some future career (say in a private accounting firm), because there is an opening in a unionized (and thus protected) occupation. Many people have evaluated and selected job opportunities based on the promise of future payouts, erroneously failing to discount the deferred benefits, instead believing that there is a 100 per cent chance of receiving their full value. However, the assumption that these future benefits will all be delivered has turned out to be wrong.

It's as simple as this: cheques that were written thirty years ago are, today, impossible to cash, in essence leaving government and some corporate defined-benefit pension schemes little more than Ponzi schemes.

Although in some jurisdictions legislation is afoot to bring the off-balance-sheet items on to the bottom line, companies and governments alike are right to be nervous about the implications of this, once the full scale of the predicament is revealed. For certain, the pension revelation will have serious implications for their credit ratings, share prices and the overall costs of debt that these entities are carrying, never mind the expected debt levels of Western countries on the back of the financial crisis bailout. Forecasts for US debt share of GDP in 2010 are estimated to approach 100 per cent, up from just over 60 per cent five years ago. For the UK, the debt ratio projections stand at over 70 per cent in 2010, an increase from 40 per cent in 2005.

In contrast, China doesn't have a state-run pension system. In fact, it doesn't have any mispriced options languishing on its national

balance sheet in any form. There are growing calls for China to establish a system of national healthcare and other pension-plan-like safety
nets. For example, the Chinese president, Hu Jintao, has been calling
for the acceleration of urban and rural social security coverage, stat-
ing that 'the development of social security is essential to maintaining
social stability and harmony, and maintaining economic growth',
further adding that 'the government should also work out an ultim-
ate solution to cover all the country's residents under the social
security system by increasing the beneficiaries of basic medical insurance, new rural cooperative medical system, unemployment insurance,
work injury insurance and other security regulations step by step.' In
2009 the Chinese government announced plans to spend more than
US$120bn on the first phase of a ten-year overhaul of the healthcare
system. The plan is, by 2011, for every village in China to have a
clinic, and by 2020, China says, it wants all its citizens to have access
to affordable, basic medical services.[6] China is minded to learn from
the mistakes of the US and other industrialized nations, and ought to
make any system a funded one, rather than an intergenerational one,
which risks collapse even faster given China's one-child policy. Ultimately the failure or success of a pension plan, and whether it lives or
dies, depend on what is actually done with the funds a pension agency
has.

LABOUR LOST

In addition to the quantity of labour, the West also faces the challenge
of labour quality. Across most metrics of labour quality, the West has
prided itself as being home to the most educated, most skilled, most
inventive and even the most productive people on earth. This position
is no longer assured.

The West (Britain and America, in particular) has spent the better
part of the last three decades dismantling its traditional industrial
bases (steel manufacturing, shipbuilding), and abandoning its once
undisputed edge in training, science and technology, in favour of the
more sanitized service industry. The net result, unsurprisingly, is the
decline of the West's manufacturing capacity.

Take London. Between 1960 and 1990, London's industrial base shrank dramatically. Whereas in 1960 manufacturing accounted for over 30 per cent of London's wealth, by 1990 this figure had collapsed to just 11 per cent. Within just thirty years, two thirds of manufacturing jobs disappeared, leaving only 500,000 working in the industry.[7]

From British Leyland's bus plants, to Whitefriars glassworks, to the soap manufacturer Pears, to Hoover, maker of its eponymous vacuum cleaners – no manufacturing company was safe. London was not even the hub of Britain's manufacturing; this scene of devastation was replicated right across the industrial heartland of Britain. Across the nation between 1979 and 2006, the numbers employed in the manufacturing industry fell 50 per cent from 7 million, to just under 3.4 million.

The decline in manufacturing jobs on the shop floor has had much more to do with changes in the West's negligent attitude towards a future in science, information technology and engineering disciplines than any of the outside economic factors which have been blamed for this deterioration. Of course, Chinese companies can manufacture goods more cheaply, and hence there were always going to be strong arguments for Western economies to cede the manufacturing sector (not least among which is comparative advantage); however, they ought to have fought more aggressively in the areas where they did have a comparative advantage (more on this later).

In the United States, the number of engineering graduates at the bachelor (undergraduate) level peaked at approximately 80,000 a year in the mid-1980s; this fell to around 65,000 a year approaching the new millennium. By comparison, in 2008 China had around 3.7 million engineering students – even on a proportional basis (accepting that China's population is four times the size of America's), it is a marked difference. As far back as 1999, over 70 per cent of first degrees in China were in science and engineering. Whereas, according to a 2009 *Forbes* article, the US prefers lawyers over engineers by 41:1![8]

The closer one looks, the scarier the picture gets. By 2004 the United States ranked seventeenth among nations surveyed in the share of eighteen- to 24-year-olds who earned natural science and engineering degrees; in 1975 it had ranked third. Obviously quality matters, so the West arguably has a reprieve – though in all likelihood, not for long – as the quality of science graduates in China and the Rest is yet to reach Western standards.

Nevertheless, in the West engineering has become passé. Whereas in the 1950s and 1960s America's best and brightest largely ended up getting their hands dirty producing goods, and working away at the coalface of invention, by the 1990s the top tenth of talent rushed into the service industry – banking and consulting the preferred options. Graduates used to be doers (as engineers and diplomats in the 1950s and 1960s State department and oil companies); then they became corporate managers at oil companies and technology companies such as IBM, in the 1970s and 1980s; then they became talkers, as investment bankers and management consultants, and finally as speculators as hedge fund and private-equity managers in the 1990s and 2000s, to today.

The 2004 *Science and Engineering Indicators Report* delivered to President George W. Bush with its companion piece, entitled *An Emerging and Critical Problem of the Science and Engineering Labour Force*, cites a 'troubling decline in the number of US citizens who are training to become scientists and engineers, whereas the number of jobs requiring science and engineer training continues to grow'.

Across the Atlantic, the story is not much different. There is no more striking example of the pendulum swing against the natural sciences than the disturbing report made during the 2004/2005 academic year by the University of Glamorgan, School of Technology. As part of an exercise to promote engineering as an academic and career option, recruitment representatives from the department visited seventy schools in the UK, meeting approximately 1,500 sixth-form (senior high school) pupils, and noted that the most frequent response to the opening question, 'What does an engineer do?', was 'Engineers fix cars/washing machines'.

How extraordinary to think that in twenty-first-century Britain, so-called well-educated students have not been taught to know what an engineer does – presumably because their education system does not deem the engineering profession as relevant to today's Western society.

If you picked up a boy's annual published any time between the 1930s and the mid-1960s, you would most likely find in it articles about engineering feats, suspension bridges, railways and planes, even descriptions of how an atomic bomb works, but not so today. Open the equivalent today and it's football teams and boy bands that grace the pages. James Dyson the British inventor put it this way: 'As a child, I pored over *Eagle* magazine cut-aways that delved into the workings of everything from Bloodhound missiles to offshore oil rigs ... it was the innards that intrigued and inspired ... what happens between childhood and adulthood? We stamp it out of them. Engineering gets stigmatized and we encourage our kids to become 'professionals' – lawyers, accountants, doctors ... Engineering is almost a dirty word. We're told it's "old industry" and that we are a "post-industrial nation".'

Never mind that China produces fourteen times as many engineers as Britain. This lackadaisical attitude towards science and engineering permeates the political structure of the industrialized West. One has to go almost as far back as Thomas Jefferson, the third US president (1801–9), who was an inventor, horticulturist, archaeologist and palaeontologist, to find a president with an engineering or science background.

Apart from the Science Minister, Lord Drayson, appointed in 2009, no engineers are represented at the highest levels of the British government. In contrast, Hu Jintao, the current Chinese president, graduated in hydraulic engineering from Beijing's Tsinghua University, and Wen Jiabao, the Chinese prime minister, is a postgraduate engineer.

In the United Nations Educational, Scientific and Cultural Organization's (UNESCO) 2005 Science Report, China contributed almost 15 per cent of world researchers, the US around 23 per cent (surprisingly close given the relative differences in average economic standards). China had 3.22 million people engaged in science and technology, with 68 per cent (around 2 million) as scientists and engineers. These are important statistics inasmuch as there is a widely held view that there is an important, positive and strong link between the production of scientists, technicians and engineers in a country and its level of economic growth and development.

Of course, on a proportional basis China isn't doing that great (it has over a billion people – 20 per cent of the world population), but this aggregate figure belies some of the leaps and bounds in research, experimentation and publication occurring in the fields of science and technology, which we will come to in the next chapter.

Taking a step back, one may question whether deindustrialization and the (inevitable) loss of manufacturing jobs truly matters. It may, after all, simply be a natural consequence of economic progress – an artefact of the swift migration of manufacturing jobs from richer countries to poorer ones.

In the classical economics literature it is often argued that there exists a clearly defined trajectory of economic growth, whereby countries pass from one dominant economic phase into another, three phases in all; broadly speaking this runs from agriculture, to manufacturing, to services – each stage roughly coinciding with improving income levels – so in places where the agriculture sector dominates the economy (such as in Africa) incomes tend to be much lower than in countries where services reign (e.g. the US and Western Europe). Of course, to a large extent this is a false distinction; in practice, economies are a mixed bag of all these sectors – for instance, pretty much every country has people employed in its agricultural sector – but, to be sure, at any given time in a country's economic evolution one of these sectors will be dominant. For what it's worth, there's arguably a fourth sector – innovation around research and development (R&D) and cutting-edge technology; it's more apposite to deal with this later.

Nevertheless, deindustrialization – the term used to describe the transition away from manufacturing to, say, services – is often perceived as evidence of economic decline, as manufacturing provides fewer jobs than it used to and the share of manufacturing in total employment in richer countries falls. For example, the share of manufacturing in total employment in industrialized countries fell from 28 per cent in 1970 to 18 per cent in 1994, leaving less than one worker in six in America in manufacturing, and in Europe one in five. British manufacturing remains a shadow of what it used to be. In the past decade alone, the UK's manufacturing share of GDP has halved from 22 per cent to 11 per cent today. And since the financial crisis in 2008, the US has lost more than 22 million jobs in manufacturing and construction; given global competition they are unlikely ever to come back.

Western governments need to recognize that just as they have ceded their manufacturing base to new economic upstarts (China, India, Korea, Taiwan, etc.), their service sector is destined to go the same way. Most Britons will have had first-hand experience of India's increasing role in globalizing service industries such as internet providers, telecommunications, banking and R&D. Call centres that were once housed in Milton Keynes, UK, have sprouted up across India. It's not just telephone companies or IT back office functions. There has been a growing trend for American investment banks to choose to hire Indian firms to handle financial modelling and comparable analysis.

Meanwhile Western policymakers seem to have been caught unawares – failing to plan for this eventuality, so that what happened to their manufacturing industry would happen to their service industry.

Perhaps, having lost the first battle, their biggest failing was that rather than look forward to the one area that could have propelled them out of their subsequent economic woes, they still looked back to fight on the manufacturing turf – a battle, if fought without protectionist policies, they would always lose. Where should they have looked instead? To the area where they had, and in large part continue to have, a comparative advantage – R&D.

Of course even if they had wanted to innovate in R&D, they had signally neglected the very areas of higher education – engineering, science, technology – that would have been required to realize this strategy. Just when expertise was needed, it wasn't there. Only substantial commitment to R&D, whether it be in fuel and energy consumption innovation, communication technology or transport, can counter the onslaught from the emerging world in manufacturing, and help restore the West's lost leadership in the economic race.

Over time, the right noises have been made; calling for retooling and re-education of the Western workforce to make it more globally competitive, and move it from old-fashioned manufacturing to new, cutting-edge frontiers – wherever they may be – from cassette recorder, to Walkman, to CD-player, to iPod. But these have not been enough.

According to the US National Science Foundation, manufacturers performed US$169bn of company-funded R&D and US$18bn of federally funded business R&D; companies in the non-manufacturing industries performed US$73bn and US$8bn, respectively. Specifically, major federal outlays in manufacturing sectors included computer and electronic parts (US$8.838bn), and aerospace products and parts (US$5.040bn), while outlays in non-manufacturing sectors went to professional, scientific and technical services, including architecture and engineering, computer systems design and scientific R&D services (US$7.608bn).

In notional dollar terms, billions clearly continue to pour into R&D. However, in the main, government policy and private investment in innovation have been left wanting, perhaps dissuaded because of the inherent uncertainty of R&D – never quite sure whether it will lead you down the garden path or a cul-de-sac, or to the next great, ground-breaking invention.

Western society has spent thirty years attracting the best and the brightest into consulting, financial services and banking – but now that these businesses have imploded in the 2008 crisis, what will these people do? And more importantly what will the new generation of the best and brightest be equipped to do, having been raised in a world that has valued service skills over the attributes that drive manufacturing innovation, and which made the West the industrial giant it has been?

A ROCKY ROAD AHEAD

Looking ahead, for America in particular, if present trends are left unchecked, the outlook for the labour market is bleak. By most census forecasts, America's minority (non-white) populations will be the majority before too long. Minorities, now one third of the US population, are expected to become the majority in 2042. By 2023 minorities will comprise more than 50 per cent of all children. The working-age population is projected to become more than 50 per cent minority in 2039 and be a 55 per cent minority in 2050. That year is also when America's population of children is expected to reach a 62 per cent minority. Already, some of America's largest states by population are 'majority-minority' – a term used to describe a US state whose racial composition is more than 50 per cent non-white. These include Hawaii, California, New Mexico and Texas.

Clearly the US is poised for substantial transitions in its demographic make-up. Yet, despite these projections, and despite the fact that it is impossible to de-link these statistics from the fate of America as a whole, it is these very groupings that remain the least educated and least skilled. America's 15,000 school districts and 100,000 schools are doing a poor job of educating America's kids, especially low-income and minority children, who are three grade levels behind by the age of nine, and less than half of whom graduate from high school.[9] Those who do graduate are seven times *less* likely to graduate from college. In Washington, DC, which has a large minority population, only 12 per cent of eighth-graders (twelve-year-olds) read at their grade level, and only 9 per cent end up going to college and graduating within five years. In 2007, when Michelle Rhee, chancellor of the District of Columbia Public Schools system of Washington, DC, and most fearless public education heroine, took up her post, academic measures were miserable. The National Assessment of Educational Progress (NAEP) that year found that 61 per cent of Washington DC's fourth-graders had below-basic reading skills, i.e. they could barely read; and 92 per cent of the city's eighth-graders were basic, i.e. below grade level, in maths. Districtwide, there was a 57-percentage-point gap in reading between Blacks and Whites, with fewer than 30 per cent of African American students reading at grade level, compared to 87 per cent of whites. As if that was not enough, the city's high-school dropout rate was around 50 per cent, and just 9 per cent of entering ninth-graders ever graduated from college. In an April 2009 report entitled 'The Economic Impact of the Achievement Gap in America's Schools', the global consulting firm McKinsey summed it up best: 'These educational gaps impose on the United States the economic equivalent of a permanent national recession.' The report goes on to note that if the gap between Black and Latino student performance and white student performance had been narrowed, GDP in 2008 would have been between $310 billion and $525 billion higher, or 2 to 4 per cent of GDP. Naturally, all things constant the magnitude of this impact will be substantially higher in the coming years given the forecasted demographic shifts that mean

Blacks and Latinos will become a larger proportion of the US population and workforce.

Quality matters, and much of the evidence suggests that while developing countries are encouraging and fostering meritocracy, their Western rivals are increasingly approaching academe with an egalitarian flare – more access (of course, with the benefit of widening educational opportunity) even if at the expense of quality.

Indeed there is a growing concern that an 'anti-meritocratic' style of education may be becoming increasingly prevalent in more developed countries, places like the UK and Europe, where there is resistance to seeking out or identifying smart students because in so doing the system is identifying the weaker students. This can be contrasted with the competition for places and brutal streaming in countries like India and China, where the exercise of academic culling is ongoing.

The relevance of education goes beyond the process of learning itself. Education plays an undisputed role in laying the path for economic success as well as ensuring social stability. It's not far-fetched to suggest that a lack of educational opportunities can lead to poor economic choices, hence a lack of social mobility, a lack of hope, which can lead to the worst kinds of social disruption and disaffection.

Economists have long acknowledged the role of aspiration and the belief that one can have a better life than one's parents, and one's kids a better life than oneself, as key to a working capitalist model.

Globalization has had its benefits, but it has also upped the competition. As a consequence, unskilled workers in developed markets have (and could continue to see) less hope as a result of more competition, as companies become global and aim to do better by allocating labour (and capital) globally even more effectively.

The ongoing challenge for emerging nations, on the other hand, is to continue to include the very poor in their plans for growth as well as to focus on becoming meritocracies, as without this broad-based approach these countries face the perennial risk that the emergence of a (smaller) very wealthy class can give rise to high levels of crime and violence among others who have little to aspire to. It is how emerging states handle this challenge that will ultimately differentiate them.

Where labour is concerned, the situation can be summarized as follows: the Rest win hands down when it comes to supply of labour versus demand; their billions swamp the opposition. Over the years, the Rest have also proven their mettle in management of human resources – turning base metal into gold. What does China not produce? True, it has some work to do in organizational skills and management. For sure, there may be quality issues around degree awards, but the Chinese are catching up, and they are catching up fast. They are well aware of their deficiencies and are working hard at harnessing the range of skills that they need to match then overtake the West.

Which goes a long way to explaining why a recent report from the Organization for Economic Cooperation and Development (OECD) finds that the US has lost its lead in education. According to the OECD, the US has fallen in the rankings 'not because U.S. college graduation rates declined, but because they rose so much faster' elsewhere. The US now lags behind some sixteen countries in Europe and Asia in the proportion of 24-year-olds with bachelor's degrees in the natural sciences and engineering. In the 1960s, the US had the highest high-school completion rate in the developed world; by 2005, the US ranked twenty-first. In terms of college completion, the US ranked second in 1995; a decade later, in 2005, it ranked fifteenth.

Bob Compton's 2009 documentary film entitled *Two Million Minutes* does not make easy watching. As the official website states:

> Regardless of nationality, as soon as a student completes the 8th grade, the clock starts ticking. From that very moment the child has approximately . . . Two Million Minutes until high school graduation . . . Two Million Minutes to build their intellectual foundation . . . Two Million Minutes to prepare for college and ultimately career . . . Two Million Minutes to go from a teenager to an adult.

This study shows that when American students are matched against their Chinese and Indian counterparts on academic performance and the amount of time spent on academic pursuits, it is clear that the US is failing. The *Economist* magazine underscores this in a separate article. On average the American school year is 180 days, in Asia more than 200 (South Korean kids spend more than thirty days more in school; this works out to an additional year in school compared to their American peers by the time they leave high school). It does not end there. American school days are shorter and children spend thirty-two hours a week at school (far lower than many European children who spend roughly forty hours a week at school), and whereas American school children devote just one hour to homework a day, Chinese children dedicate more than three times that amount to it.

The urgency in a 1983 report by the US Department of Education entitled *A Nation at Risk* was clear: 'Our one unchallenged pre-eminence in commerce, industry, science and technological innovation is being overtaken by competitors throughout the world ... the educational foundations of our society are presently being eroded by a rising tide of mediocrity that threatens our very nature as a nation and a people.' But save for relatively small efforts such as the 'No Child Left Behind' programme, this clarion call has been largely ignored. The Trends in International Mathematics and Science Study (TIMSS) seems to back this up. In 1995, 1999, 2003 and 2007 TIMSS compared the mathematics and science achievements of US fourth-grade and eighth-grade students with those of students in other countries. In the most recent rankings, US fourth-grade performance was trending downwards in both mathematics and science.

It's not just the US. The third phase of the Programme for International Student Assessment (PISA), released in 2008, shows that the trend in the UK is equally disturbing. Every three years the PISA tests 400,000 fifteen-year-olds from fifty-four countries in mathematics, reading and science; testing the knowledge and skills young people need to compete in the globalized modern world. In reading, the UK has dropped from seventh in 2000 to seventeenth place in PISA's 2008 international rankings, and in mathematics it's fallen from eighth to twenty-fourth place. The trend is clearly disturbing.

A MISALLOCATION OF LABOUR: PRICE SIGNALS

In June 2009 Real Madrid, the Spanish football club, paid Manchester United US$80m for Cristiano Ronaldo, dubbed one of the world's greatest footballers. In Spain, his salary comes to £180,000 a week (around US$286,650 in October 2009 dollars), up from his English earnings of £120,000 per week. Across the Atlantic, the take-home pay, for the year 2009/2010, of Kobe Bryant, the famed basketball star of the Los Angeles Lakers, is expected to be around US$23m (i.e. around US$442,000 a week). Contrast this with the average UK salary of £24,000 (i.e. £463 a week, and US earnings averaging around US$45,000 a year (i.e. US$884 a week).

If asked, many people in the West would baulk at the salaries of sport personalities, but would nevertheless keep their emotions in check and chalk these fantastic earnings up as the understandable and inevitable result of the free market.

What many fail to appreciate is that these stellar salaries come at an enormous cost; not in terms of the cash parcelled out to the supremely talented few, but in terms of the wider social cost that the average Westerner has to bear. These incomes, while barely believable, have become part and parcel of Western culture because, as the advertising slogan goes, they're 'worth it'. To be fair, there are Indian cricketers who command high salaries, but nothing like those of their Western counterparts.

What we see here – the propensity for high salaries in ostensibly non-productive areas – is another example of the misallocation of labour, further contributing to the economic demise of the West; yet another nail in the West's economic coffin, the significance of which is barely acknowledged, and scarcely understood.

But what exactly is the relationship between these high salaries for the lucky few and the West's continuing economic decline? How can what Ronaldo or Kobe Bryant earn possibly hurt anyone else? How could their good fortune lead to the West's misfortune?

In their 2005 bestseller, *Freakonomics: A Rogue Economist Explores the Hidden Side of Everything*, Steven Levitt and Stephen Dubner describe the payout structure for drug-dealers in the Southside of Chicago, whereby the top echelons earn millions of dollars while the foot soldiers pocket only a few hundred a week. The foot soldiers are prepared to work for their small amounts in the belief that one day they might get lucky and earn the large amounts. The potential pot at the end of the rainbow is the allure. But for the majority, like most pots at the end of rainbows, it's a fantasy.

In the minds of the hundreds of foot soldiers, the payout looks like this: the small probability of making it big, multiplied by the amount of cash they can potentially rake in, is larger than the greater likelihood that they won't make it big, multiplied by the cost of failure (i.e. getting arrested, injured or even killed). This is the lottery effect – the value of a dream.

Whereas people seem to understand that this is how the drug world's pay scheme works, what is not acknowledged is just how much of this is mirrored in more legitimate spheres. Very much like the drug world's foot soldiers, thousands of young kids across the West, often with the sincere encouragement of their parents, aspire to be the top basketball, football or tennis players – wherever their nascent skill appears to direct them. What they in almost all cases (after all, only a few make it to the big leagues) refuse to accept is that they won't get there. For every David Beckham or Michael Jordan there are a thousand disappointed wannabes that nobody ever sees. There is clearly an externality to society of having a larger number of people attempting to make it to superstar level and failing, and not developing widely usable skills.

It would seem that there is a good case for governments to adopt a policy here, arguably one that places a 'special' tax on high-income earners (sports people, etc.), from which payments can be made to subsidize the many thousands of aspirants who don't make it to the big league. Conceptually, this 'high-earners tax' would not be so different from the environmental tax levied on industrial companies. As this higher proportion of tax is diverted from the salaries of top players to a communal pot, not only would their incomes decline, but also fewer people would be lured into these areas. The Nobel Prize-winning Ronald H. Coase's theorem would say we should assign the cost of this externality to one of the actors and let the cost of the externality be traded. Another example could be to place a special tax on the very institutions such as FIFA, NCAA and so on that are creating the high earners.

Of course, it is not just sports people and athletes and Hollywood actors who are benefiting from the irrationalities of salary pricings. Chief executives in publicly traded companies and hedge fund managers have also come under fire. There is, however, an important difference, which is that if you don't make it to the top 10 per cent of

CEOs, hedge fund traders and the like, you still have a decent level of education and transferable skills in mathematics and business that can ostensibly benefit society as a whole. In other words, the cost of a 'failed' hedge fund manager is a lower deadweight cost to society than that of a failed basketball player or footballer.

The practical difficulty is persuading parents to make the decisions; those which are in the best interests of their children, and of society as a whole. Of course, across much of the developed world there exist legal structures to protect education systems and ensure that children attend schools and meet the required levels of academic attainment. In practice, however, standards are falling short. In a stinging attack in October 2009, Sir Terry Leahy, the then head of the supermarket chain Tesco – Britain's largest employer – lamented UK education standards as 'woefully low' and remarked on how 'employers like us are often left to pick up the pieces.'[10]

As regards the payout structure, it is not just that kids and their families discount the probability of failure and overestimate the probability of success; it is also that they are able to discount the costs of taking the gamble as the costs of the bet are almost always borne by society as a whole – regardless of the odds. Most worrying for the West's long-term economic prospects are the costs of the 'also-rans' who, having devoted all their formative years training to achieve sports 'gold' (which they will never attain), have often only the most basic survival-level reading, writing and arithmetic skills.

In the Conference Board 2006 paper subtitled *Employers' Perspectives on the Basic Knowledge and Applied Skills of New Entrants to the 21st Century U.S. Workforce*, the employers' assessment of high-school graduate entrants in the US was mournful. In key categories, employer respondents assessed the entrants as follows: 53 per cent found high-school entrants deficient in mathematics, 70 per cent found them deficient in critical thinking, 70 per cent in work ethics and professionalism, and 81 per cent in written communication. No wonder the authors titled the paper *Are They Really Ready to Work?*

Here we have a situation where not only is Western society encouraging millions of children to fix their eyes on virtually unattainable endeavours that arguably have no broad social value (unlike, say, the lawyers, doctors, teachers, engineers they could train to become), but also the costs of producing a society of sub-performing and disappointed youth are borne by society as a whole, to no productive end. What the West is left with are coming generations of underachievers who are about to face competition in the labour market from the Rest that will undoubtedly test them, if not outperform them, on every productive level.

What does Western society want? Experts in basketball or experts in astrophysics? More investment bankers, or more scientists and doctors? Like capital, optimal labour allocation is critical for the well-oiled functioning of an economy; the point is to make allocation work in the best way. So in the same way that the US government is happy to underwrite free options for financial institutions in the form of subsidies that have yielded 'too much bank credit' and 'too much housing' without the potential for broad social benefit, there is a real risk that lax labour policy and the existing (albeit privately driven) incentive structure spawns many more wannabe sports stars and celebrities than healthcare professionals or teachers. Is this really what we want?

Such has the misallocation of labour been that there are now grave concerns that, even as industrialized countries recover from the financial crash, the West will find it hard to keep up with rising international standards. From food technologists, to nuclear power engineers, to head teachers to doctors and nurses, vacancies exist in the post-crisis period. In 2009 the chief executive of the UK's Recruitment and Employment Confederation, Kevin Green, put it like this: 'If we have got shortages even during as bad a recession as we have had in forty years, what the hell is going to happen to the labour market on the other side of this?'[11]

The problem extends beyond poor-quality graduates. The most aptly qualified are making career choices that do not necessarily feed a broad-based pipeline of productive contributors to the economy. Take a look at what is happening to graduates of the illustrious Massachusetts Institute of Technology in regard to the careers they choose. The data reveal that of the undergraduate population 27.2 per cent end up in finance, 15.6 per cent in software and information services and 12.9 per cent in management consultancy. Masters level students also favour management consultancy and finance, with 19.3 per cent and 14.3 per cent choosing careers in these fields respectively. Software and info services take up 13.6 per cent. Engineering graduates and biotechnicians are all heading to Wall Street. It seems more and more people want to be a hedge fund investor instead of a teacher, doctor or engineer. According to US census data, in 2000 10.5 million people in the workforce held at least one college degree in a science or engineering field. Of this number, only 31 per cent (3.3 million) were directly employed in science and engineering occupations.

FOREIGNERS NEED NOT APPLY

In 1996 the University of Chicago was forced to hire an immigration lawyer to make the case that their newly appointed finance professor, the British-born, Harvard-trained Nicholas Barberis, was a 'genius' and as such deserved a special visa from the US government, in order to take up his post. Chicago won the case, but had the university not contested it, Barberis would not have got his work permit.[12] As of January 2010, under the new US Electronic System for Travel Authorization, all Europeans must pre-apply online for visas to enter the United States. Authorization can take up to seventy-two hours. And there are cases of foreign students who, graduating in the top ranks of their classes at American universities, take a short holiday before commencing a new job in the US, but, when the time comes to return to the United States, find their visas are denied.

Over the past ten years, there has been a growing trend for the government to restrict the movement of foreigners into the United States. Just look at what has happened in patterns of the H1-B1 visa category – professional visas available to foreign nationals who have a job offer in an occupation requiring specialized knowledge.[13] Although computer-related applicants take the largest share, other specialist categories include medicine, architecture and education.[14] Effective from 1 January 2004, the number of visas to be issued under the H1-B1 category was capped at 65,000 annually.

There is broad acknowledgement, both inside and outside the US, in industry and academia, that visa restrictions are putting America at a severe competitive disadvantage. One of the conclusions of a study prepared by McKinsey and Company in 2007, for New York City's mayor, Michael Bloomberg, found that restrictions on professional and business visas were one of the biggest problems to be overcome if New York was to retain its status as a world financial centre.

Situations like the one in which an investment firm located a derivatives operation in London, simply because the Chinese national whom they hired to head it could not get the required visa, are driving American companies abroad to get access to the people that they need. While politicians urge a tough stance in the name of protecting American jobs, evidence abounds that hiring foreigners contributes to domestic job creation.

It's not as if America is restricting the influx of foreign students to come to the US to study. UNESCO notes that students born outside the USA continue to account for a substantial portion of US science and engineering degrees, with Chinese- and Indian-born students in graduate programmes in 1999 accounting for about 35 per cent and 25 per cent the total, respectively. The report goes on to note that in 1999 foreign students earned almost 50 per cent of all PhDs in engineering, mathematics and computer sciences, and approximately 35 per cent of PhDs in the natural sciences. For sure, American institutions are gaining by the school fees they charge, but the trouble is that once they are qualified, at the precise time when these graduates can best contribute to the growth of the US economy, their visas are denied and they are barred from employment.

In an October 2009 *Wall Street Journal* article entitled 'Immigrant Scientists Create Jobs and Win Nobels' the president of the Massachusetts Institute of Technology, Susan Hockfield, laments the current anti-immigrant situation. She points out that although eight of the nine people who shared that year's Nobel Prizes in chemistry, physics and medicine are American citizens, four of the American winners were born outside the United States and only came to the US as graduate or post-doctoral students or as scientists. She highlights the fact that of the thirty-five young innovators recognized in 2009 by *Technology Review* magazine for their exceptional new ideas, only six went to high school in the United States. From MIT alone, foreign graduates have founded an estimated 2,340 active US companies, which employ over 100,000 people. Annalee Saxian, of Berkeley, estimated that over 50 per cent of entrepreneurs and heads of start-ups in Silicon Valley were non-American-born, and over 25 per cent Asian-Indian. Nationwide, she concludes, in 2005 immigrant-founded companies produced US$52bn in sales and employed 450,000 workers. Despite these facts, immigration policy is not moving in their favour.

This myopic and aggressive stance that endorses labour protectionism is clearly to the economic detriment of the United States, and playing straight into the hands of its competitors. Putting aside the fact that America's success was built on the wealth of its immigration, this strategy of turning in on itself, particularly in light of its worsening education and academic record, is as blind as it is foolhardy.

While attempts to redress America's labour problem, such as President Obama's announcement that 3 per cent of GDP is to be invested in American science and technology, are perfectly sensible, these initiatives are too little to have a meaningful effect on the situation. Moreover, they do relatively little while visas for the world's best and brightest are still being denied.

More protracted and stringent visa policies and application processes will undoubtedly serve to discourage an increasing number of foreign students from attending US universities, particularly students from the largest student pools such as China and India. Already the trend is observable. The US Department of State recorded a decline in the number of applications for student (F) visas, from a peak of 320,000 in 2001 to 236,000 in 2003.

Although foreign students are still enrolling in US universities, many more are choosing to take their talents elsewhere. For example, the number of PhDs in natural sciences and engineering awarded by Asian institutions is growing rapidly. In 1998, on a par with the USA, Asian institutions granted around 20,000 PhDs. Moreover, and more importantly, the UNESCO report points out that in many instances the quantitative increase in the number of Asian PhDs awards has been matched by a concurrent increase in the quality of graduate education in leading Asian universities.

In 'What Makes a University Great?', Jamil Salmi suggests that there are three factors: a high concentration of talented teachers, researchers and students; sizeable budgets; and a combination of

institutional freedom, autonomy and leadership. True, tertiary institutions in the emerging Rest might not yet boast high degrees of each of
these factors, but it would be short-sighted to dismiss them outright
on this basis, as important strides are constantly being made to
improve them. In the same week, in February 2010, that the British
government announced that they were slashing university teaching
budgets by £250m in the 2010/2011 fiscal year, the UK's *Guardian*
newspaper ran a story pointing out that the Chinese government now
spends at least 1.5 per cent of its GDP on higher education. And even
Saudi Arabia, not known for prioritizing education, sets aside around
26 per cent of its non-military budget towards the education of its
citizenry.

In *Let Their People Come: Breaking the Gridlock on Global Labor
Mobility*, the economist Lant Pritchett offers a number of ways of
supporting labour migration from poor countries to rich, while also
making this politically acceptable in rich countries. These include
greater use of temporary worker permits, permit rationing (this is
already in place to some extent in many rich countries) and the reli-
ance on bilateral rather than multilateral labour agreements.

The US investment bank Goldman Sachs makes the further point
that a surge in immigration over the past decade has boosted America's foreign-born population to 40 million (out of roughly 350 million
people). The wave of immigrants is thought to have accounted for
about half of the growth in the US labour force in this period, and
increased GDP growth by around half a percentage point per year.
This is no bad thing. Yet, already, the report notes, the rate of immigration to the United States has started to slow, in large part reflecting
the clampdown on immigrants and immigration by more aggressive
public policy. The net result of lower immigration flows will not only
be to reduce America's labour force growth, but over time there will
also be a decline in the country's potential GDP growth rate.

America's structural labour problem revolves around the fact that
her workforce is becoming increasingly uncompetitive in a globalized
world. Increasingly her labour, and that across much of Europe, is
relatively ill-trained, reluctant to work to the extent of wage-earners
in other (emerging) markets, and willing only to operate under high

expectations around remuneration (pensions, healthcare), that make them costly for competing businesses.

This structural labour problem has been unfolding over the past 30 years. However, it has been conveniently masked by a series of macroeconomic events: the dot-com boom, the rise in the surfeit of debt that led to the credit crises, and the consequent emergence of a government spending bubble that is currently ongoing. Each of these events hid the true consequence of a structural labour problem by substituting other forms of income – whether it be capital gains, debt or government transfers – for more traditional gains in salary and wages. As such, strong household consumption, and the subsequent short term gains in retail and service sector jobs, deflected attention away from the core labour market problems going on in the background, thereby postponing any real attempts to redress the true problem.

Taken in its totality, the labour issue is not just about the marked decline in quality of the people who are needed to fuel the private sector – the engineers, scientists, entrepreneurs and industrialists – but also about the striking increase in the numbers of people moving into the public sector, their rising levels of compensation (which in the US has outpaced that of the private sector), and the concomitant decline in productivity (more on this issue in the next chapter).

In 'Public Sector Unions and the Rising Costs of Employee Compensation', Chris Edwards points out that the average financial compensation in 2008 in the US public sector (referring to state and local governments, not the federal government) was higher than private sector remuneration by thousands of dollars. Since 1980 average public sector compensation has been significantly outstripping private pay) and public expenditure is rapidly increasing (with healthcare, pension, unemployment and poverty spending all on the rise).

The Edwards study is an important one in that it considers the trends in state and local government compensation since 1950, and because state and local compensation represent a sizeable portion of the overall US economy. According to the Bureau of Economic Analysis, state and local workers (teachers, college instructors, police officers, healthcare administrators, and many other occupational groups) account for around 20 million of the 23 million civilian government workers in the United States. In 2008, the total cost of wages and benefits for state and local workers was $1.1tn, which was half of the $2.2tn spent in total by state and local governments.

In this regard, there is also, of course, the pressing matter that compensation costs will almost certainly rise, and substantially so, in coming years as a result of growing pension and healthcare costs. Already such public sector benefits have a pronounced effect on overall public sector compensation. The Bureau of Economic Analysis data show that average compensation in the private sector was $59,909 in 2008, including $50,028 in wages and $9,881 in benefits. Average compensation in the public sector was $67,812, including $52,051 in wages and $15,761 in benefits.

Although there has been some public acknowledgement that something fundamental needs to be done to deal with the structural problems in the labour market (for example, the US government's target, announced in 2009, of 3 per cent of GDP to be invested in American science and technology), on the whole these concerns have been met by insufficient and inadequate policy action. All things being equal this leaves America, and countries across Europe, facing a brutal choice. Either the living standards of a vast proportion of people living in the West will have to be reduced – and dramatically so – or these governments, and the US government in particular, will have to establish a very large, very expensive, welfare state.

Not just any welfare state, however. Of course, welfare states can function effectively if they are well-engineered, well-developed and self-financing (Germany and countries across Scandinavia are evidence that this can be the case). Instead, the US is on a path towards the worst form of welfare state, one borne of desperation that rapaciously feeds on itself. America's fast-growing population – and indeed that of the West as a whole – of unskilled, unemployed and disaffected citizens is at the core of the threat to the country's wealth and economic stature. Any economic system requires a skilled and innovative labour force – something that Western economies are fast running out of.

5

Giving Away the Keys
to the Kingdom

TFP IS THE KEY

On 12 November 2009 an article in the *Economist* magazine proclaimed that 'productivity growth is perhaps the single most important gauge of an economy's health'; continuing with 'nothing matters more for long-term living standards than improvements in the efficiency with which an economy combines capital and labour.'

Thus far, this book has considered two key pillars of economic growth: capital and labour. In standard economic growth theory the third critical constituent is known as total factor productivity (TFP) – an ingredient which accounts for effects in total output not caused by inputs. TFP is thought to explain up to 60 per cent of growth between economies, and as such is often seen as the real driver of economic growth. It is therefore a prime indicator in forecasting patterns of economic growth in years to come.

Whereas capital and labour are seen as factors over which a country has a degree of determination, TFP is the catch-all phrase given to contributing factors over which there may not always be direct control – e.g. geographical factors (terrain and the weather). It also includes rule of law, property rights, human rights, freedom of expression, etc. Perhaps less obvious is the inclusion of technological growth and efficiency – regarded as the two biggest sub-sections of total factor productivity – which countries, although they may strive after them, cannot be assured of achieving. In much the same way that money drives capital accumulation, and people and skills drive labour output, TFP is brought about by efficiency (doing the mundane better and faster) harnessed to invention. To a *very* large extent the West's pre-eminence has been all about its inventions.

THE TIDE OF TECHNOLOGY

James Watt: first reliable steam engine (1775). Eli Whitney: cotton gin, interchangeable parts for muskets (1793, 1798). Robert Fulton: regular steamboat service on the Hudson River (1807). Samuel F. B. Morse: telegraph (1836). Elias Howe: sewing machine (1844). Isaac Singer: improves and markets Howe's sewing machine (1851). Cyrus Field: transatlantic cable (1866). Alexander Graham Bell: telephone (1876). Thomas Edison: phonograph, incandescent light bulb (1877, 1879). Nikola Tesla: induction electric motor (1888). Rudolf Diesel: diesel engine (1892). Orville and Wilbur Wright: first aeroplane (1903). Henry Ford: Model-T Ford, assembly line (1908, 1913).[1]

These inventors from the Industrial Revolution and beyond radically transformed how the world works and how we live. What they have in common is that they were born in the West, though pre-industrial history tells us that the monopoly on invention was not, *per se*, limited to the US or the West. (China had also been a font of invention in her original heyday.)

Nevertheless it is undisputed that for much of the twentieth century it was the West that piled on innovation after innovation, thus maintaining its technological hold over the rest of the world. Sir Timothy John Berners-Lee (inventor of the World Wide Web), Bill Gates (the founder of Microsoft), and Larry Page and Sergey Brin (the genius behind Google) have all carried on this tradition. But the scientific and technological monopoly the West once enjoyed has now been well and truly breached. Indeed, in the recent past any new technology would almost certainly have come from the United States. Not so now.

TECHNOLOGICAL FEATS

The middle of the last century saw Japan emerge as a leading technological innovator in the car industry, electronics and steel manufacture.

Perhaps the most memorable invention was the 1979 creation of the Walkman, which revolutionized for ever how the world listened to music. Since then, the emerging Rest have also, in one form or another, been making their presence felt in technological and medical spheres for decades. A few examples:

Chien-Shiung Wu, known as the 'First Lady of Physics', was a highly respected Chinese physicist who worked on the Manhattan Project at Columbia University (believed to be the only Chinese person to do so), where she helped develop a process to enrich uranium ore.[2] Then there is the controversial Chinese-born Qian Xuesen, one of the founders of the Jet Propulsion Laboratory at the California Institute of Technology, who played a central role in the development of missile technology and rocket science, who died in 2009. In 2008 India's Chandrayaan-1 successfully landed near the Moon's south pole, forging Asia's reputation in space exploration.

The West may have secretly hoped that such incursions into what had previously been areas of Western invention and innovation would end in humiliating failure; that, unable to handle the complexities of new technology, in trying to emulate it emerging countries would suffer the same fate as the Russians when they built the near carbon copy of the Anglo-French supersonic jet Concorde, the Tupolev Tu-144 (also known as 'Concordski'), which ignominiously crashed at the Paris Air Show in 1973. If nothing else, even the ill-fated Concordski episode should have served as a warning – after all, it *did* fly and stayed in commercial use for the Russians until 1978.

Over time, efforts to usurp the West's technological edge have grown much more fierce and insistent, and evident in mainstream technology as well as in medical science.

It was Christiaan Barnard, a South African doctor working in Groote Schuur, a South African hospital, in December 1967, who carried out the world's first successful human heart transplant.[3] In September 2009 scientists in Thailand announced that their experimental HIV vaccine had, for the first time, cut the risk of infection. And today in India, in an enviable feat of process innovation in the area of healthcare, Dr Devi Shetty's clinics perform more than double the number of cardiac bypass surgeries than the Cleveland Clinic, a US leader. In 2008 Dr Shetty's surgeons also performed more than twice the number of paediatric cardiac surgeries than Boston's well-known Children's Hospital. Estimates are that Dr Shetty's group perform around 12 per cent of India's cardiac surgeries, all at a fraction of the cost in the United States. No wonder, according to a report by the consulting firm Deloitte, some 6 million Americans (up from 750,000 in 2007) are expected to travel to other countries to access affordable medical care.[4]

China and Peru are leading the pack in stem cell research. Mexico is considered a major centre for so-called 'stem cell tourism', with a number of treatments now available under the aegis of the International Stem Cell Institute.[5] Laser eye surgery, based on the lasik technique, now a commonplace operation, was pioneered by a Colombia-based ophthalmologist, José Barraquer, in 1950 in his clinic in Bogotá, and perfected by the Russians in the 1970s. But never mind the past, let's look at the future.

STEALING THE WEATHER

In the run-up to the 2008 Olympics in China, Beijing's Weather Modification Office tracked the region's weather via satellite, radar, planes and a super-computer. Using two aircraft and a battery of artillery and rocket launch sites around the city, weather engineers shot silver iodine and dry ice into the incoming clouds so that the rain could be flushed out before it reached the Bird's Nest arena. Any rain clouds that happened to get through were seeded with chemicals that shrank the droplets, thus ensuring that the rain would not fall while the clouds passed over.

The Beijing Weather Modification Office is just one part of the National Weather Modification Office that manipulates the weather across the whole of the country. China's weather engineering programme is the largest in the world – 1,500 weather modification experts, in charge of thirty aircraft and their crews, as well as 40,000 part-time workers – farmers in the main – who are there to man the 7,000 anti-aircraft guns and 5,000 rocket launchers to shell the clouds. (It was in fact American scientists who in a laboratory made the crucial breakthrough, in 1946, of creating and controlling the rain, but implementation matters.)

The implications of being able to control the weather for China and the world are stupendous. With this technology vast regions of land can be rendered fertile and the implications for drought reduction, flood avoidance and food production are theoretically limitless. Just think what implications the ability to control the weather could have militarily.

One only has to remember the Allied D-Day landings in Normandy in the Second World War, and the nail-biting decision General Eisenhower had to make on the advice of the weathermen, to appreciate what a life-and-death difference weather can make. In the months running up to the Normandy invasion, the weather had been relatively settled, but when the decision had been made to invade in June, the weather outlook had become much more gloomy. As history books tell us, the Allied military strategists planned everything – the troops, the equipment, the artillery, checking the dates of the high tide – but the one thing they could not plan for was the weather. China's weather mastery at the 2008 Olympics is just a prelude to what she might be able to achieve.

While this has been going on, three disturbing trends around technology and innovation have emerged in the West to undermine its position:

First, Western technological advancements are being stolen, misappropriated or simply handed over to the rest of the world . . . for free. Second, even when technological acumen is not stolen, monies earmarked for research and development are being reduced, leading to a lack of technological investment in innovation and the key areas of America's industry that need it most. Third, a lot of the money left over is redirected to endeavours that have arguably little benefit to society as a whole.

STOLEN, MISAPPROPRIATED, TRANSFERRED

Over the last three decades of the twentieth century the West has experienced an aggressive transfer of its technology to its most virulent competitors. Of course, there is no harm in other countries being good at technological know-how (in a global world, benefits can be had by all); rather, at issue is making sure that those who invest in the R&D – in this case mainly the industrialized West – get the right price for the technological innovation. Espionage and copyright breaches have meant that the transfer of technology from West to the Rest has largely been for free. The technology transfer that has ensued has been in part willing, and partly not.

The Concordski episode demonstrated that technology could and would be appropriated and put to use. But this insight was surely nothing new. Industrial espionage was a major factor throughout the Cold War, and is continuing in the most potent of forms today.

The US government is thought to field up to 40,000 attempts *each day* by Chinese hackers to access its information technology systems. A spy network dubbed Ghostnet, believed to be controlled from China, is alleged to have compromised nearly 1,300 computers used at NATO, foreign ministries, embassies, banks and news agencies across the world.[6] In April 2009, citing current and former US National Security officials, the *Wall Street Journal* reported that cyberspies had penetrated the US electrical grid and left behind software programmes that could be used to disrupt the system. Allegedly the spies were in China, Russia and other countries, and were believed to be on a mission to seize control of the US electrical system. This is just the tip of the iceberg.

In August 2009 *Foreign Policy* magazine cautioned that the US will lose its battle in cyberspace without a leader at the helm. The article goes on to note that in 2009 China celebrated the tenth anniversary of the publication of *Unrestricted Warfare*, a popular policy book written by two colonels in the People's Liberation Army on how China can defeat a technologically superior opponent with dominance in electronic warfare. Today China has an estimated 100,000 hackers capable of stealing R&D on weaponry and incapacitating the command and control systems needed to deploy most modern armies that depend on these platforms. In 2007 Jonathan Evans, the Director-General of MI5 (the British national Security Service), alerted 300 businesses that they were under Chinese cyber-attack.

The rise in technology espionage against the West by the Rest permitted rival companies across the emerging world to make the same goods at even lower costs. The West's proprietary technology was proprietary no more, which would, at least in part, explain why the number of patent lawsuits against Chinese 'innovators' more than doubled from 7,500 in 2003 to 17,500 in 2007. And even though China has opened more than fifty courts to deal with intellectual property cases, the headline in an article published in the April 2008 *Economist* magazine tells it all, '850,000 lawsuits in the making: Doing business in China'.[7]

WILLING AND ABLE

Superior know-how should have always given the West a leading edge. But it didn't. Even when technology has not been stolen, it's been given away. Western companies fell for the allure of low costs of production, and set up shop across the emerging world in droves. But what the West had not bargained for was the (allegedly illicit) transfer of their intellectual property, which was tacitly condoned.[8]

Has the West been guilty of a cultural narrow-mindedness that saw emerging countries only behind a plough? Perhaps thanks to a long-embedded perception of its own cultural superiority, the West viewed these emerging countries as essentially backward, simple and rural; certainly, unlikely to ever become serious economic competitors. Behind an ox they posed no threat to the West, but manning robotic-arm production lines they pose a daunting challenge. The rose-tinted view saw any economic progress in the emerging states merely as an opportunity to expand Western markets rather than as a threat to those markets. The emerging countries would become additional consumers of Western goods.

ALL THINGS TO ALL PEOPLE

There is another way in which the West is losing its technological edge – in the realm of R&D investment. As detailed earlier, the R&D that the West has funded over decades is continually being given away for free. This act of seeming generosity, while appearing to be in the interest of all, comes at an enormous cost and acts to the detriment to the global society as a whole. An efficient system of R&D works best when the returns and benefits recouped from the proper selling on of today's technology can be used to finance tomorrow's innovation. But in a system of freebies, there are no returns to finance future breakthroughs.

Yet the West in all its munificence has continued to give numerous free gifts to the world. It has policed the sea lanes and forged relatively higher social and environmental standards, and the US has near single-handedly contained the spread of communism while rebuilding Europe. In 2007, for example, defence spending as a share of GDP was close to 4 per cent in the US and around 2.5 per cent in the UK. In China (what will possibly be the world's second-largest economy in 2010) military spending as a share of GDP hovered close to just 1 per cent.

America's largesse is often portrayed as a moral crusade, but, whatever the case, all this costs money, lots of money. Nowhere is this more evident than in the pharmaceutical industry.

Each year, the drug industry spends billions of dollars on developing drugs on a variety of diseases – HIV-Aids, cancers, cardiovascular complications, etc. Even after running exhaustive trials in laboratories, on animals and finally on human patients, many attempts fall by the wayside before an effective drug reaches the shops. In some cases the process of trial and error can take more than a decade. However long it takes, it's a harsh fact that only a small proportion of R&D research becomes an actual drug sold over the counter.

Today, the undisputed leader in global pharmaceutical R&D – certainly in terms of money spent – is the United States.

According to the UNESCO 2005 Science Report and the UNESCO Institute for Statistics, the world devoted 1.7 per cent of GDP to R&D – that is roughly US$830bn. North America's share of world gross expenditure on R&D was 37 per cent (mainly America, which alone had 35 per cent). Europe was at 28.8 per cent, and ranked below Asia, which stood at 31.5 per cent – for reference, Japan contributed 12.8 per cent and China was at 8.7 per cent. China's contribution was up from 3.9 per cent in 1997. Latin America (2.6 per cent) and Africa (0.6 per cent) were for the most part irrelevant.

A 2005 report suggests that the United States spent an estimated 5.6 per cent of its total health expenditures on biomedical research, more than any other country. But government subsidies of industrial R&D have declined substantially from highs of 40 per cent in 1953 to just 10 per cent in 2000. According to *Business Monitor International*, in 2008 the per capita pharmaceutical expenditure in the US was US$1,018.2 compared to just US$27.6 per person in China. France, which ranked second behind the US in pharmaceutical spending on a per capita basis, spent over US$200 less at US$784.[9]

In 2001, the total funds for industrial R&D in the US comprised US$181bn and US$17bn (totalling US$199bn in current dollar terms) split between company and federal funding respectively. In 2000 industry is thought to have funded 66 per cent and performed 72 per cent of R&D in the US. Aside from the federal government and private industry funding, other institutions such as universities, state governments and non-profit organizations also participate in R&D to some (albeit a lesser) degree. According to UNESCO, private industry in the US has come to dominate the performance of R&D, with a tenfold increase occurring between the US$18.9bn it spent in 1953 and the US$199.6bn in 2000. But it's not just private money that funds the R&D. For the past several years, the amounts earmarked specifically for federally funded research and development centres have hovered around US$5bn a year. Of the twenty-one most important drugs introduced between 1965 and 1992, fifteen were developed using knowledge and techniques from federally funded research.[10]

Although the US remains the leader in R&D spend, the federal share of national US expenditures on R&D has been on a steady path of decline, moving from around 65 per cent in 1965 to about 25 per cent in 2000. Government subsidies of industrial R&D have also declined substantially, from highs of 40 per cent in 1953 to just 10 per cent in 2000.

Despite all this investment, and despite the fact that most drugs are closely guarded by patent rights, which are supposed to protect the developer and their invention for at least fifty years (Pfizer, the owners of the patent for Lipitor, a cholesterol treatment and the top selling drug in history, own their patent only for fourteen years (1997–2011)), many drugs find their way into the emerging markets as low-cost generics. These imitations are consumed by and manufactured in emerging countries for a fraction of the overall cost incurred to develop and make them. These imitations absolutely do cannibalize the markets for the drug manufacturers; not just today, but also tomorrow – as the cheap replicas flood the very regions in which there is most demand.

For many drug manufacturers, devoting billions of dollars in time and money to developing the right drug for the right problem, what this means is that they are never able to recoup their full costs. Put another way, Western countries often feel obliged to subsidize the health of the world, without demanding that the rest of the world share some of the costs. When it comes to the pharmaceutical industry, profit appears to be a dirty word. While these companies may still be making money, they face constant pressure to minimize profits in favour of handouts, thereby reducing the resources needed to fund further R&D.

The traditional Western companies have been unable to stem the tide of drugs being parcelled out at knock-down prices. Across the globe, the poor (very rationally) buy generics because they are the cheapest. And whether or not the big American and European pharmaceutical giants cut their drug prices is immaterial – it will make no difference. They will never be able to undercut the Indian, Brazilian or Chinese companies.

Why then not have a factory in Brazil or elsewhere where costs are low? The bottom line is because these companies cannot make enough money to support a decent return. In 2009, the head of Britain's leading drug maker, GlaxoSmithKlein, lamented that the amount of profits the company made from the least developed countries was less than US$10m (£5m) set against the actual costs of R&D and distribution which run into billions.[11] This is unsustainable, and in the end everyone loses. Already Western drug companies, which remain at the forefront of innovation in the medical field, are spending more time concentrating on HIV-Aids variants that pervade the Western world, and which will pay, over those common in poorer and emerging countries. In doing this there is a collective waste of resources, as companies start doing the same research around, say, cancer, heart disease, similar strains of HIV-Aids, etc.

Over the long term, America and the West cannot afford to be guardians and subsidizers of the world; and as with other global public goods, they should take a more aggressive stance in making others help underwrite the true R&D costs. At the moment, the Rest have all the upside and effectively no downside. However, there is a lot of downside for the West. This free rider problem around R&D contributes to a situation where the United States is running a sustained, and arguably unsustainable, current account deficit. While the US pays the full price for goods and services that it imports from China, etc., it earns only a fraction of the costs that could and should be earned from many of its pharmaceutical (and other technological) exports. All adding to a worse trade deficit. Nonetheless, there are movements in the right direction to remedy these imbalances.

On 9 February 2007, alongside the Bill and Melinda Gates Foundation, the governments of Canada, Italy, Norway, Russia and the United Kingdom committed US$1.5bn to launch the first Advanced Market Commitment (AMC), a contract designed to speed the development and availability of a new vaccine. Such Advanced Market Commitment contracts intend that the market for vaccines, pharmaceutical medicines and drugs (particularly for drugs that tend to be neglected by the largest (private) R&D budgets) be comparable in size and predictability in developing countries to those in industrialized countries. Clearly a welcome innovation in the healthcare field.

The West believed its economic superiority would always win – it was wrong. The technology that was conceived and built for the West's advantage has ultimately been used against it, and taken for a song. Has the West been inveigled into this? Forget industrial espionage, or the exodus of Western companies to lower cost havens, at home Western titans of industry fell asleep at the wheel. It's not just that the Chinese stole the technology which helped increase their productivity, nor that US companies transferred their plants and technologies (which invariably would contribute to the problem); it is also that Western companies have, over time (willingly), ceded their leading position.

INNOVATION MYOPIA

On 18 November 2008 the heads of the three American car giants, General Motors, the Ford Motor Company and Chrysler, lodged a desperate appeal for a bailout package to the US Congress. The three companies – once among the most powerful corporations in America – were reduced to appealing for cash from the government. How could this happen? In large part it boils down to a wilful and resolute blindness with regard to technological innovation.

These companies had for years seemingly all but ignored market trends and environmental changes and battled against cleaner fuel standards. America's big three sleep-walked through the transformational decade while their foreign competitors – Nissan, Toyota – spent time and money producing cars that catered to the tastes and needs of the twenty-first century. Even as early as the 1950s, with the American car industry so dominant, the historian David Halberstam noted that 'the [car] industry's engineers were largely idle as their skills were ignored. Thus, during a time when the American car industry might have lengthened its technological lead on foreign competitors, it failed to do so. Instead, the industry fiddled with styling details', offering new fins and different colour combinations for every annual model change. General Motors' top designer, Harley Earl, described this culture as 'dynamic obsolescence'.

It is therefore no surprise that the fortunes of their Eastern rivals flourished as the earnings of their American counterparties floundered – to the point when in autumn 2008 General Motors warned that it could soon go bust, which in fact it did, a few months later; in time for Christmas. Over a multi-decade period, successive leaderships had managed to lead the car companies from the front of the pack to bottom billing.

Of course, there is an argument that Ford, Chrysler and General Motors were simply reflecting the American psyche of more, bigger, and the unassailable belief that one could have anything without any consequences (a strategy that had worked for some time). Similarly revealing, what the car companies asked the US Congress for was just further evidence of their unwillingness to face reality.

At the time of their plea for a US$25bn cash injection from the US taxpayer in 2008, it was abundantly clear that whatever money they got (US$15bn was subsequently approved by the US Congress on 8 December 2008) would merely help postpone the demise of these companies. Chrysler and General Motors admitted as much when they revealed that they needed US$7bn and US$4bn, respectively, by year's end, just to stay afloat. Almost certainly no cash would be directed to what was really needed – R&D. If anything, the US motor industry's decline has run in parallel with the decline in its R&D investment. It is this as much as any economic downturn that led these three giants of American industrialization down this path in the first place.

What other explanation, but wilful blindness, could there be for car companies marketing the gas-guzzling Hummer, or monstrous SUVs, during a period when much of the world had gone compact and eco-friendly? The most glaring example in the motor industry is the way American automobile companies failed to anticipate the demand for the cleaner, smaller, environmentally friendly electric cars.

In the last century the West led the world in innovation, but who will do so in the next?

You only have to look at the number of US patents that have been awarded to Asian inventors to see how the balance is shifting. Patents and licensing activity are considered one of the main indicators of technological development. True, the US lead remains large, but rival countries from the Rest are catching up. In 1978 there were only thirteen patent applications from South Korean inventors. In 2008 there were 8,731. Patent filings in China increased 33 per cent in just one year, between 2004 and 2005, making it the world's third-largest. And between 1991 and 2001 the number of Chinese patents granted at the United States Patent and Trademark Office (USPTO) rose by an amazing 373 per cent (from 63 to 293), as compared to 73 per cent in the US (from 51,703 to 89,565); of course, these numbers are tempered by the fact that China is starting from a rather low base, while the US starting point is higher. Nevertheless, the increasing number of patents being filed from developing countries is a strongly growing trend. One can only suspect that the emerging nations will come to lead the world in innovation. There is, of course, little to say that this in itself is a bad thing.

SOMETHING'S GOING ON
IN THE KITCHEN

Just as capital has been misallocated, and labour has been misallocated, technology is also being misallocated.

There is no doubt that technological gains over several centuries have been the engine that has powered the West's economic dominance. However, there is clearly a point when it can go too far – a point of diminishing returns when the value garnered from increased efficiency no longer benefits society as a whole; in fact, it may come at a cost.

Think of a kitchen where utensils, condiments and crockery are lying everywhere. This leaves the cook spending a good half of his time looking for things instead of cooking. It makes sense, therefore, for him to order things: to have the pots and pans in one place, the spices in another, and the knives in another. He can lay his hands on things quickly and get to work.

There does come a point, however, where the value of him organizing his workplace adds little additional value to his ability to cook. Having the saucepans with their handles pointing at 45-degree angles, and condiments in the condiment cupboard arranged in descending order of size with all labels facing forward, may superficially look more efficient, but the time spent making it so adds a layer of additional cost that far exceeds any efficiency benefit that it might bring to the cook.

In a similar vein, technology has made trading in stocks and bonds a very efficient and quick business.

If trader A wishes to sell a share in General Electric at US$15.00, technology has made it possible for him to find (or not) a suitable buyer B in a matter of seconds, and the deal will be done promptly, executed through a computer. But technology can go too far, and what is known as high-frequency trading is a case in point.[12]

Back to the case of trader A and trader B. There was a simple transaction between two people which had taken approximately five seconds. What financial institutions have done is to create super-fast computer systems that work so quickly they can see trader A's intention to sell and trader B's intention to buy before they see each other.

These high-frequency traders can then step in, buy the stock and sell the stock all before the 'normal' transaction will have happened; and all the while making money by charging both the seller and buyer for their uninvited yet completely legal role. A consultancy company, the Tabb Group, recently estimated that high-frequency trading accounts for as much as 73 per cent of US daily equity volume, this figure being up from 30 per cent in 2005. In the US, bank IT spending will reach US\$43.5bn in 2009, up from US\$42.9bn in 2008, according to Celent, LLC, a Boston-based research firm.[13]

So what has this technology done except provide an intermediary with the opportunity to make more money – quickly. To what end technological advancement? Society bears substantial costs on at least two fronts: the fees paid by the trading exchanges to the brokers for stepping in could be better used for productive investments; and the promise of high rewards for building the bigger, faster and more technologically advanced mousetrap will divert the most gifted, talented and creative minds from areas such as solving the energy problem, cancer research or food production from which society as a whole (as opposed to just a handful of people) can benefit. This is not an anti-libertarian argument; it's an elucidation of how all of society can potentially be made better.

So, going back to the kitchen, not only can the obsession with the hyper-efficiency of the financial markets offer incremental benefits that are at best marginal (the notion of diminishing returns), but it could also carry (societal) costs.

In the last decade US productivity has improved, yet over roughly the same period China has posted the world's fastest productivity gains on record. Although the US undoubtedly remains among the global leaders in technological development, which drives efficiency and productivity in both labour and capital utilization, the worrying emerging trend is around increasing investment in productivity gains, where benefits accrue to a relatively small segment of the population, very often with no direct or broader societal benefits. For example, billions of dollars are now directed towards substantial investment in technological areas, such as high-efficiency trading (with ostensibly narrow economic benefits), in lieu, say, of investment in important sectors such as energy efficiency, food security or healthcare.

HEALTHCARE

While technology is largely being deployed to the financial sectors, rapidly emerging over the horizon is what Sir John Oldham, a physician and UK government adviser on long-term healthcare issues, calls a 'tsunami of healthcare needs'.

He estimates that between 2010 and 2050, there will be a 252 per cent rise in the number of people who are sixty-five years old or older in the industrialized West. Almost simultaneously he expects that there will be a 164 per cent increase in people with diabetes in the West, with the largest increase in Type II diabetes, which is primarily linked to lifestyle factors such as food intake. And as if that were not enough, between 2010 and 2014 (just four years from the time that this book has been written), 60 per cent of the existing cohort of diabetes sufferers (i.e. the majority) will have more than one long-term condition, including, but not limited to, chronic heart disease, chest maladies, muscular ailments, vascular problems or neurological complications. So although we are extending people's lives, the length of time that people will be ill will also be longer. Already in the UK 75 per cent of in-patient stays involve long-term conditions.

The cost burdens of this are staggering. And the demographic shifts are unforgiving. In 2010, 70 per cent of the health- and social-care costs in the UK are due to people with long-term conditions, and two thirds of emergencies are associated with these conditions getting worse. Data on Alzheimer's disease are similarly sobering. In 2010, the total estimated worldwide costs of dementia are US$604bn. About 70 per cent of the costs occur in Western Europe and North America. According to the US-based Alzheimer's Association, the number of Americans aged sixty-five and older who have or will have Alzheimer's disease is projected to increase from 5.1 million in 2010 to 13.5 million in 2050. Over the same period, the costs of care of sufferers is expected to soar to a staggering US$1tn. As people live longer the associated costs of such age-related afflictions are bound to be economically debilitating. A McKinsey report forecasts that by 2065 US health costs will represent 100 per cent of the country's GDP, with Japan and the major European countries achieving the same numbing statistic soon after. Because by its very nature such an equilibrium cannot exist, something is going to have to give.

With the current state of affairs the options seem clear, although not easily digested. In years to come governments will be forced to spend less on health, and politically have to face the backlash that would ensue from such a decision. Linked to this, other (publicly) funded sectors of the economy would inevitably have to suffer, be they education, infrastructure or national security.

Another option, in no way less unpalatable, requires a far-reaching and fundamental transformation that would see what John Oldham describes as less healthcare management in hospital and more health-care management on the part of the individual. A tall order indeed given social norms and the culture of fast-food and comfort eating in which the West has been inculcated.

In 2010, estimates suggest some 40 per cent of first-grade pupils (around the age of six) are obese. Obesity is the biggest driver of diabetes and with that often comes heart disease, kidney disease and other chronic ailments. Across the industrialized West many medical practitioners agree that this generation of six-year-olds will be the first to live *less* long than the generation that preceded them.

For economies, not only are there substantial cost implications arising from the cash outlays needed to cater to a generation that will be afflicted with long-term medical conditions at a disturbingly earlier age, but there is also the cost of lost output as the Western economies become less economically competitive with a more incapacitated workforce.

The challenges the West faces today suggest a complete revamp of the status quo is desperately needed. Governments have a clear respon-sibility to ensure their citizens attain some semblance of a basic education, comprising reading, writing and basic arithmetic. However, not everyone needs to learn integrals and calculus. And where high maths skills are required – say in jobs in businesses and industry – the private sector will almost certainly step in to pay for people to acquire them.

Considered together, the unnerving directions being taken in healthcare and education make a case for an overhaul of the academic curriculum across much of the industrialized West. Moreover, these ominous trends call for less of an emphasis on broad-based learning and more of a stress on healthy living and the basic elements of finance. Back to basics.

The looming healthcare tsunami also makes the case for government to consider another form of the Coase theorem discussed earlier, one where higher taxes are imposed on food today with the full knowledge and anticipation of the enormous associated healthcare costs that are guaranteed tomorrow.

ENERGY EFFICIENCY

It's not just education and healthcare that are causing headaches for policymakers across developed economies. There are very real and warranted concerns around energy, and what is rightly seen as an over-reliance on fossil fuels. The political ramifications of the West's oil dependency require a separate book to be written, but suffice it to say there are many detrimental effects attached to such an addiction. And while this book cannot offer a detailed treatise on the energy question, it's fair to provide some indication of the issues inasmuch as they have direct links to the theme of economic growth running through this book.

Like all good economic problems there is always a demand side and a supply side to contend with. The energy question is no different, with many on the demand side of the debate suggesting higher taxes as one way to curb demand for the spectrum of oil products. However, in a world which could see as many as 2 billion new entrants to the middle class by 2030, curbing energy consumption is a hard sell, never mind that Western politicians will almost certainly find it difficult to wean their own citizens off their addiction to multiple cars per household and other oil-related habits. All in all, today's prospects are for energy demands only to increase.

Naturally, the debate on energy also has a supply side dynamic. And on this side the debate has roughly evolved to be between energy manufacturing (mainly fossil fuels – coal production, natural gas and nuclear plants) and energy farming (including wind farming, solar energy and biofuels).

The main problem with fossil fuels is that they produce carbon by-products which are considered harmful to the climate and to living creatures. Carbon capture and storage (CCS) (in which carbon dioxide is captured from, say, large fossil fuel power plants and stored away from the atmosphere) can help mitigate the deleterious effects of fossil fuel emissions, but it is very hard to accomplish this in a cost-effective way. Which is precisely why the case for substantial resources aimed at technological research into CCS is so compelling. Meanwhile the well-documented problems associated with energy farming – energy supplies can be intermittent and unreliable, and are difficult to store and transmit over long distances – mean that, despite the noise around these alternatives, investment in such renewables cannot actually yield the best returns, and they continually prove to be among the most cost-ineffective despite receiving vast government subsidies.

Not so for nuclear energy.

While the calamity of the 1986 Chernobyl accident will for ever be etched into history, there are many rational reasons to look to nuclear energy as an alternative energy source. For one thing, on a relative basis, it's still considered the safest of energy sources, without the carbon by-product concerns arising from fossil fuels, not to mention that nuclear power can run for twenty-four hours a day with no disruptions, and just one nuclear molecule provides many hundreds of times of kilojoules of energy than its closest competitors.

Yet today, despite the pressing energy question, the US government does not fund anything meaningful in the nuclear field. Worse still, decades of the stigma attached to nuclear energy means that there has been little US investment in the nuclear engineering field to groom scientists who can advance research and practices in this area. Meanwhile, in 2010, it is thought that as many as 50 per cent of the power plants being built in China are nuclear-based, and even France gets almost 20 per cent of its electricity from nuclear sources.

In effect, the US, in particular, needs a Manhattan Project-style plan for energy. It is not just lagging behind in the public policy debate on nuclear energy; even if there were to be an about-face in thinking, it does not have the labour and technical know-how to put nuclear energy sourcing on track in a short time.

The 2010 BP oil spill on the US coastline and the ever-present geopolitical concerns caused by US dependency on oil sourced from some of the world's most politically unstable and despotic nations are reminders of why billions of dollars of investment in technological alternatives and into solving issues around energy storage, transmission, waste and cost reduction are so very critical.

SECURING FOOD

Around 1 billion people go hungry everyday.

The good news is that we have made significant strides in combating this ill, as this absolute number has remained stable while the world's population has rocketed from just 3 billion in 1960 to almost 7 billion today (the number going hungry is expected to remain roughly constant as the global population heads towards 9 billion by 2050). In other words, as a proportion of the total, fewer people are starving.

Nevertheless, for this 'bottom billion' a very pertinent question remains: does the world (developed and developing countries) have the ability to keep food production growing fast enough to offset forecasted global population increases? There seem only two real answers to this question.

One is deforestation and land-clearing to allow access to the earth's remaining arable land for people to grow food on. Of the billion people who go hungry globally each day, the highest concentration, some 300 million people, live in sub-Saharan Africa. But one third of the world's untilled arable land is also in Africa, suggesting there may be scope to redress the hunger situation there somewhat (building infrastructure and the establishment of transparent land-tenure and property rights would go a long way to solving Africa's food woes). Nevertheless, given the state of the environmental debate today, there is virtually no scope for a cool-headed discussion of such a proposal, thereby rendering it moot.

The other obvious option is technology. It's pretty clear that agriculture yields have to rise in order to cater to food pressures. In the 1960s staple crop yields in the West were rising by 3–6 per cent a year; in recent years they have collapsed to 1–2 per cent, with the yields across the most impoverished countries languishing around flat.

Technological advances – like them or hate them – can remedy this.

To be sure, agricultural yields are rising, just slower than population growth. The problem is that real technological advancements and efforts to combat hunger (and, as we will see shortly, disease) are stymied by people who have a romantic view of agriculture (and very often little scientific education), meaning their opposition to technology is very dangerous for the hungry poor. These people would recoil in horror from living their grandmothers' lives – they wouldn't want her attitudes, her modes of transport, her modes of communication or her medicines. But they continue to push for her methods of food production, with what appears to be little regard for the consequences. Ultimately, therefore, solving structural food crises is not just about increasing technological investment in agricultural production, but is also about the need for a fundamental attitude shift.

FROM HERE ON IN

In December 2008 comScore, a global internet research firm, reported that the world had reached one billion online users. According to its report, China was the country with the largest online audience, with 180 million users, surpassing the US at 163 million.

By comScore's estimates, around 55 per cent of the world's internet users are in the developing world (41.3 per cent in Asia–Pacific, 7.4 per cent in Latin America and 4.8 per cent in the Middle East and Africa); the balance is shared between the US (18.4 per cent) and Europe (28 per cent). This may simply be due to the fact that these populations are larger, and substantially so, but the speed and penetration of the technological connectivity spreading across the emerging lands cannot be denied. And these figures are rapidly climbing. We have already discussed how all this technology feeds into the growth story. It is essentially by increasing productivity, of capital and of labour, and increasing efficiencies in the economy.

The crucial catalyst has been the ability of labour in the developing world to absorb and deploy technology. Indeed, it is not just how many engineers a country has that matters, but rather how productive they can be. Even with the best education and know-how, without the hardware to increase productivity and raise output (and lower costs), even the most skilled labour force can be rendered impotent. Total factor productivity growth boils down to scientific innovation, the adoption of new and existing technologies, and technological assimilation to ensure improvements in production. Which is why the advent of the computer age has permanently transformed the speed and efficiency with which the average worker can produce anywhere in the world, but most of all in the emerging countries.

Data from the OECD going back to 1990 suggest that TFP growth across the most industrialized countries – the US, Japan, Germany, Britain and France – has been an anaemic 1 per cent a year. Meanwhile, the UBS economist Andrew Cates estimates China's TFP average annual growth between 1990 and 2008 to be 4 per cent – importantly, the world's fastest productivity gains on record. India too shows strong TFP growth (close to 3 per cent) over the same period. China's TFP growth is so remarkable it is almost twice as fast as South Korea and Japan at their peak economic growth periods.

There is more bad news for the West. In the past, total factor productivity increases were matched by a rise in wages, and these increases would lead to a boost in consumption, and investment, and these would spur greater (quality) economic growth. In the past twenty-five years, however, less pass-through has occurred and, in fact, Western wage increases have tended to lag behind productivity gains. This has meant that rather than TFP gains accruing to the providers of labour (i.e. wage-earners, through salary improvements), they have accrued to the owners of capital. The owners of capital have taken these productivity gains and, in turn, have lent the money to the providers of labour (in the form of debt). So, instead of labourers having increased purchasing power due to wage increases, labourers have increased their purchasing power through the accumulation of debt. This was certainly true in the case of the US, where wage-earners borrowed heavily to purchase houses and finance consumer consumption, neither of which went to fundamental growth improvements.

It is for this reason, and others outlined previously, that TFP and technological gains have stalled in the West, whereas TFP gains elsewhere (in particular in China and the other rapidly emerging countries) have translated into higher investment. For now, anyway, there are compelling arguments that these productivity gains alone might not be enough to drive development. In his seminal book on productivity, Bill Lewis, a founding director of the Mckinsey Global Institute, argues that productivity gains, if they are accompanied by distortions, cronyism and vested interests that impede fair and open competition in emerging countries, whose companies (can) pay no taxes, ignore regulations and steal intellectual property, won't necessarily translate into per capita GDP.

In some industrialized economies public sector growth (in absolute size and compensation) has been correlated almost entirely with a decline in productivity. In the UK, for example, the extra billions of pounds funnelled into the public sector in the decade leading to 2010 did not help bolster productivity. Quite the contrary, nearly all areas have shown a decline in productivity, including in many key sectors. For example, according to the Office of National Statistics, productivity in the UK's National Health Service has plummeted from around 102 in 1997 to roughly 96 in 2004 (productivity indexed so that 1999 = 100).

While factors such as a poor skill base, dilapidated infrastructure and cumbersome legislation all contribute to poor productivity performance, it is widely acknowledged that public sector growth has played a major role in this worsening decline. At the very minimum, unless the industrialized West implements radical policies to both protect and increase its proprietary know-how, this ominous trend will continue, again to the West's long-term economic detriment.

PART TWO

Back to the Future

From East to West and Back Again

Just as the cataclysm of the Second World War revealed the fundamental shift, once and for all, in world power from Great Britain to the USA that had been going on behind the scenes for roughly a generation, so too the financial crisis of 2008 has exposed another world upheaval many decades in the making: namely, the first tangible indication that a new transference of economic power has already begun; that of the West to the East, and perhaps more crucially from the US to China. If nothing else changes, this new transference of power portends to have even greater ramifications than the last.

For the last 500 years, the powers that have dominated and, in the broadest sense, shaped the world have been Western; and as communication grew globally with technology, so too did the West's influence. Today, the global language for business, trade and collaboration is the Western-based Romanic alphabet; the West proselytizes and exports (albeit gradually) its construct of democracy as being the finest expression of political/social man. In every corner of the world people sway to Western music (think Elvis and Michael Jackson), are entranced by Western film stars, drive Western-designed cars, play Western games – cricket, football, tennis and golf – listen to Western classical composers, read Western novelists, and debate Western philosophy and thinking. The development of modern man's history over the last 500 years has, indeed, been moulded by the West.

Now for the first time in over half a millennium it is the East that is in the ascendant, China and India in particular. For the moment it is precisely in economic terms that this change is most visible – but make no mistake, sooner or later, other changes to the ways things are done will be made too.

Think of the changes that happened between 1900 and 1950. Think then of the changes that took place from 1950 to 2000, cultural, social, all driven primarily by Western perceptions, Western inventions, Western goals. The next fifty years are not likely to be the same.

The renowned historian Niall Ferguson popularized the term Chimerica to describe the shift in power from a monopoly of the US to a duopoly of China and America. A perceptive word, by a perceptive man, but in the words of Ronald Reagan on the campaign trail for his second term as US president: 'You ain't seen nothing yet.' Chimerica is just the beginning. China is undergoing a second revolution. It had its cultural revolution in the mid-1960s, and now is in the throes of its economic revolution, and the myriad possibilities that it entails: its growing economic power, its global reach, its sense of who it is; its confidence grows daily, as does its ability to realize its ambitions. Its moment is coming, the momentum building.

Is it too late for America?

If America continues to follow the same misplaced policies as the ones outlined in the previous three chapters, the short answer to the question is yes. Economic forecasts already predict that America will cede its top spot as the world's largest economy to China by 2027 – a mere seventeen years away. The continued erosion of the quantity and quality of its capital, its labour and its monopoly in technology has set the American economy on a path of long-term, structural and fundamental destruction. It is, of course, possible to rein in the destruction, but not without solid policymaking and the implementation of hard choices.

China has not yet had an industrial revolution in the purest sense of being an innovator, instead apeing what has gone before. And, of course, while in 2027 it might hold economic supremacy, the average Chinese person will still be a good deal poorer than the average American.

However, is it simply a matter of winners and losers – a zero-sum game: if China wins, America has to lose? The Pareto Improvement theory postulated by the Italian economist Vilfredo Pareto suggests it doesn't have to be that way; it is quite possible for there to be an action in an economy that harms no one and helps at least one person.

In the global economic context, it may be possible for China to rise without America falling. Indeed, it may be possible that both can rise together. There is still a lot to play for.

But, with China in the ascendant and with the undeniable economic momentum, the question becomes: how will America play it? This is the pertinent question, but before addressing this, first a brief look at the countries of the new world order that are challenging the status quo.

'Economic activity is a source of power as well as wellbeing. It is, indeed, probably the most important source of power, and in a world in which military conflict between major states is unlikely, economic power will be increasingly important in determining the primacy or subordination of states. Precisely for this reason Americans have every reason to be concerned by the current challenge . . .'

In 'Why International Primacy Matters' (1993), Samuel Huntington was referring to the economic challenge posed by Japan. The US$846m purchase of New York's Rockefeller Group in October 1989 came to symbolize Japan's ascendancy. Had Huntington written his penetrating insight only a decade later he would almost certainly have seen a very different contender squaring up.

6

A Topsy-Turvy World

A SEAT AT THE GROWN-UPS' TABLE

A banker tells a story of an interaction with a senior Russian bureaucrat. Just months after Russia's 1998 default, a major international bank had decided to extend a loan in the hundreds of millions of dollars to the Russian government. In the weeks following the signing of the loan agreement, senior management at the financial institution agitated for a closing dinner (the customary meal which provides the lender with an opportunity to remind the borrower who's boss, and affords the borrower (in this case the Russians) the opportunity to show the lender just how grateful they truly are).

Under pressure after numerous phone calls, and a barrage of emails, the Russians finally capitulated and agreed to meet the bankers in Moscow. However, the acceptance came with a stern warning: 'We are the Russian Federation . . . we will not be lectured to.'

Over the last fifty years, the West's policies have principally been policies of exclusion – a culture of 'us' versus 'them'. In nearly all cases, the major international agencies – the organizations that set the policy agendas for world security, economics, trade and development – are dominated by the developed West, with virtually no representation from the emerging world. The G8, the boards of the IMF and the World Bank – the list goes on.[1]

Although this is now slowly changing, for whatever reason, these organizations have on the whole been reluctant to change, and the emerging world has been shut out. In 2009, to have the UK, France, Canada and Italy as permanent members of the G8, but not Turkey, Saudi Arabia, Mexico, South Africa, Brazil, India or China is not only preposterous, but also demonstrates an unwillingness to face the new reality of the modern economic world.

But now, to the detriment of the industrialized West, the emerging countries have responded by forming their own clubs. The south–south nexus (as it's termed) has meant the 'ostracized' emerging world today trades together, and plots together, with increasing disregard for the old, industrialized West.

In the spring of 2008, the most advanced group of the emerging bunch, Brazil, Russia, India and China (also known as the BRICs), announced *their* closed gathering – the first of its kind – would take place in Yekaterinburg, Russia, in 2009. The West was not invited. One of the purposes of the gathering was for the leaders of the BRICs, to 'use their economic clout to get a bigger say in how the world's financial system is run'. By the end of it they were calling for the establishment of 'a multi-polar world order'.

In a January 2010 *Financial Times* op-ed, Gideon Rachman argues that four of the world's most important democracies in the developing world – Brazil, India, South Africa and Turkey – are just as likely to side with China (or even Iran) on the big international issues as with the US. The 2009 Copenhagen climate conference was a poignant example of an increasing disregard for America. Rachman alleges that the Americans failed to fix one-to-one appointments for President Obama with the leaders of Brazil, India, South Africa and Turkey. The *pièce de résistance* was when, upon arriving for a last-minute meeting with the Chinese premier, Wen Jiabao, President Obama found the Chinese already in deep negotiations with the leaders of Brazil, India and South Africa. Worse still, and rather symbolically, the leaders had to squeeze up to make space for the American president at the table.

It is perhaps naive to lock all emerging countries into one bloc, as they could fall out or, indeed, politics could prevail and unforeseen events (both inside and outside their borders) could transform allegiances and outlooks, but for now the bulk of the evidence shows that they realize the strength of their combined weight, and their linkages – trade, financial, political – are deepening. Their partnerships are multiplying year on year in matters of food production, infrastructure and natural resources.

For example, in February 2009 China agreed to lend Russian

oil companies US$25bn in return for oil supplies for twenty years.[2] The two countries are also considering building a 4,000-kilometre (2,500-mile) pipeline from Russia's Far East Amur region to Daqing in north-eastern China.[3] Meanwhile, in May 2009, alongside a deal to increase Brazil's export of chicken and beef, China lent around US$10bn to Petrobras, Brazil's government-controlled oil company, in exchange for providing 200,000 barrels of oil a day to Sinopec (China's state-owned company) for the next ten years.[4] These sorts of deals – enormous in their scope – are becoming increasingly common between countries outside the West.

In July 2008 Russia's state-controlled gas company, Gazprom, announced its plans to buy *all* of Libya's future volumes of oil and gas exports – i.e. in perpetuity.[5] In recent years China has gained much notoriety for the staggering infrastructure and natural resource investments made across Africa and the Middle East.

The naked grabbing of land and natural resources has, of course, implications far beyond financial transactions among the emerging countries. The Gazprom approach is clearly an attempt to seize Europe's energy supplies, China's involvement in continental Africa (and elsewhere) is obviously made in anticipation of the world's future dwindling food supplies (after all, China itself is only 7 per cent arable land). China's headstart has given it an indisputable lead in the control of Africa's land mass, which represents one third of remaining untilled arable land on Earth.

And, of course, China's purchase of Peru's Mount Toromocho, composed of 2 billion tonnes of copper, is yet another strategic move to corner the natural resource market.[6] In the first four months of 2009, China overtook the US as Brazil's biggest trading partner, and by the summer of 2010 the same was true for Chile. The West is witnessing undisguised manoeuvres to command and control global economics, which is undoubtedly the precursor of geopolitical dominance.

The emerging countries, replete with cash, are spreading it liberally. It's not a simple matter of buying up the world's resources and being king of the world's supermarket: they have successfully put the Western countries in a position of subservience by making them debtor nations – in hock to the Rest.

China now lends the United States 23.4 per cent of its total borrowing (US Treasury securities worth US$800.5bn as of July 2009);[7] at the height of the 2008 financial crisis Russia lent €4bn (almost US$6bn) to Iceland in a bailout,[8] and Brazil gave US$10bn to the International Monetary Fund.[9]

By feeding the West's seemingly insatiable appetite for debt, the Chinese have masterfully manufactured the West's goods and provided them with the very cash (in the form of loans) with which to buy them; they have locked the West into a stranglehold of debt and dependence from which it will be very difficult to escape.

America might have thought itself clever in charging an entrance fee to Chinese goods, in the form of loans. But this has proved shortsighted: it is after all America that is drowning in debt, and whose citizens are consumed by consumption. It would have been a different matter had America borrowed domestically, and used the cash to make goods that kept Americans (and not the Chinese) in employment. But it didn't. America let China in the door, and like the old Levant parable of the Arab's tent and the camel outside, it has found itself out in the cold, and the Chinese moving in.

So aggressive and domineering has the approach of the Rest been in recent times that the West has started to retaliate – wherever and whenever it can. June 2009 saw an opening salvo when the US and Europe launched co-ordinated action against China because it had unilaterally decided to restrict its exports of raw materials – coke, silicon and zinc.[10]

So what has got the West's goat? It is not simply the stark realization that it has lost the monopoly it once had in capital, labour and technology, but more that, while they baulk at the belligerent if not ruthless approach the leading Rest are adopting to solidify their leads, in the light of their own route to economic greatness their objections ring somewhat hollow. The best the countries of the West can hope for in a globalized world is that they become one of many at the top table, but given their current economic path even this is not a racing certainty.

The emerging frontrunners have been quick to point out, with a generous helping of *Schadenfreude*, the West's glaring and humiliating economic and financial position. At the World Economic Summit in Davos in 2009 the world heard the Chinese and Russian leaders take turns in lambasting the West, and America in particular, for its role in bringing the global economy to its knees, and pointing out the precariousness of America's future economic position.

In a speech mocking the US role in the financial debacle, the Russian prime minister, Vladimir Putin, said: 'I would only like to remind you that, only a year ago, from this rostrum, we heard the words of American representatives about the fundamental stability and cloudless prospects of the US economy. But today, the pride of Wall Street – the investment banks – have practically stopped existing.'[11]

Perhaps in anticipation of these embarrassing and censorious lectures, no senior US government official was in attendance – the first time in recent memory.

WHAT HAVE THEY DONE TO DESERVE THIS?

The Nobel Laureate Milton Friedman once remarked:

> The great virtue of the free market system is that it does not care what colour people are; it does not care what their religion is; it only cares whether they can produce something you want to buy. It is the most effective system we have discovered to enable people who hate one another to deal with one another and help one another.[12]

Post-Second World War capitalism has fed and watered the world. It has improved people's health, increased longevity, given people work, educated them, clothed them and enfranchised them. All the benefits that you, the reader, enjoy, the job you have, the books you read, the car you drive, have been delivered to you courtesy of the market system – capitalism. Even the breakfast on your table is made possible through an intricate web of enterprise, labour and means of production that only capitalism (for all its faults and iniquities) can deliver.

Yet despite its beguiling attractions, countries have always grappled with a choice. Indeed, thirty years ago emerging countries faced two distinct alternatives: capitalism or communism. If they chose capitalism – which many of them did – they had to choose which type (the economic results of taking the other path have been broadly disastrous – see Cuba, much of Africa, and North Korea).

This is not the place to give an overall critique of the capitalist creed; it is, however, the right place to highlight the gradations across the capitalist system, inasmuch as each variant has profound implications for capitalism's ability to deliver economic prosperity in the new economic order. Indeed, the form of capitalism that countries chose would prove crucial in setting their economic paths to date and determining their prospects for economic growth tomorrow. But, perhaps most significantly, the type of capitalism they adopted would be critical in sheltering these economies from the vagaries of the financial markets in the 2008 credit crisis; and it would put them in a position to bail out those countries that had adopted the more virulent strain of capitalist system which had hitherto played the leading part on the global economic stage. These also put countries like China in a position to launch aggressive strategic campaigns such as global commodity requisitioning.

Contrary to popular belief, that all forms of capitalism are the same, historically the capitalist matrix has been broadly defined by three main varieties.

The first type is based almost solely on laissez-faire economics, and is perhaps the purest form of what Adam Smith had envisaged. This is the model adopted by the US, and to a lesser extent the UK (though, of course, the UK has a government-funded National Health Service), which even in times of economic stress believes in the edict, as voiced by the British prime minister, Margaret Thatcher, to the House of Commons in April 1988 that come what may 'there is no way in which one can buck the market.'[13]

The second approach is one of relatively high-tax, state-based support for public goods (a type of good where everyone benefits, but costs cannot be allocated to one person, e.g. a street light), but where the private markets are largely left to their own devices. This is the model favoured by much of continental Europe, and hence why income tax rates are generally higher in places like Scandinavia, France and Germany than they are in the US. It is from this tax base that everything from railways to pension systems is heavily state-subsidized.

The third form of capitalism is where the government has a firm hand in pretty much everything. This command-style regime is, in essence, the model adopted by China and the other stirring economies.

While in this case the government would not necessarily run or control a bakery, it would dictate the price of the bread. Very often this balance is achieved through a combination of stringent rules and regulations, and orchestrating a fine balance of macroeconomic policy. The architects of the East Asian miracle got this point. China's Deng Xiaoping, Singapore's Lee Kuan Yew and South Korea's Park Chung Hee all in their individual ways came to the consensus that an economic model couched in capitalistic thinking, laced with a hefty dollop of government intervention, was the way to go. This pragmatic approach was famously articulated by Deng Xiaoping at the 1961 Guangzhou conference when he said: 'I don't care if it's a white cat or a black cat. It's a good cat so long as it catches mice'; he was taken by all to mean that a country's productive life was of paramount importance, and not whether it adopted a communist or capitalist ideology.

Asia was not the only place where this new model of capitalism was rolled out and took hold. Sheikh Al Maktoum, the visionary behind Dubai, took this reclaimed land from obscurity to being the largest man-made harbour in the world, with a 2005 GDP registered at US$37bn for a population of just over 1 million people. Although it must be said (and 2008 certainly proved) that an economy largely built on tourism and an over-leveraged financial system must be on shaky ground (this would come to pass – see Dubai at the end of 2009).

Beyond Asia and the Middle East, the late 1980s movement of *perestroika*, the free-market economic overhaul that swept away the USSR's long-held shibboleths and defined the rise (and eventual fall) of Mikhail Gorbachev, had been the mantra adopted by a succession of Eastern European countries. But perhaps the finest moment came when, under President Boris Yeltsin, communist Russia capitulated to the heady allure of the capitalist model, briefly descending into an unshackled state of unconstrained and freewheeling oligarchs, until reined back in by the very visible hand of the Vladimir Putin government.

THE FORK IN THE ROAD: A CASE FOR STATE-LED DEVELOPMENT

Although it is impossible to know their exact thinking at the time, history would have warned China (and other emerging countries) of the consequences of unfettered capitalism – the hyper-inflation of the Weimar Republic, the 1929 Wall Street Crash and the ensuing Great Depression, and indeed booms and busts dating as far back as 300 years ago with the Dutch tulip mania of the seventeenth century and the South Sea bubble of the early eighteenth century, and the series of panics that marked the progress of the Napoleonic Wars.

The case for a government-led capitalistic approach (and for not allowing the free market to run roughshod) has seen no more compelling evidence than the 2008 credit crisis. In academic circles and on the financial circuit a broad consensus was reached as to the immediate causes of the crisis – excess borrowing (which Chapter 3 detailed extensively) coupled with inadequate regulation.

The Federal Reserve Chairman, Alan Greenspan (for decades referred to as the central banker to the world), had, over his nineteen-year tenure, taken the view that the most efficient marketplace was one governed by the least amount of formalized instruction. This almost inevitably resulted in a more freewheeling culture steeped in a belief that man's inherent goodness would, in itself, regulate the system – any necessary restraint would come from within rather than from without. What became brutally clear in 2008 was that self-restraint was the one thing the market could not be trusted to exercise.

Nothing would have bolstered the view of the emerging Rest of the need for and efficacy of state-led capitalism than the 2008 financial crisis.

In the Davos conference addressed by Russia's prime minister, Vladimir Putin, the Chinese premier, Wen Jiabao, underscored the view that a system based on 'excessive expansion of financial institutions in blind pursuit of profit' and an 'unsustainable model of development, characterized by prolonged low savings and high consumption' was not the way to go. Although he was careful not to name names, clearly he was referring to the United States.

The purpose here is not to pick apart the workings of the financial system (or what underpins it) upon which the West has come to rely (the financial literature is littered with these rebuttals). Rather, this discussion is simply to remind us that while the West seemed only too willing to ignore these inconvenient truths and brush aside the difference between theory and practice, the Rest apparently seemed all too aware of the free market's limitations and of the part that government must play in an irrational world; that, not just because of the weakness of financial models but for perhaps a whole host of macroeconomic reasons, government's role should be central – it should be the protagonist.

The 2008 financial crisis reminded the world that there are at least two occasions when even in an economy operating under a free-market system a government must step in and act. One is when there is market abuse or a breach of the law. The other is when the markets malfunction: for example, private markets can fail to provide public goods. Public goods exist for the benefit of everyone, but no one person wants to bear the cost of providing them – think of services such as education, healthcare, national security or infrastructure (though whether even some of these are public goods is a matter of debate). Here governments can, and do, step in to provide what private markets otherwise would not.

This book has already detailed how both the quality and the quantity of American education investment has been severely diminished over recent decades. And there has been no shortage of debate on the pros and cons of national security funding in the US, nor on health-care questions and the fact that as many as 50 million Americans (around 20 per cent of the country's population) had no healthcare insurance until the Obama administration instituted a nationwide healthcare scheme. And of course the mounting costs of continuing wars in Iraq and Afghanistan mean that national security and national interests are never far from the minds of policymakers and citizens. Not so infrastructure. Yet it is in this sphere – critical for the functioning of any economy – that America is vulnerable, and China is going for broke.

The state of America's infrastructure and the relative lack of focus in the area are well known. Yet government focus and financial commitment are exactly what this sector so desperately needs.

The collapse of the I-35 Bridge in Minneapolis, Minnesota, in August 2007, and the breach of the levees in New Orleans during hurricane Katrina in 2005 are just two examples of widespread weaknesses in the infrastructure of the US. In regular reporting the American Society of Civil Engineers dutifully catalogues numerous others. In published research the Society states that America's infrastructure overall is close to 'failing' and warrants a grade 'D'. It also states that around 30 per cent of America's 590,750 bridges are 'structurally deficient or functionally obsolete' and that it would require spending of US$9.4bn a year for twenty years to put them right. This is just for bridges.

The American government's role in paving the way for entrepreneurship and economic growth by laying down infrastructure dates back to the days of the cowboys. In *Bold Endeavors: How Our Government Built America, and Why It Must Rebuild Now*, Felix Rohatyn makes a lucid and compelling argument for the role of government in providing infrastructure. He details how government policy led the way for the public works which played an integral part in shaping America's economic destiny, from the Transcontinental Railroad, to the construction of the Erie Canal, the Reconstruction Finance Act, the Tennessee Valley Authority and the creation of the interstate highway system that modernized America; to the extent that in the nineteenth century the US army was deployed to protect the workers who laid down the infrastructure.

While there is growing acceptance that, as Rohatyn puts it: 'America's roads and bridges, schools and hospitals, airports and roadways, ports and dams, water lines and air control systems – the country's entire infrastructure is rapidly and dangerously deteriorating', the question that must be asked is where is the money going to come from to remedy this situation, and remedy it fast? Indeed money for infrastructure – certainly private cash – seems targeted towards vanity projects, leaving many New Yorkers hard pressed to name the last time Manhattan or any of the five New York boroughs had a new bridge or tunnel. Yet the city's sports teams – the Mets, the Giants and the Yankees – have each recently built a new stadium.

It is not just the US that is suffering from a dilapidated and debilitating infrastructure. According to *Britain after Blair – a Liberal*

Agenda, UK businesses argue that the state of Britain's transport infrastructure is not just one of the principal obstacles to improved productivity, it is also a clear impediment to business investment. In a survey for the Confederation of British Industry (CBI), 51 per cent of companies said that the reputation of the UK as a place to do business was being significantly harmed by transport problems.

The Obama administration's American Recovery and Reinvestment Act of 2009 includes US$45bn to spend on transportation infrastructure projects, doubling the federal budget for this purpose, and the private investor Warren Buffett's 2009 US$27bn bet on US railways are steps in the right direction, but relatively small steps all the same. After all, the 2009 American Society of Civil Engineers' *Annual Infrastructure Report* estimates that the US will need at least US$2.2tn over the next five years to remedy the structural failings and deficiencies across the country's public works system. Worse still, in 2005 the Society said it would cost US$1.7tn to fix what's broken; that's a US$500bn increase in the price tag (from US$1.7tn to US$2.2tn) in just four years – a very disturbing trend; and one likely to gather momentum in the years to come.

Meanwhile China's infrastructure roll-out is legendary. Projections from the *Economist* magazine suggest that between 2006 and 2010 China will have spent US$200bn on its railways alone; the largest investment in railroad capacity by any nation state since the nineteenth century. In addition, the Chinese government will oversee the construction of 300,000 kilometres (187,500 miles) of roads in its rural areas, as well as nearly a hundred new state-of-the-art airports over the next decade.

As for trains, one story suggests that, by 2020, 50 per cent of the world's high-speed trains will be operating in China, at speeds of 250 kph (over 150 mph) across 18,000 kilometres (11,250 miles) of track. Already Shanghai, China's financial capital, has the Maglev, the trans-rapid, super-speed, contactless magnetic levitation train system which, at a top speed of 430 kph (nearly 270 miles per hour), is the fastest train in the world. It was built in just four years. China's infrastructure today may have started from a low base, but the point is that it is in the government's focus for sure.

IN SEARCH OF POLITICAL FREEDOM

The West has believed in and relied upon a model couched in terms of political freedom (specifically individual freedoms and democracy), as well as a financial ethos based on a rational, complete and relatively certain world, a world where individual freedoms propel people to act in a self-interested way, which in turn would (should) lead to self-regulation, which would keep the markets in check. Until 2008, this seemed the way to go. Francis Fukuyama's 1992 polemic *The End of History* encapsulated this view, that the Western model had been tried and tested and there was no better one.

The Rest have taken a more cynical (but perhaps the more realistic) view of the world in which we live. Their political and economic systems are guided by a dogged belief in the state, and a suspicious apprehension as regards the behaviour and motivations of the individual. They believe that, left unshackled, individual human greed would always lead to equilibriums that benefit the few at the expense of the many – and of society as a whole. They point to the income inequalities of the West, and indeed the cronyism and vested interests within their own societies, and feel justified in their stance. They observe the irrationality, incompleteness and uncertainty of the world and grow even more confident in their conviction that, in the case of a shock, only governments can be relied upon to put together the plans that could save an economy from destruction, and that only a strong government would ever be able to steer a country out of a crisis. The backlash from the 2008 fall-out and the calls for nationalization, more governance and stricter regulation may have bolstered their view. How peculiar it seems that the West, so focused on individuality, would choose to ignore the risks and vagaries of human nature, whereas the monolith that the West knows as China appears to have factored them in.

Of course, it may still be too early to call; we need to wait and see how China does if and when it achieves Western standards of living. There is, after all, an argument that the greatest danger of 'fat tails' (i.e. low-likelihood, high-impact risks) remains in emerging countries precisely because their political institutions are most vulnerable, and their style of governance has not been tried and tested over long periods of time. There are clearly many inherent problems with Western-style institutions and economies, political agencies and incentive structures – most of which boil down to agency risk and/or under-informed decision-making. This is not necessarily so in the emerging world.

Take the all-important natural resource sector. Measured by their reserves, the thirteen largest oil companies in the world are owned and operated by governments – emerging market governments. State-owned companies such as Saudi Arabia's Saudi Aramco, the National Iranian Oil Company, Petróleos de Venezuela, Russia's Gazprom and Rosneft, the China National Petroleum Corporation, Malaysia's Petronas and Brazil's Petrobras control more than 75 per cent of global oil reserves and production. Of course, state-ownership of oil across the industrialized West is simply non-existent. The Western oil majors – ExxonMobil, BP, Shell – are all in the hands of private share-holders. Moreover, big as they may appear, they only account for 10 per cent of the world's oil production and 3 per cent of its reserves.

Then there is the matter of savings. The sovereign wealth funds of the emerging world, discussed earlier, are government-led, ensuring that the national savings decisions are at the most senior political levels in the interest of the state at large, over and above purely indi-vidual motivations. Of course there are entrepreneurs in these regions whose intention is maximize their own profits and who are motivated by self-interest, but there is little doubt that they must work in a con-trolled framework where public welfare as a whole is paramount. Of course, Chinese equity investment has not been a unilateral slam-dunk success, but the important point is that sovereign administered funds are pools of capital 'owned' by governments acting in the inter-ests of the broader population – and in this case very different from the piles of private capital familiar in the West.

Even at the very personal level, the line between private and public decisions is blurred. What Westerners would regard as the sanctity of the individual, much of the Rest regard as the domain of the state. China's well-known one-child policy introduced to alleviate economic and social pressures (the Chinese authorities claim that since its inception in 1979 this policy has averted at least 250 million births up to 2000) is just one example of how the leading emerging countries seem to leave little to chance.[14] In 2008 China's National Population and Family Planning Commission stated that the policy would remain in place for at least another decade.[15]

And while Westerners complain bitterly about being captured on closed-circuit television (CCTV) surveillance cameras, Singapore has established the Social Development Unit, a government-led match-making organization whose mission is 'to promote marriage among graduate singles, to inculcate positive attitudes towards marriage among all singles, and to bring about the formation of strong and stable families in Singapore'.[16] In over twenty years of playing cupid, the state agency has been responsible for nearly 30,000 marriages. The brave new world.

In the emerging world the state's reach seems to know no bounds; the collective state is paramount and takes precedence over any individual, contravening the Western dogma that the individual is king.

In a competitive and brutal world order, such as we have today, it is foolhardy to expect the Rest to abandon their aggressive strategy that has, thus far, proven to be successful – one has only to look at the economic El Dorado the Rest have discovered.

THE YING OF THE WEST VERSUS THE YANG OF THE REST

Previous sections looked at the evolution of GDP across countries over the centuries, providing a picture of who was in the ascendant and who was on the decline. However, in order to better understand why countries' aggregate GDPs are in the position they are in, it's best to break GDP down into its respective component parts.

A country's economic ability to produce wealth (its gross domestic product – GDP) boils down to one simple equation: $Y = C + I + G + (X - M)$. Many will recognize this as the most fundamental, most simplistic and most basic of all macroeconomic formulas. But this very simple tenet encapsulates, in the most straightforward way, what the West did wrong and what the Rest did right. It is, in fact, the easiest way to explain what is a very complicated story. Let's look at the formula a little more closely.

Y represents a country's GDP, i.e. its income. Its GDP is made up of the following: C stands for consumption, the amount the population spends (individuals, not government); I represents the total investment in a country (both public and private); G reflects the net position of government, i.e. its revenues (taxes, etc.) less its expenditure; and (X – M) is the country's exports less its imports. For example, a country with consumption of US$200, investment of US$100, a net government position of US$500, exports of US$400 and imports of US$200 (i.e. a net external position of US$400 – US$200 = US$200), will have a GDP of US$1,000.

Each country's GDP is governed by this sum (including how a country relates with other economies). An examination of this formula will also explain how the industrialized world found itself in free-fall, while the Rest were on the up. This has not been accidental. And although economics may appear to be a capricious affair, it is striking how effectively the Rest have been pursuing their long-term goal of economic success. There is little doubt that these countries are now firmly ensconced on the path there.

Consumption

If there is one thing that has come to define the twentieth-century Western mindset it is unfettered consumerism. The story of the American consumer has been one of how he has been encouraged by all and every means possible to increase his insatiable appetite. There is nothing inherently wrong with consumption *per se*. Indeed, looking at the GDP equation above, an increase in consumption feeds into the GDP (or income stream) of an economy in a positive way – higher consumption means higher GDP.

What happened in recent decades is that a combination of low interest rates, easier credit and the rapid growth in all forms of asset prices (between 1997 and 2006 American home prices increased by 124 per cent) fuelled and financed the West's consumption boom in a cycle that gathered momentum. For example, the rise in house prices enabled many homeowners to use the increase in their house values to refinance their homes with lower interest rates and to take out second mortgages, and, in tune with the times, they used this unlocked cash for a consumer spending spree. US household final consumption expenditure as a percentage of GDP was, in 2007, 70 per cent, compared with about 35 per cent in China and 54 per cent in India. Despite China's standing in the world – it is the world's second-largest economy – it ranks only fifth in consumption, and for this reason its consumer spending has been labelled 'anaemic' in the *McKinsey Quarterly*.

In 2009 China had a savings rate of 51 per cent of GDP – one of the highest in the world, compared to just US$1.6tn in the US economy (13 per cent of its GDP), which, incidentally, was six times the size of China's. These estimates of aggregate savings (government saving, plus corporate savings, plus household savings) provide just a glimpse of the very distinct and divergent savings paths that these two countries have chosen. (As part of the post-financial-crisis deleveraging process, US savings are now on the rise.) Looking at the more disaggregated savings picture reveals an even greater chasm between them.

Chinese household savings, for example, were a lofty 30 per cent of household income. Compare this against a negative (after-tax) savings rate of 0.4 per cent of US households, which means to say that the average American household was not saving at all – happy days. Of course the problem is that this is not a statistical blip – the chasm has been growing for decades. As Stephen Roach, former Chief Economist at Morgan Stanley, put it in 2006: 'The two major players in the global economy, the US and China, are operating at different ends of the saving spectrum. Thrifty Chinese have taken savings to excess, while profligate Americans have spent their way into debt.'[17,18]

The sub-prime market saga is today well known, but commentators on the whys and wherefores of the financial crisis routinely, and mistakenly, claim that US private consumption increased at the expense of gross private domestic investment, which is simply not the case. The questions surrounding consumption are twofold: does consumption rise at the expense of investment? And does consumption rise at the expense of trade (more specifically, the trade balance)?

Investment

Much like private consumption, private sector investment in the US rose in an upward trend from US$1.389tn to US$2.136tn in the years 1997 to 2008.[19] On closer inspection it is clear that headline figures belie the true picture; much of this investment boom pooled in the housing sector, contributing to the home sector bubble.[20]

The fact is, consumption did not occur at the expense of total aggregate investment. The problem was that the quality of the investment was poor: too much of the investment was targeted at the most unproductive sectors. This investment in unproductive ventures that produced no cash stream meant the US was inevitably set for a fall. Investing in plant, roads, railways and machinery is one thing – these are cash-yielding assets which add to the economy – but paintings, holidays and all forms of housing are very much another; these convenience-assets produce nothing, yet production is what economic growth is all about.

Commentators and policymakers appear overly concerned about consumption as a percentage of GDP but this is a red herring, and simply focusing on US consumers buying too much stuff is missing the true and core problem. An increase in consumption as a percentage of GDP is neither a good nor a bad thing by itself. What is important is what accompanies it. Indeed, one person's consumption is another's income.

To illustrate this: imagine for a moment that the US government creates a national healthcare system; then individual consumption would most likely drop because currently health spending forms part of consumption. However, the government portion of GDP changes (i.e. government spending); it goes up if the cost of delivering the healthcare is greater than the taxes levied to pay for it, and thereby increases the deficit. Conversely, government spending would go down in the (unlikely) case that public healthcare delivery is cheaper than the taxes levied and, of course, nothing would really change from an accounting standpoint, assuming that the government can deliver services as well as the private sector (suspend disbelief on this fact).

In a similar vein, imagine what would happen if the US government got out of the defence business altogether and all army, navy and air force personnel were immediately hired by private security forces. The immediate reduction in the public payroll would be reflected as government spending going way down, and (private) consumption going way up. In either of the cases presented, a change in consumption as a percentage of GDP on its own means little; it's the relative change in the components of GDP that matters.

Indeed, if consumption goes up, and investment goes down, the situation is worthy of grave concern. The UK economy in the 2000s is a screaming example of this. Yet over a number of years in the US, consumption has gone up, but, while investment has generally been flat, it has at times even gone up!

The problem for the US is that the rise in consumption as a percentage of GDP was not offset by investment or by a change in the government percentage, but by the trade balance growing. Much of the subsequent increase in income leaked offshore. What this means is that solving the US consumption problem in itself is only a part of the problem – the larger problem, indeed where policy should focus, is solving the trade problem.

The trade balance

Henry Ford was known for paying his factory workers above the going rate, and when asked why he did this he famously proclaimed something to the effect that: 'I want to pay my workers more so they will buy my cars.'[21]

In much the same vein, America's consumption boom need not have been detrimental to its economy had not the benefits accrued somewhere else. Indeed, if Americans had largely consumed American goods manufactured by American workers (even if debt-financed), then the net effect could have been positively beneficial. The data are telling in that the increase in US consumption actually came at the expense of the trade balance (the difference between exports and imports). As far as America is concerned, the problem has been that its higher levels of consumption, witnessed over recent decades, have helped secure growth and employment for China and not for Americans at home. In other words, American consumption has generated income that has not seeped into American pockets. This is not an argument for protectionism; it's a statement of reality.

In 2007 China and America traded goods worth over US$400bn between themselves; this was up from US$5bn in 1980. Take a look at the telling differences in the trade balances (exports minus imports). In 2006 the US had a yawning deficit of 6 per cent of GDP – the low spot of a near decade-long cycle that see-sawed between –4.3 per cent in 2000 and –5.3 per cent in 2007.

In the meantime, China's external position has been nothing if not buoyant. In 1970 China's trade share of GDP was just 5 per cent. Although signifying that China was selling much more than it was buying, this positive trade balance was nothing compared to its peak in 2007 where, after a multi-decade positive run, the country's trade book stood at a colossal 75 per cent of GDP. Which is precisely why, in 2009, China was ranked number one in world exports, beating Germany to the top spot.

All this has not gone unnoticed by Western citizens and policymakers. Despite the accompanying threat of manufacturing job losses, the 'Buy American' slogans, the rantings of US opinion formers, such as the TV pundit Lou Dobbs, and even the charges levelled against the Chinese for unsportsmanlike play (commentators have long voiced concerns at how China has maintained and manipulated its currency to its trading advantage; keeping its fixed exchange rate weak – as Western countries once did – and not allowing a natural currency appreciation to occur, which, in turn, makes relatively cheaper Chinese goods more attractive to foreign buyers – more Chinese exports, a stronger Chinese trade balance).

Comparative advantage versus volume-maximizer

The core problem is that the US is following trade guidelines set out in economics textbooks some 150 years ago – the law of comparative advantage. Comparative advantage puts forward the notion that ideally an individual, company or country should produce the goods or services where it has the lower opportunity cost, and can produce them most efficiently. The notion of comparative advantage is nice in theory, but only works when all countries (individuals and companies) play by the same rules. The practical reality is that this is not the case. And while there are gains to be had from trade when there is no reciprocity from a trading partner, the ideal scenario is one in which countries trading together are each doing what they best do in the most cost-effective and efficient way.

Indeed, Asian countries, led by China, have tended to play a trade game of absolute advantage, where individuals, companies and countries produce goods and services at a lower absolute (not relative) cost than another. Like many other emerging countries China is a volume-maximizer, not profit-maximizer, in that it needs to maximize volume to drive jobs in an effort to ultimately maintain social (and political) stability.

Which is why China doesn't just want to make T-shirts and radios, toys and trinkets, and trade them for operating systems and aeroplanes; China wants to make everything. On the whole, volume-maximizers tend to pursue absolute advantage, not the competitive advantage posited by Western countries. The US needs to realize this fact and adjust international and trade relations to address it. More on this pertinent issue later.

Government spending

Finally, there is G, the government fiscal position.

Whereas by 2008 most industrialized nations were running fiscal deficits in the order of 4 per cent of GDP (the US at −4.1 per cent, Japan at −3.4 per cent, the UK at −3.5 per cent), China boasted a double digit fiscal *surplus* in the same year, as well as for the better part of the last decade. Compare this with the West's performance. Between 1992 and 2001, the average US fiscal deficit was 2 per cent – a prelude to the following six years of burgeoning government funding shortfalls (in 2010 the US fiscal deficit approached a worrying 11 per cent of GDP).

Suffice it to say that running a deficit is not in itself a bad thing (in fact, many economists have argued it's a harbinger of long-run growth), the important point is whether or not the country is able to finance it. Given that Western nations borrowed heavily from places like China it is no surprise that they have become heavily beholden debtor nations. In 2009 America's financial position was precarious:

it was running the greatest fiscal budget deficit since the Second World War.

The tax revenue the US federal government collects (about 17 per cent of GDP) pretty much offsets the government's spending on defence (even in 2008 Joseph Stiglitz estimated that the costs of the Iraqi war alone were US$3tn – almost one third of the US GDP), health and pension benefits (social security, Medicare, Medicaid, veterans' benefits), and interest payments on debt.

The rest is financed by borrowing. Education, infrastructure (roads, railways, bridges, water, transport and tunnels), science and techno-logical innovation, the courts and legal system, aid to foreign countries, security, clean energy and the climate change agenda are financed with borrowed money. This is a good place to segue into another metric: debt.

THE DEBT CLOCK

In 1989 a real estate developer, Seymour Durst, anxious to highlight the rising national debt, unveiled a billboard-sized clock near New York City's Times Square which did just that, second by second, twenty-four hours a day. Those who cannot get to New York can log on to www.usdebtclock.org for an equally sobering experience. What is on display is the total value of America's national debt burden at any given moment.[22]

At the time of writing in spring 2010, the US total debt (defined by the US Federal Reserve as the total debt of US households, businesses, state and local government, financial institutions and the federal government) stands at US$55tn (US$54,799,285,524,321.22, to be precise). With estimates that the US national debt has been rising at a US$3.6bn a day since 2007, one thing is for sure: by the time anyone reads this it will be a whole lot bigger. Meanwhile at around US$12tn the outstanding US national debt implies that every American citizen bears a debt burden of around US$40,000 (remembering that the aver-age US take-home (after-tax) pay is around US$45,000, that means he or she has been working for a notional US$5,000). So basically every American would have to work for a year for free to cover this debt.

Put another way, America's outstanding national debt is fast approaching the total annual GDP value of the country, which stands at US$14tn, and is likely to have surpassed that figure by the time this book is on the shelves. Unsurprisingly, Durst's original debt clock has had to be replaced to accommodate more noughts.

The culture of consumerism that ensued after the age of relative thrift could only be sustained by unprecedented levels of debt. The stark reality of debt pervades not only the government, but also individual households. In practical terms, because this meant that both Western governments and individuals were spending more than their revenues, it left them no choice but to borrow to plug their shortfall. And borrow they did.

During these years Americans spent US$800bn per year more than they earned. By 2008 household debt had grown from US$680bn in 1974 to US$14tn in 2008 (the size of the total American economy). US household debt as a percentage of income rose to 130 per cent during 2007, versus 100 per cent earlier in the decade, and nearly quadruple the 36 per cent of 1952. The average US household owned thirteen credit cards, of which 40 per cent had debts outstanding (this was up from 6 per cent in 1970).

Clearly the stigma associated with having (unsustainable) debts has long passed. People forget that in mid-nineteenth-century Britain people would be imprisoned for such debts, and would not be released until they paid them off.

Between 2001 and 2007 the US public debt burden grew from US$3.32tn to US$6.51tn dollars, i.e. a 96 per cent rise in just six years, and an increase from 33 per cent of GDP in 2001 to 47 per cent in 2007. As discussed in earlier chapters much of the US debt financing came from China and Japan, whose largesse (albeit at a fee) accounted for 23 and 21 per cent of the US liabilities, respectively, according to the US Treasury Department's 'Major Foreign Holders of U.S. Treasury Securities' (2009). All the while China was running pretty lean with its debt share of GDP at a meagre 16 per cent, and Russia's was merely 10 per cent of GDP in the run-up to the global financial crisis.

Hindsight is truly 20/20, and looked at in the cold light of day anyone can see that these figures are preposterous. The US is not alone in this quagmire. According to the *Financial Times*, 'in cash terms, the [UK] government expects to borrow more in 2009 and 2010 than the entire borrowing of centuries of British governments between 1692 and 1997.'

Of course, one can borrow as much as one likes, as long as someone out there is prepared to lend. The trouble arises when no one is willing to lend to you anymore, and lenders' largesse comes to a screeching halt, leaving you with debt, and lots of it; Iceland 2008 being one recent national example.

Debt works its way into the GDP equation through how governments and individuals finance their activities. And although apparently absent from the formula $Y = C + I + G + (X - M)$, the level of interest rates dictates the amount of consumption and investment by individuals and government. So as interest rates rise, for example, the corresponding level of investment is thought to decline (the higher interest rates reflecting again the higher cost of borrowing, which ostensibly discourages investment) and vice versa. In a similar vein, as interest rates plummet, savings decline and consumption rises, as individuals, reluctant to lock up their cash for little reward, spend their money instead.

It is worth remembering that although in credit crisis parlance debt has taken on a bad name, it has (and will always have) a vital role in a functioning market economy. It is, after all, the lifeblood of finance, offering borrowers the chance to invest in projects that they otherwise might not (for example, the use of credit cards is one way for entrepreneurs to acquire capital for their start-ups; it is believed that the search engine Google was originally financed by such means), and governments the opportunity to fund today the public works (roads, railways, etc.) that otherwise could take a lifetime to finance, and, of course, are an integral part of a country's success tomorrow.

One might wonder why the Chinese were not more outraged at the extravagant boom in US consumption, and the reckless low-quality investment in the housing market – they were lending them the billions of dollars after all. Likewise the Japanese and Middle Eastern states, which meant that in total these countries had the US government on the hook for close to an eye-watering US$2tn.

The answer is clear, certainly where China is concerned.

First, it was vendor financing. Thanks to their bloated coffers, the Chinese were willing to provide subsidized loans to the United States, loans which helped fuel consumption underwritten by debt – credit card debt, consumer loans, car loans, school loans, etc. The Chinese should have been concerned, but there was so much more for them to gain (at least in the short term). In return for China's funding of this orgy of consumption, US consumers and consumption helped keep Chinese factory production lines moving and millions of Chinese employed; a political coup for any government, but especially so for China with its development agenda which would need to see its millions of citizens put to work in order for it to succeed.

Remember, because of the sheer size of its population, and the need to maintain political stability, China has adopted the stance of a volume-maximizer. The more product it can push, and sell outside its borders, the better for the country as a whole. It matters little if the product is sold at non-market (i.e. distorted) terms, or even if it makes no profit at all; this suits China, and the Western rationale of profit-maximization falls by the wayside. In a nutshell, because there was something very valuable for China to gain it would never have bitten the hand that fed it. The US International Trade Commission estimates the 2008 bill for imports to the US from China at US$337.8bn, in other words that is the revenue China could forfeit if it lost its US consumers.

The second reason harks back to the earlier discussion on the downside of guarantees. Although many millions of Americans had borrowed for what became possibly the biggest unproductive bubble in history, the US government had given iron-clad guarantees to China and other lenders that they would get their money back, come what may. Even when 'come what may' happened – Fannie Mae and Freddie Mac's near utter collapse – the Chinese didn't call and demand that these institutions reduce their risk; they simply called the US government and reminded them who was boss, urging them to place guarantees on the Chinese debt the US held. The US obliged, placing itself further in debt to the Chinese. Before the Chinese are pilloried and accused of being unfair for demanding guarantees, it is worth remembering that even at the individual level most Americans behaved in a similar manner.

Though it is true that many people might have spotted house prices looking frothy back in 2005 or 2006 and got out of the market by selling housing REITs and housing stock positions, what did they do? They took their money and placed it in their bank accounts, never once asking the banks what they were doing with it. Why should they? After all, their deposits were government-guaranteed. What the world later found out, of course, was that virtually all the banks had bought into the very market (the housing market) from which the deposit holders had tried to escape.

A GLIMPSE INTO THE CRYSTAL BALL

People say one of the best ways to gain a deeper understanding of the Chinese psyche is to understand Xiangqi, a two-player board game akin to chess which is known to draw thousands of spectators.[23] Apparently, the game gives a good glimpse into how the Chinese think and develop strategies over the long term. A perhaps altogether less cryptic way to understand the Chinese economic strategy is to read the Eleventh Five-Year Plan for National Economic and Social Development of the People's Republic of China.[24]

Here, laid bare, is a fourteen-point plan penned by China's National Development Reform Commission. The overview covers all the key sectors one might expect – science and education, the environment and security, as well as topics traditionally less synonymous with the China story, such as democratic politics and institutional reform. Whatever China's detailed strategy of attack – and details are characteristically scarce – one thing is evident: it is doing something right.

Although the economic policies of the Rest have not necessarily been identical (for example, India has remained more closed to global trade than, say, China), if we look back on the past thirty years the economic outcomes of the most dominant emerging players have been broadly similar. While private savings have increased among the Rest, they have decreased in the West; as government budgets skyrocketed to surplus in the Rest, in the West fiscal deficits ballooned, and as trade balances moved more and more positive in the Rest, rising imports left gaping holes in Western trade positions. Besides this, across the emerging markets the development approach has been deliberate and systematic – nothing has been left to chance. Most important of all, the majority of forecasters agree, the strategy has been effective.

At the turn of the century, Angus Maddison postulated that China could overtake the USA and reach pole position as the largest economy on earth before 2020. The American investment bank Goldman Sachs earned fame (and notoriety) for similarly startling projections in 2001 and 2003, when in its published research it described China as on the path to the top of the GDP league table. Brazil, India and Russia were not far behind. In fact, by Goldman Sachs estimates, these four countries are expected to be in the top five largest economies by 2050.

Although China's income per capita surpassed India's in 1986, in many ways India is the one to watch. Some forecasts have India becoming one of the world's three largest economies within the next thirty years, and the only BRIC economy able to sustain its growth at over 5 per cent throughout the next five decades.

Already, with 450 million people in 2009, India has the largest middle class in the world – more than all the European populations added together. The burgeoning Indian middle class will contribute, of course, to the 2 billion new members estimated to join the ranks of the global middle class by 2050. In 2006 the US share of world GDP stood at 26 per cent. It had, in the preceding two years, been trounced by the emerging economies that now represent nearly a third of world GDP.

What does this all mean?

In the early summer of 2009 the newly appointed American Treasury Secretary, Tim Geithner, addressed a roomful of Chinese students at Peking University on the continuing financial crisis. When, in an attempt to reassure them of America's probity, he told them that China's official holdings of Treasury bonds were safe, the statement was met with open laughter. Faith in the almighty dollar seemed no more.

The decline in the reputation of the American greenback is not confined to a few unruly students but goes right to the top, and not just in China. At the same World Economic Forum in Davos where they had been quick to point out America's hubris, China's premier, Wen

Jiabao, demanded better regulation of major reserve currencies, while Vladimir Putin castigated the world's over-reliance on the dollar as 'dangerous'. The governor of the People's Bank of China, Zhou Xiao-chuan, has suggested that the dollar be replaced as the world's reserve currency (albeit by the IMF's Special Drawing Rights – a basket of the world's leading currencies – the US dollar, the euro, the Japanese yen and the British pound sterling).

Although the US dollar remains the currency of choice around the globe (accounting for around 65 per cent of the world's foreign currency reserves in 2010, though this figure is down from the nearly 85 per cent of FX reserves in 1973), when we look at the history of sterling the trend is ominous. At the end of 1899 sterling accounted for approximately 64 per cent of FX reserves; by the end of 1913 it accounted for approximately 48 per cent of FX reserves.

Not even a century ago the British pound was the world's favoured currency.[25] It was superseded by the US dollar. Looking just thirty years ahead, it is not hard to conceive of a world where other currencies are equal if not superior to it in strength. With three quarters of all currency reserves owned by the emerging economies (China itself has one third of the entire reserve pool), it is no wonder that speculation in the foreign exchange markets is rife that a new currency will emerge controlled by the leading rising countries.

There are those who regard the prospect of the Chinese renminbi becoming the world's reserve currency as remote in the foreseeable future. They argue that central banks around the world are likely to keep most of their reserves in US dollars, as much of global trade remains denominated in dollars. They also argue that America's allies in Asia and the Middle East are unlikely to dump the dollar as they gain comfort from the shelter of America's military umbrella: a political as much as an economic decision. There is the view that China's economy has some growing up to do before the renminbi becomes the currency of choice. Specifically, its bond markets and its currency regime still lack the size, depth and convertibility to rival the US dollar. And in making the decision to 'hold or unload' there is something to be said about a country's or region's price stability/inflation, property rights and political stability. Yet there have already been signs to the contrary.

Many saw the 2009 US$50bn loan that China made to the IMF as its clearest signal yet that its currency – the loan was to be made in China's local currency, the renminbi – was gaining in international stature. There have been other signs.

In 2009, as a way to provide seed money to its trading partners, the People's Bank of China signed a total of 650bn renminbi (US$95bn) in bilateral currency swap agreements with six central banks: South Korea, Hong Kong, Malaysia, Indonesia, Belarus and Argentina. Meanwhile China is in discussions with other central banks to make additional swap agreements and will most likely expand them to cover all the country's trade with Asia. China's strategy to raise the status of the renminbi in international trade and global finance is well and truly underway.

No more a world where the greenback is the world's favourite currency, instead it would be the redback. Think about it. Foreign exchange, share prices, the price of copper, the price of oil, all in Chinese renminbi.[26]

7

All is Not Lost

BETWEEN SCYLLA AND CHARYBDIS

Homer's *Odyssey*[1] describes two grotesque monsters, dwelling on either side of the Straits of Messina. Scylla is portrayed as having six heads sitting on long necks and twelve feet. She inhabits a dark cave, and regularly attacks and eats sailors passing too close to her lair. On the other side of the strait, Charybdis has an enormous gaping mouth, into which he draws vast quantities of water and then creates dangerous whirlpools by belching throughout the day. While passing through the straits Odysseus has to decide which monster to confront; he opts to lose only a few sailors by passing Scylla, rather than face the whirlpool of Charybdis and risk the loss of his entire ship.

Like Odysseus, it seems the West must choose which monster to confront: if it does nothing, it faces swift economic oblivion; if it continues to pursue wrong-headed policies, although its survival may be prolonged its economic demise will be inevitable.

According to the 2009 Rasmussen polls 37 per cent of Americans don't expect the US to be number one by the end of the century. And nearly half of those polled (49 per cent of Americans) say America's best days are in the past.[2] And according to the Pew Research Center for the People & the Press, in December 2009 just 27 per cent of Americans said the United States is the world's top economic power. China now holds that position, said 44 per cent of those polled.

In theory, the world (including the West) should be happy about the possibility that the incomes and livelihoods of hundreds of millions of people will be meaningfully improved – and converge with those of the industrialized West. After all, broader world growth offers the possibility of bigger economic markets, broader technological progress, less global poverty and more of the world's population living better lives. The problem, of course, is that we can't all be winners. Natural resource limits and constraints remind us that this is so. Setting aside the depressing statistics for a moment, there are, nevertheless, reasons to remain sanguine. Despite the battering from the financial crisis, it's not necessarily all over for the West.

On the plus side, the US remains the largest single economic zone in the world. It still represents nearly 30 per cent of world GDP, meaning it is starting from a position of relative power. It remains the biggest manufacturer, is home to some of the world's best universities, is the most economically competitive, and is ahead on generating profits. It still maintains the lead in transparent and credible institutions – and in terms of the rule of law, though it is far from perfect, it remains one of the leading countries in the world. For many millions, the opportunity set remains better in the West. It still offers the best standards of living (the water they drink, the air they breathe) for its citizens even in the most heavily populated conurbations, such as New York, London or Paris, and on balance a place like America is arguably still, all round, the best endowed in terms of natural resources.

Emerging countries are undoubtedly converging with the richest economies, and fast. Merrill Lynch and Capgemini expect the Asia–Pacific region to overtake North America as the largest concentration of wealthy people in the world by 2013. That noted, emerging countries have a number of hurdles to clear in order to achieve economic supremacy. Their cities are bursting at the seams with their inhabitants, their infrastructure is creaking, and they are choking with pollution. Also, gaping income inequalities, debilitating diseases and political uncertainty all add to their problems.

FROM GLUTTONY TO GLOBAL CONSTRAINTS

In the summer of 2008 Nigeria faced a severe power shortage. The country was reportedly only managing to produce 6,000 megawatts of power for its 150 million people. By contrast, each year South

Africa, facing a critical energy shortage of its own, produces almost 40,000 megawatts of power each year for just 60 million people. Nigeria is clearly in deep trouble. But the acute power cuts are not confined to Africa, or even just the emerging world, as the rolling power cuts and blackouts in California and Texas have proved. Power shortages exist on a global scale, and any efforts to lay down and/or modernize electricity and power production themselves require a consistent and reliable power flow; sadly this does not exist.

US$27tn. That's the International Energy Agency's estimate for what it would cost the world to remedy its chronic power shortage. This number is roughly equivalent to twice the total value of the US GDP today.

British researchers forecast global energy demand will increase by 50 per cent by 2030. The rising pressure on energy resources is well known. In 2002, for example, the United Kingdom became a net importer of gas; this, after decades of being one of the world's leading exporters of oil and gas as well as being able to satisfy its own domestic demand. Already Europe imports 30 per cent of its gas from Russia, having depleted much of its own resources. Today, with just 5 per cent of the world's population, the US uses 25 per cent of the world's energy.

Naturally, the security implications of industrialized countries being beholden to poor oil-based emerging economies is enormous. Yet the US remains dependent on energy imports from arguably some of the most unstable countries on earth – Angola (3.2 per cent), Iraq (6.3 per cent), Venezuela (8.4 per cent) and Nigeria (9.6 per cent), to name a few. To make matters worse, because only a handful of countries export energy, aside from Norway, all prosperous countries already are energy importers.

As oil-exporting countries (and indeed the rest of the emerging world) continue to create their own middle classes that demand (domestic) energy, the global picture becomes even more precarious. In a 2004 publication, *The BRICs and Global Markets: Crude, Cars and Capital*, economists from Goldman Sachs saw China's oil demand increasing to a 16.5 per cent share of global oil demand from roughly 9 per cent over the following twenty-five years, this growth exacerbated by the rapid rise of the middle class; their estimates are that over 200 million people in the BRICs could have incomes over US$15,000.

But energy demand is only half the story – the other half is the very real concern that supply is not likely to meet this. A report by the UK Energy Research Council said worldwide production of conventionally extracted oil could 'peak' and go into terminal decline before 2020 and that there is a 'significant risk' that global oil production could begin to decline in the next decade. US oil production peaked in 1970 and gas in 1973.

The International Energy Agency (IEA) has also raised alarm bells. In 2008 it projected a near 50 per cent decline in conventional oil production by 2020 and a significant potential gap between supply and demand by 2015. According to the IEA's *World Energy Outlook 2008*, in order to meet the world demand forecasts for oil in 2030, 'some 64 million barrels per day of *additional* gross capacity – the equivalent of almost six times that of Saudi Arabia today – need to be brought on stream between 2007 and 2030.'[3]

The picture is even bleaker. Global efforts underway fall short of what is needed. Investment in oil production (particularly (Western) government-sponsored investment) has been inadequate. Even with the geopolitical risk of energy resource constraints, the IEA still suggests that an expenditure of at least US$450bn per year is needed to sustain oil production and to increase overall output to 104 million barrels per day by 2030.[3]

Today, Saudi Arabia is the largest oil-producing country in the world, and Russia the second largest; together they produce just over 9 million barrels of oil a day. Yet America imports 11–12 million.

The global consulting firm McKinsey claims that a US$170bn a year programme which targets cost-effective opportunities in energy productivity could halve the growth in energy demand, cut emissions of greenhouse gas and generate attractive returns. Yet, energy substitutes – nuclear power, hydro, biomass and renewables – do not put much more than a dent in oil demand. Moreover, even the best and most aggressive efforts towards 'green growth' are superseded by immediate oil and energy demands and the geopolitics of food production and transportation needs today.

The bottom line is this. Given where forecasts for resources are (energy, land, water) there is no way that one billion Chinese can live like 300 million Americans. *Ceteris paribus*, this is not possible; but it is exactly Western standards of living that the Chinese (never mind the hundreds of millions of people from other emerging states) are striving for.

AN UPHILL BATTLE

In a report entitled *Global Challenges – Our Responsibility*, the government of Sweden identified six other major obstacles that the world faces and which could impede progress over the next century. These are: oppression, economic exclusion, migration flows, climate change and environmental issues, conflicts and delicate political situations, and communicable diseases and other health threats. Quite clearly, each of these subjects warrants its own detailed study, but nevertheless the broader point is not to be missed, that they can all be seen as trademark characteristics of the emerging world. Each and every one of these is seen as a hindrance to the unbounded 'rise of the Rest', a drag on economic growth and prosperity.

Oppression is still, to this day, viewed by many as the defining characteristic of the emerging world. Even in countries where democracy ostensibly reigns, many of the freedoms taken for granted in the West are, in the emerging world, constrained or denied. Freedom of expression, freedom of the press, freedom of movement, freedom of assembly and even freedom of economic pursuits – all have their gradations of constriction. It was, after all, only in 1977 that India, the world's largest democracy, saw the forced sterilization programme initiated by Sanjay Gandhi to limit the country's population growth. Thousands of men with two children or more were (in return for a transistor radio) forced to undergo a vasectomy, but such was the determination of government officials and police officers to meet their targets that thousands more – unmarried young men, women and political opponents – were also sterilized.[4]

Meanwhile, conflicts are raging across the emerging world – be they in Pakistan, Iraq, Afghanistan, or flare-ups like the 2009 Muslim uprisings in China. Millions of young people struggling to find work and facing few economic prospects at home has got to be a formula for political unrest and even full-blown war. Countries like Uganda, with a population of 32 million and a median age of fifteen years, and Iran, around 65 per cent of whose population are younger than thirty years of age, are just two examples out of many in the emerging world where demographics will play a defining and damaging role in a country's prospects if opportunities (i.e. their youth) are not properly harnessed.

And yes, economic exclusion is a harsh fact of life, with income inequalities (measured using a Gini coefficient, where a low Gini coefficient on a scale of 100 indicates a more equal distribution, and a higher Gini coefficient indicates a more unequal distribution) remaining significant across the emerging world: China, 41.5; India, 36.8; Brazil, 55.0; Russia, 37.5. The United States is not much better than these countries, with a Gini coefficient of 40.8.

As for environmental concerns, the continuing face-off between India and China, propelled to a large extent by water shortages, should be seen as a prelude to many more serious theatres of conflict that are bound to emerge around questions of water, energy, land and basic human survival. In what some see as the early signs of a water war, China is thought to be considering rerouting the Brahmaputra River to its Yellow River, which would have devastating effects on the land and people of Bangladesh and India.[5] Meanwhile the International Energy Agency predicts that 97 per cent of the increase in carbon emissions between 2009 and 2030 will come from non-industrialized countries – and 75 per cent from China, India and the Middle East alone. The Great Smog of 1952 killed around 12,000 people in London in just five days. Left unchecked, the pollution risks across the emerging world will be much more devastating.

Malaria, cholera and HIV-Aids are endemic to the poorer countries, but in recent years the world has witnessed a spate of new health threats in the form of SARS (Severe Acute Respiratory Syndrome), bird flu and swine flu (although it is fair to say that the threat has not always been borne out). Each of these communicable diseases originated in pre-industrial, rapidly emerging economic environments where, because of overpopulation and in agricultural smallholdings, humans and animals freely mix. While there have been casualties, none of these easily transmitted diseases has mutated sufficiently to take a global hold, but one has to imagine that it's only a matter of time.

With oppression, wars, environmental issues, health concerns, Neo-Malthusian resource constraints (land, water, energy), and many across the emerging world lacking job prospects, large-scale migration seems inevitable. Today, some 200 million people (3 per cent of the world's population) live outside their country of origin; the very real fear is that unless these problems are addressed, these global migratory patterns and the number of displaced persons will only grow. Included in this number, the United Nations estimates that, as of 2008, there are approximately 42 million forcibly displaced people globally, including 15.2 million refugees.[6]

In his celebrated 1994 article 'The Coming Anarchy', in the *Atlantic Monthly*, Robert Kaplan takes a bleaker view. He makes a compelling argument for how 'scarcity, crime, overpopulation, tribalism and disease' will be the death knell of the developing world, dragging down the rest of the world with it. A global cataclysm.

THE THREAT OF OVERPOPULATION

The human toll could be devastating: remember, the fourteenth- and fifteenth-century plague cost France 66 per cent and Britain 50 per cent of their populations at the time.

Without such a virulent pandemic, a global famine or the outbreak of the Third World War, current forecasts are for the world's population to be over 9 billion by 2050. British government advisers put the global populace at 8 billion (a 33 per cent increase from around 6 billion today) by 2030. China already has forty cities with populations of a million people or more. The knock-on effects of such a huge global population are a real hazard on many fronts.

In terms of urbanization, and urban migration, some predict that 70 per cent of people worldwide will live in cities by 2050. Already in China estimates are that around 20 million people move from the rural to urban areas each year (at this flow rate, a rough back-of-the-envelope calculation suggests that 200 million new jobs will be required in the next ten years). And by 2035, around 40 million people are expected to crowd into Lagos, which is the largest metropolis of Nigeria but is a collection of islands of less than 1,000 square kilometres (625 square miles).

True, population forecasts are much bleaker for the richer, older Europe. Without mass migration, Eurostat projects that the European Union population (currently at around 500 million) will grow at a reduced rate, with the population forecast to start dropping in 2010, and falling to around 444 million by 2050. Meanwhile, according to the US National Intelligence Council publication *Global Trends 2025: A Transformed World*, nearly all the population growth over the next twenty years will come from Africa, Asia and Latin America, and less than 3 per cent from the West. Already 50 per cent of Africans are eighteen years old or under, and there are 47 million orphans. The political pressures of having so many young people entering the workforce or needing land for subsistence is very real.

Population dynamics invariably have large implications for the demand for food and water, expected to increase by 50 and 30 per cent respectively by 2030. Researchers continue to highlight the vulnerabilities associated with food security. In the UK, for example, which today produces 60 per cent of its own food, predictions are that in just twenty to thirty years the average UK diet will very much resemble that of the Second World War, when there were rations on everything from meat, to bread, jam, sugar, tea, cheese, eggs, milk and cooking fats. This is the outcome of a double-whammy – more demand for food driven by burgeoning populations coupled with the scarcity of inputs (water, arable land, etc). As populations rise, a natural result of this economic growth and decline in poverty is a greater demand for more protein-based foods – e.g. meat and dairy products. This adds to pressure on water (it takes 1,000 litres to grow a kilogram (2.2lb) of wheat) and pressure on land (it takes up to nine kilograms of grain to produce one kilogram of meat).

The logic goes like this: there is a finite amount of arable land in the world and there's more and more competition to get it. It's not just private sector individuals, companies and funds leading the charge to purchase land from governments in the remaining fertile areas around the globe. In an article entitled 'The New Colonialism: Foreign Investors

Snap Up African Farmland', *Der Spiegel* highlighted just a few such transactions: the Sudanese government has leased 1.5 million hectares of prime farmland to the Gulf States, Egypt and South Korea for ninety-nine years. Kuwait has leased 130,000 hectares of rice fields in Cambodia. Egypt plans to grow wheat and corn on 840,000 hectares in Uganda. With 80 per cent of the world's remaining untilled arable land in Africa it's not just about competition, but about security, with the side effect of food inflation as food scarcity becomes a relative certainty.

In terms of political vulnerabilities, Eurasia Group's Global Political Risk Index ranked the stability (from 0 to 100, where low scores are weaker performers and high scores better performers) of twenty-four emerging markets based on the ability to absorb internal or external shocks and crises. The most stable countries (with an index value greater than 80) possess most of the following characteristics: efficient state institutions; a high degree of political institutionalization; a high degree of political legitimacy among the population; sound economic performance and policies; absence of significant anti-state opposition; only rare instances of political violence; low levels of social, ethnic and religious tensions; and infrequent humanitarian disasters. Perhaps unsurprisingly the high scorers (scores in parentheses) include Hungary (77), South Korea (76) and Poland (74), and the low scorers Pakistan (42), Nigeria (46), Venezuela (51) and Iran (51). Furthermore, other rankings place poorer economies as some of the most dangerous countries in the world; in order: Somalia, Afghanistan, Iraq, Democratic Republic of Congo (DRC) and Pakistan.

Companies that offer political risk insurance help mitigate investment risk by providing insurance to possible investors against adverse government actions or war, civil strife and terrorism across different countries. In this way, the political risk insurance industry provides a market-based ranking of the riskiest countries in the world.

No one ever said it would be plain sailing, but the Rest have something the West hasn't got – the political mettle to drive the decisions that they need to take to keep their societies afloat. Taken together, the challenges present a gloomy picture of how the Rest's march to progress could well falter and stall. But as the next section will discuss, though emerging countries are vulnerable, their difficulties are not insurmountable.

A POLITICAL IMPERATIVE

August 2009 saw in Ziketan (a town of 10,000 people in the Qinghai province of China) the outbreak of one of the most virulent and least common forms of plague – the pneumonic plague. The Chinese government acted swiftly. By sealing off the town and quarantining its citizens, the Chinese authorities reacted in much the same way that they always seem to react to events that affect the country as a whole – unilaterally and decisively; and in a way in which, some would argue, the greater good of society trumps the desires of the individual.

Meanwhile, compare what was happening in the same month in Britain, where authorities were struggling to cope with an outbreak of swine flu. Although medical experts warned the government of the dangers of handing out the anti-flu drugs too liberally, the government, fearing the backlash from the voting population, chose to distribute drugs that were not only unnecessary but also might encourage the virus to mutate and return in an even more devastating form. Said Professor Robert Dingwall, a member of the Committee on Ethical Aspects of Pandemic Influenza: 'It was felt . . . it would simply be unacceptable to the UK population to tell them we had a huge stockpile of drugs but they were not going to be made available.'

Herein lies the essential difference between the mindset of the Rest and the mindset of the West. In places like China, the state is paramount and its government acts in the interest of and for the greater good of China as a whole, even if at the expense of the individual. Western governments, in contrast, have embedded in their very foundations that the rights of the individual supersede all.

Through political strong-arm tactics and apparatus, developing countries can and do make the harder, tougher decisions, and have the authority to implement them in less time than their Western counterparts. In the US, for example, the political decision-making process must go through Congress, the Senate and the Office of the President in order for a law to see the light of day. As this book is being written, the president of the United States is touring the country trying to drum up support for a healthcare programme which could benefit millions of Americans, but is facing, among other things, stiff opposition from vested interests and their supporters. Arguably this is democracy at work, but at tremendous cost.

In Britain, it can take years of inquiries and public debates to get planning approval to build motorways, power stations or most major infrastructure projects (it has been six years since the UK government's White Paper on building Heathrow airport's third runway was published, and it still hasn't been built).

In either case, and indeed for much of the West, the decisions that are made can be swiftly modified or overturned by newly elected governments of different political persuasions, holding different political views. Consistency in policymaking only lasts – and is guaranteed – as long as the incumbent government is in power. In the US, the political imperative (never mind the lobbying) means that with Congressional and Senatorial elections on a two-year cycle, there are elections to be fought and won every twenty-four months (with a presidential race every four years – and the risk of change in policy direction).

Frankly speaking, the constitutional framework that has defined the US for the past three centuries and is the pride of its people is not likely to be amended in order to hand more power to the state. Yet arguably more power, more flexibility and fewer committees are exactly what is needed. What sense does it make in the depths of the financial crisis – a state of economic emergency by most accounts, which brought the country and the world to its knees – for the president of the United States to have to build consensus around a desperately needed fiscal stimulus package before he and his advisers can act? In November 2008, the Chinese stimulus package, which amounted to US$586bn (4tn renminbi), to combat the financial crisis was implemented in a matter of days. China's stimulus package amounted to nearly 15 per cent of annual economic output spread over two years.[7,8] Similarly, at the onset of the bird flu in the mid-2000s, China is thought to have killed 2 million birds in a matter of days to avert its spread, whereas because of political haggling and process the United States struggled to kill even one.

A strong case can be made for the streamlined decision-making of the Chinese, and indeed of many other emerging markets – certainly for the speed with which policies can be taken and implemented. But the question remains of whether democracy and the sanctity of the rights of the individual elevated above all else will prevail. Remember, arguments for some of the most atrocious acts and policies have utilized economics and the good of society to make their case – in practice, however, history tells us freer populations tend to be more productive over time.

THE GLOVES ARE OFF

For the past 500 years, Western economic dominance has been a story of ruthlessness and self-interest. Its military power, its global hold, its influence on the world, have been the history of its trade, or rather the history of its single-minded ability to extract from other countries, other continents, other peoples, the material, land and people that would drive its economy forward – and in other words make them rich. Though it passed from one state to another, be it Venice or Holland, Spain, France, Great Britain or the United States, be it in 1760 or 2006, through wars, pestilences, political upheavals, the West maintained its iron grip – implacable in its determination to extract from the Rest whatever it wanted, regardless of its costs.

Examples of the brutal reality of their demands are everywhere: thus the British waged a cynical and cruel Opium War in China, launched solely to protect the lucrative drug trade to China which was debilitating thousands of the Chinese people (a war of which even a young Gladstone said: 'a war more unjust in its origin, a war more calculated to cover this country with permanent disgrace I do not know.'[9] Thus the history of Africa was one of slavery, slavery imposed not simply by the British and Americans (between 9 and 12 million) but by the French and Dutch too – creating a virtual monopoly on cheap labour. Oil, wheat, spices – whatever the West wanted, the West got; the West's demands, the prices it was prepared to pay, were paramount. Nothing else mattered. Countries and populations could go to the wall in furtherance of Western needs and wants.

In his book *Capitalism and Colonial Production*, Hamza Alavi estimates that between 1793 and 1803 the resource flow from India to Britain was around £2m a year (equivalent to billions today), which he notes 'has not only been a major factor in India's impoverishment . . . it has also been a very significant factor in the industrial revolution in Britain.'

No story is more illustrative of the pattern than that of the Egyptian cotton trade. In the middle of the nineteenth century Britain's cotton was primarily supplied by the American South, King Cotton, the backbone of the Southern economy. This trade suffered a huge setback during the American Civil War. Imports plummeted. Britain and France turned to Egypt, investing heavily in cotton plantations. The Egyptian government too took out substantial loans with European bankers and stock exchanges. The Egyptian cotton trade flourished. However, when the American Civil War came to an end British and French traders abandoned the Egyptian market without a moment's hesitation, precipitating Egypt into a financial collapse that ended in the country declaring itself bankrupt in 1882.

It may not have seemed obvious at the time, but this undisputed position of Western economic superiority changed for good when, in the middle of the twentieth century, American and Western policy-makers made a conscious decision to open up their economies to the free movement of goods and services.

In the run-up to the 1950s, Western economies – led by the United States – were largely mercantilist, opting to maintain a stranglehold on the economy by restricting the flow of capital and labour across their borders. Trade was just one weapon in their artillery. Acts like the American Smoot–Hawley Tariff which 'imposed an effective tax rate of 60 per cent on more than 3,200 products and materials imported into the United States' littered Western legislation. Even before this the United States Tariffs of 1824 and Tariff of 1828 protected American interests in the face of cheaper British commodities, including cotton goods.

Although intended to protect the economic welfare of its own people, and a useful tool in a government's political appeal, trade tariffs were anathema to more libertarian economic thinking, which believed in the merits of free markets. The godfather of this economic religion known as Ricardian advantage was Adam Smith, and decades later at Bretton Woods it was given form and legitimacy.

WELCOME TO THE REAL WORLD

In the first three weeks of July 1944, a meeting was held at the Mount Washington Hotel in Bretton Woods, New Hampshire, USA, that would change America's fortunes for ever. Over 700 delegates from some forty-four countries resolved to establish a framework for a global system of financial and monetary management. John Maynard Keynes, the pre-eminent British economist, and Harry Dexter White, at that time the US Secretary of State, led the discussions which laid the foundations for three organizations: the International Bank for Reconstruction and Development (commonly known as the World Bank), the International Monetary Fund (IMF) and the International Trade Organization. All were designed to restructure international finance, establish a multilateral trading system and construct a framework for global economic cooperation.

The free-market doctrine espoused by Ricardian thought would have worked fine as long as everyone, each country, played fair and by the rules of engagement. These were basically that each nation would build, grow and produce the goods and services that it did best. It is known as comparative advantage and assumes that, while acting in their individual interest, countries will never seek to take unfair advantage by manipulating the policy tools that they have in their hands. An assumption with little basis in reality, hence the WTO's less than stellar performance record.

There is a long history of governments – Western ones included – taking no notice of the rules of the game. Indeed, the very countries which were so vigorous in setting up the open markets system were among the first to break ranks.

The aftermath of the Bretton Woods agreements saw a range of policies, known as 'beggar thy neighbour policies', used by Western governments that sought to benefit one country at the expense of others. For instance, by slapping on trade tariffs and quotas on imports such as under the Smoot–Hawley Act, America was able to (at least temporarily) increase domestic jobs and undercut foreign manufacturers. In a similar vein, in 2002, President George Bush imposed tariffs (of up to 30 per cent) on imported steel products to help support American steel companies.[10] And President Barack Obama's administration in 2009 imposed trade barriers on the import of Chinese tyres.

Exchange rate manipulation is another example of how policy has been very effectively utilized by governments to further their own ends. By keeping their currencies artificially strong, policymakers were able to combat domestic inflation, at the expense of their competitors, whose invariably weaker currencies spawned their own inflation.

These practices are not a thing of the past. Even today, the West pursues self-interested policies at the expense of developing countries, be they the US$300bn US farm subsidy programme, the European Common Agricultural Policy[11] or the European aeroplane-manufacturing industry which all involve billion-dollar handouts each year. And in the aftermath of the financial crisis, in the US, trade protectionism is once again being touted as a necessary tool.

These naked displays of self-interest at any cost have not been lost on the Rest, and China in particular. China has seen how effective these manipulative measures have been and has honed them to a fine art. There has, of course, been a long-running feud between China and the West over China's part in keeping its currency (the renminbi) favourably and artificially low in order to boost its exports. The West's numerous protests have proven largely ineffectual. China remains doggedly undeterred. All told, while an appealing tool to exert leverage in the short term, protectionism has rarely been effective in the long run.

China is also seen to have perfected its skill in pursuing what are termed 'race to the bottom' policies. Here the government seeks economic dominance by continually undercutting its rivals. For example, in the competition for low labour costs across much of Asia, and indeed the whole developing world, China will continually undercut the labour costs of its rivals until none of them can go any lower and its competitors are put out of business. In the most extreme form of this game, the winner, with all competition virtually erased, becomes an effective monopoly and can now raise the price of her goods. For now, China's comparative costs versus other Asian countries say it all: according to the World Bank's World Development Indicators, in 2006 the compensation of employees as a percentage of total outlay was 28 per cent in Sri Lanka, 11 per cent in South Korea, 31 per cent in the Philippines, and just 5 per cent in China.

As mentioned earlier, the result of this iterative tit-for-tat match has been that China has become a volume-maximizer with a near absolute advantage, as opposed to profit-maximizers using comparative advantage, favoured by classical Ricardian theory. What this in effect means is that China cares more about the number of Chinese it has in employment (a volume proposition) and less about the profit earned. Like so many times before, America's predicament cannot solely be laid at China's door; its fate is also partly self-induced. So, theories aside, what should America do? It has to cater for and court its increasingly non-competitive and ill-educated population, and needs to ensure that jobs are being created (in 2009/2010, US unemployment hovered around 10 per cent; and closer to 20 per cent when you include the underemployed) – job creation is key.

In a world where not all players abide by 'the' set of rules, you have to fight fire with fire, which is precisely why, much to the chagrin of many pure comparative advantage theorists, the din for greater protectionism in the West (and in America in particular) continues only to grow louder. There's not much point playing as a free marketeer when the reality calls for some protectionism in order to survive.

While China has not always played fair (and perhaps has no intention of doing so – why would it? It's not in China's interest), the opening of the US capital markets on the back of the Bretton Woods agreement laid the foundations for when US corporations would become more powerful than the US government itself. This transfer of control helped seal America's fate.

The purpose of government is to take control – to pass laws, fight wars, sign treaties (trade and otherwise) and, most importantly, act on behalf of its citizens. Over the centuries, for better or for worse, this is what Western governments have done. But with the passing of the Bretton Woods accord, something else happened that was not foreseen. Slowly but surely power drained away from America's government and fell into the hands of the corporations. As America's might blossomed, so did the power, reach and financial muscle of its top companies. In 1955 its corporations were already behemoths: General Motors (#1), US$9.82bn revenues; Exxon Mobil (#2), US$5.66bn; and US Steel (#3), US$3.25bn.[12]

But, unlike governments, companies do not act on behalf of the population at large; they act on behalf of their shareholders.

When US policymakers decided to open its capital account, thereby allowing the unfettered movement of capital through its borders, this set America up for a big fall. Now any returns on American capital invested abroad would end up in the pockets of company shareholders, and they had no obligation to invest their money domestically for the betterment of America; they could just put their money in private secure bank accounts abroad. That's the beauty of globalization.

In search of cheaper labour, multinational corporations could and did set up plants thousands of miles away, creating jobs for the Rest and not for the West. The only thing companies were interested in was the company's profitability and therefore the shareholders' return on capital. Even more removed from their home country at large.

What started out as a series of perfectly sensible and seemingly innocuous policy decisions has morphed into what GavKal Research calls 'platform companies' – corporations (mainly US) that exist to design and sell concepts in the West, but where all the heavy lifting – labour-intensive manufacturing, shipping, construction, etc. – has been outsourced to the Rest. This works as long as there is no illicit transfer of intellectual property.

The US needs to make sure the benefits of its consumption accrue to the broadest number of its citizens. For the past several decades benefits have accrued back to the US via profits to platform companies often in the form of returns on capital. Whereas the benefits accruing on labour and mind (i.e. ideas/knowledge) go to the rest of the world, the benefits accruing to the West (on capital) benefit only a small minority (of share-holders) and are not broadly redistributed. But it does not end there.

More worrying is the fact that the returns accrued on capital go to companies and the wealthy – the two parties most likely to leave the country.

Once again, there are returns, huge returns, to the capital of the US companies involved. However, once again, these returns rarely accrue to US state coffers. Consider, in contrast, the state-owned sovereign wealth funds across the emerging world, which collect any positive returns on capital earned and distribute them for the benefit of the whole country as they see fit. It is not uncommon to hear of large-scale infrastructure, schools and hospitals being built out of cash streams from these public pools of money.

Although not impossible, it will be difficult for the US to get its Ricardian-infused policy genie back in the bottle.

OUIJA BOARD: GUIDE TO THE FUTURE

In the game of Risk players re-create a battle for world domination. By controlling armies, the goal for players is to capture territories from each other, thereby and ultimately eliminating all the other players. Like real life it is truly a risky game; a game of probabilities.

Economically the world stands something like this: the US and much of Western Europe are running out of capital, their labour dynamics are damaged (ageing population and falling academic standards) and their grip is loosening more and more on the monopoly they once held in technology. The rising Rest, led by China, but by no means on its own, have money in the bank, a superior labour outlook and a drive to take the technological lead.

How might the world look in thirty years? Here are four possible scenarios – all of which are centred on the most important economic axis between China and America.

Scenario 1: the status quo

If nothing else happens, and growth and structural economic changes continue on the current path, it's a virtual certainty that America, as well as most advanced European economies, will, by the end of the twenty-first century, trundle along and most likely become, at best, second-tier economies. Hard as this is to swallow, difficult as it is to fathom, and as unacceptable as this notion may be, *ceteris paribus*, this is a dead-on certainty.

This jaundiced view is supported by many of the economic forecasts, such as those of the investment bank Goldman Sachs, which claims that of today's economic leaders, only the United States will be among the five largest world economies (the others being China, Brazil, India and Russia) as soon as 2050.

Over the past half-century the Rest, led by China, have embarked on deliberate, systematic and highly effective strategies which have emphasized saving over consumption, and productive investment as opposed to underwriting the cost of global policing (such as patrolling international waters and peacekeeping), as the West has so often done. While the West was busy devising strategies to dominate the world, exporting its ideology, fighting international wars, suppressing communism and propping up its allies (whatever their persuasion), and swamping the world with financial and military aid to bolster its sphere of influence, the Rest were biding their time, building up their defences, adapting the West's economic rules, and preparing to outwit it and emerge as the heirs to the world economic throne. All signals point to this approach continuing.

The West is used to turbulence and conflict. In fact its political systems, its economic dynamic and its rhetoric thrive on it. Post-Second World War Western democracies (and the US in particular) have been eager to engage the world in all types of invasion – military, political, ideological and even financial. They patrol the seas, finance wars, insist that their political, social and economic way of life is the model to adopt. It is willing, to use President Kennedy's famous phrase, 'to pay any price, bear any burden, meet any hardship' to see its importance writ large upon the world stage. But the economic costs of this strategy are mounting, and mounting fast.

Military wars, ideological wars, religious wars, cold wars – we have seen them all. But there has been another war, as long and as drawn out as any, which has required plans and strategies, enticements, treaties, alliances, friends and foes, but the significance of which the West has been unwilling (or simply unable) to recognize: this is the economic war, from which would emerge winners and losers – and from today's vantage point the losers over the long term are the West, and the winners are the Rest. Of course, people in the West could came to think of this as not necessarily a bad thing, since globally more people are better off.

Without a dramatic reset, the economic war seems over; there appears to be a victor and a vanquished, but it may be that the battle has been won and not the war. And that, like the great generals of the past who regrouped and redirected their troops at the bleakest hour, the West too has options which could save it from oblivion. But without something to jolt it into action, it would appear that it's game over.

Scenario 2: China falters

In 2010, America was still the world's largest economy, the most innovative, the most technologically dynamic. And while China is giving America a run for its money, the question is for how long can China keep its amazing economic performance going? It's already been thirty years, could it be longer?

There are many commentators who believe that China's winning hand has been overplayed and that its path to economic superiority is by no means assured. In an article in *Foreign Affairs*, Josef Joffe scoffs at the recent wave of articles spelling out the decline of America, arguing that it remains in pole position and that it's not just economics which matters, but rather that 'it takes a country that is not just rich, but also democratic and free'.

In *Foreign Policy* magazine Minxin Pei dismisses the thesis of a decline of America and the dawn of a new Asian age as hype, proclaiming that it will be many decades before China, India and the rest of the region take over the world. He rightly points out that although Asia produces roughly 30 per cent of global economic output, because of its enormous population its per capita GDP is only US$5,800, compared with around US$48,000 in the United States. Moreover, he continues, even at current growth rates, it will take the average Asian seventy-seven years to reach the income of the average American: the average Chinese needs forty-seven years and the Indian 123 years.

Reading the tea leaves

It is true that on a number of fronts China is beginning to mimic the West – arguably to its detriment. For instance, China is building a society around the automobile, but with UN forecasts that 50 per cent of its population will be living in cities, one would think a public transport strategy would be more apposite. And as regards reports that China is looking to establish a pension fund system that mirrors the burdensome defined-benefit schemes of the West – it would be better advised not to go down that route.

The real challenge for China appears to be less its economics (it largely seems to have got that right) and more how its government will evolve as a manager of the country's economic direction. Will it be able to maintain its command economy centralized hold, or as it grows ever more powerful and complex will it, like a successful large corporation, increasingly devolve its responsibilities to satellite fiefdoms. In its current state, its stakeholders are its party members, its management the Chinese politburo, and its executive board the Chinese policymakers who meet once a year to debate and outline the strategy for the country.

Over time, the latter approach has proved its worth, not least because of its inherent ability to combat the misallocation of resources while implementing focused solutions – something successful companies are extremely adept at. Of course, the experience of the USSR has shown that there is an inherent risk of implosion in too rigid a centralized political system.

According to long-term BRIC projections made in 2010 by Goldman Sachs, it could take just seventeen years for China to become the biggest economy in the world (i.e. in 2027). To highlight China's ascendancy consider that at the first publication of the BRIC thesis, in 2002, Goldman Sachs argued that the increase in China's dollar GDP has been effectively the same as creating two new Indias, a new Italy, nearly a new France or the UK. Now, in a review of their numbers, Goldman Sachs economists point out that China's GDP has risen by almost US$4tn since 2000. In fact, China has created another seven Indias (at its 2001 size), nearly three Italys, more than two

Frances, and even close to one third of a US of the size it was in 2002. Meanwhile, the combined GDP of the BRIC countries is thought to have risen by more than US$6tn to close to US$9tn, from US$2.5tn at the beginning of the decade. By comparison, the US is thought to have added US$4.5tn over the same period.

In 2010 China overtook Japan to be the world's number two economy. By Goldman Sachs estimates, in order to take the number one spot by 2027 (with a GDP of around US$21tn) China needs to grow by around 10 per cent per year in dollar terms. Yet even with these astounding growth rates and forecasts, China has a long way to go. It's the difference between a billionaire who merely has to preserve his capital fortune (analogous to being the United States), versus a millionaire (the emerging Rest) who has to grow his capital at a rapid rate to come anywhere near the levels of the higher capital plains. Of course, there is also the perennial question of whether this growth can be accompanied by job creation and, if so, in what sectors – public or private, permanent or transitory. China has, year on year, excelled at delivering sustainable Ricardian growth? the pertinent question is will it, over the longer horizon of time, be able to deliver more Schumpeterian-type growth? Named for the Austrian economist Joseph Schumpeter, this form of economic growth, termed 'creative destruction', rests on innovation and an accompanying rise of an entrepreneurial force that would bolster long-term economic growth. On whether China, and indeed many of the other recent economic upstarts, can deliver such growth, the jury is still out.

Whatever its longer-term prospects, China does not seem to need a miracle to make its near-term growth rate a reality. If you believe the growth forecasts, and face the reality of America's dire financial position, it is difficult not to be sanguine for the prospects of China and the Rest. Barring unseen eventualities, China is going to win. It may take ten years, it may take twenty, but win it will. If the West does not throw up some real resistance, and change tack on the key ingredients for its long-term strategy – it's sure to be sooner rather than later.

Scenario 3: America fights back

America, and to a lesser extent Europe, could fight back. Rather than sit back and let the apparently inevitable unfold around it without a fight, it could launch a counter-attack. This would, however, require the most radical of solutions, and the most aggressive of political wills. For tinkering on the periphery of policy by pushing for global cooperation and friendly negotiations in the hope that everyone will play fair is not likely to get America very far.

For now, the US is, quite clearly, focused on fixing her economic problems in the context of the current global framework and remaining largely open to the global economy.

Over the past two years the Obama administration has pledged sizeable investment and policy support in critical areas. The Science and Technology bill earmarked 3 per cent of US GDP to education, while the American Recovery and Reinvestment Act of 2009 assigns more than US$45bn towards transportation and infrastructure, doubling the federal budget for this purpose. And in his 2010 Carnegie Mellon Speech after the BP oil spill in the Gulf of Mexico, President Obama outlined new US policy efforts aimed at encouraging investments that would help move the US away from fossil fuel energy dependency, towards energy alternatives such as natural (shale) gas, clean energy and even nuclear energy.

While laudable on paper, the problem with this strategy as a cure to remedy America's economic ills is twofold.

First, given the scale and depth of America's problems, the strategy as outlined thus far is too narrow and small. In order to be transformational, the approach needs to be big and bold, and certainly much more aggressive. This should include a hard look at and a serious revaluation of the US's role as virtually the sole underwriter of global public goods (such as policing the sea lanes, international security, etc.).

Second, the plan to address America's economic ills while remaining open crucially relies on the rest of the world playing fair. The recent spat around global competitive devaluations is a stark reminder that issues of economic policy fairness (such as currency manipulation) fall outside the bailiwick of US policymakers.

There are risks to remaining open. For one thing, there is likely to be a further worsening of US living standards as American labour remains too costly to employ, increasingly unskilled and, therefore, globally uncompetitive.

Then there is likely to be an enlargement of a welfare state to counter the effects of the rise in US structural unemployment; as it stands, almost 45 per cent of Americans do not pay federal taxes, and since 1980 average US public sector compensation is already higher than the private sector.

Finally, the US will continue to face a widening income inequality, as by remaining open, the gap between the incomes of an educated and competitive work force in areas where the US has a global comparative advantage (such as technology and R&D) versus the large population of the unskilled and disaffected, will inevitably widen.

Policymaking will need to be fierce, innovative and radical. Yet in the American context, given the political construct, this is incredibly challenging. Take America's engagement with China, for example; it is complicated by many different factions and interest groups each pulling in opposing directions. At Finmeccanica's 5th Management Convention in November 2009, John Hamre, president and CEO of the Center for Strategic and International Studies in the US, offered a crude taxonomy of the five factions in America concerning relations with China.

First, there are Labour Democrats. These are Democrats who are close to blue collar labour and largely see China in highly negative terms, as a country that is stealing American jobs through unfair manipulation of its currency and its tolerance of sweatshop practices in its own labour force that undercut workers in the West. Second, there are the High Technology Democrats, or Silicon Valley Democrats. These are highly educated, urbane and cosmopolitan Democrats who largely are excited by China, culturally. They see the world in sweeping global terms and think China is intriguing and challenging. Third are Religious Republicans (this also applies to some progressive Democrats), who see China in a dark light and largely in terms of human rights violations. Fourth are Defence Republicans. These are Republicans who see China as the next Soviet Union and believe we need to prepare ourselves for a fight with it. And finally there are Big Business Republicans, Republicans who see China as a great way to lower production costs, and potentially as a huge market, and don't want to miss the opportunity that China offers.

These five factions align themselves and diverge, depending on the issue (they are quite divided on the question of the valuation of the

Chinese renminbi, but on the question of Europe wanting to remove Tiananmen export control sanctions all five were in strong opposition, albeit for different reasons). This is why America seems to vacillate in its positions on China, when it needs to have a firm, coherent strategy. US policies on China merely reflect the relative strength of each political faction in the American domestic political arena, and ultimately this works against the country.

Living within reason

Political machinations aside, America has its work cut out for it – and needs to put its house in order. Capital: America needs to start living within its means. This implies a reduction in debt-financed consumption – at both the government and the household level. Labour: it needs to invest once again in its people – a high-quality workforce is what built America and it will take a similarly skilled population to get it back on its feet. Technology: the US needs to plough vast sums into new technologies to increase its workers' productivity, and get serious about protecting its copyrights. All of this requires money – money that the US does not have. Of course, it's not just about money; it's also about quality policymaking – fiscal, industrial, regulatory – that together reduces uncertainty, engenders confidence and encourages investment.

Is the United States bankrupt? That is to say, is the United States at the end of its resources, exhausted, stripped bare, destitute, bereft, wanting in property or wrecked in consequence of failing to pay its creditors? These are the questions posed by Boston University's Professor Laurence Kotlikoff. The answer is sobering. He concludes that the United States is going broke, and that while remaining open to foreign investment can help stave off bankruptcy, radical reform of US fiscal institutions is vital to secure the nation's economic future.

US debt to GDP stood at 47 per cent in 2007, but after the financial crisis was forecast to be higher – substantially higher. The IMF forecasts a debt to GDP ratio of close to 100 per cent by 2019.

AmeriCAN

In the era after the financial wreck of 2008, policy discussions have concentrated on the obvious lessons, such as the need for greater regulation, through more hands-on government agencies. Less obvious lessons, perhaps, are the need for America to focus on more productive investment (as opposed to leverage speculation) and for the implementation of real, serious policies that will reverse the damage and the earlier misallocation of resources in capital, labour and technology. This requires savvy, it requires vision and it requires a long haul – does America have the mettle?

Scenario 4: America's Nuclear Options

Drastic times call for drastic measures.

There is, of course, a more aggressive way for America to fight back – particularly when it comes to sorting out its financial problems; an option that goes very much against the American grain. This is to become much more closed and protectionist, even if only until America gets her economic house in order and her rates of economic growth trend higher.

Although proposals for greater US protectionism are generally met with derision from mainstream policymakers, evidence over the last thirty years suggests that Americans have not benefited that much from the US being open to globalization.

If anything, although global income inequality *between* developed and developing countries has improved, income inequality *within* the US has worsened. According to research at the University of Chicago, while the richest 1 per cent have seen their incomes rise three times over the past thirty years that the US has been opened, the poorest 10 per cent have seen their incomes rise by a relatively paltry 10 per cent.

Moreover, in that time American living standard improvements (measured as average per capita income) have been marginal. At 2.1 per cent, average US GDP growth between 1980 and 2001, when the US was largely open, is identical to growth between 1950 and 1980, when the US was largely closed.

This type of data suggests at least that closer consideration of the possible benefits of adopting more protectionist policies is warranted.

There are compelling reasons why Americans (the results are similar across the major Western economies) have not benefited from globalization to a greater degree, such as the fact that economic gains over the past several decades disproportionately accrued to the holders of capital rather than to the providers of labour, and the fact that US households over-invested (at least 30 per cent of household wealth) in the domestic housing asset class, thereby remaining relatively under-invested in the globalization which registered marked gains.[13]

In considering which direction to take – whether to remain open or become more closed from the global economy – policymakers need to be guided by long-term (twenty-year plus) thinking, as the urgent issues impacting the world's most developed economies today are precisely long-term and structural in nature. Of course, in light of the current economic circumstances, short-term, tactical considerations are important. But, unfortunately, as ever, the myopia around the political imperative in the West mitigates against long-term thinking.

This is precisely why there is an urgent need to decouple economic thinking from short term political expediency. Pull the plug and start anew. After all, 'the future doesn't belong to the fainthearted; it belongs to the brave . . .'

A stronger variant of this theme of protectionsim is for the US to default.[14] An outright US government default is not something to dismiss offhand. Default sounds like a cataclysmic option – stock markets would crash, the cost of debt would soar, the dollar would suddenly turn into monopoly money, and there would undoubtedly be a deafening international uproar. Already in November 2009 the derivatives market was betting on an increasing chance of the US government defaulting on its bonds. According to the Depository Trust and Clearing Corporation, the volume of US credit default swaps – the derivatives that measure the cost to insure against bond defaults – have more than doubled from US$4bn in 2008 to US$10bn in 2009. But would it really be that bad for the US to default?

Western defaults have happened before (Iceland in 2008 and the UK, in all but name, in 1976, when it was forced to go to the IMF for a bailout loan), but certainly not on such a monumental scale – this is, after all, the United States, the economic leader of the world. This is not to suggest that America should default just for defaulting's sake, in order to wipe out its obligations. The attraction would be for America to wipe its slate clean and for the government to reset its financial statement. As in the case of the UK in 1976, such a default could provide an opportunity for a much needed overhaul of the domestic policy agenda, particularly the culture of leverage, as well as recasting the 'homeownership for all' strategy, and pushing for greater investment in labour and technology.

America's current financial state has, no doubt, given its policymakers the impression that their hands are tied, bound by the strictures of the lender that is China. However, they underestimate the power they have, and the strength of the symbiotic relationship that exists between America and China as the borrower and the lender, respectively.

Murder-suicide in Chimerica

A default scenario is the one China ought to fear the most. According to calculations by Standard Chartered, as much as 82 per cent of China's US$2tn in foreign reserves is in dollars, making China one of the biggest buyers of US Treasury securities, in some instances splashing out as much as US$10bn a month; in return China earns around US$50bn a year in interest from the United States, according to Brad W. Setser at the Council on Foreign Relations. Half of the US Treasury bond market is owned by foreign investors.

It is true that in the event of a US default the American economy itself would suffer if foreign investors were to desert it (for example, long-term interest rates would rise sharply and this would increase the cost of mortgage financing and the corporate bond markets, to the detriment of the US economy), but a US default like this could be viewed as a necessary and temporary reset of the economy.

The US would not be the only loser. Remember that not only would China lose the value of all the American debt it held, but importantly such a US default would, at a stroke, jeopardize China's own development strategy, which counts on the US (government and individual citizens) borrowing cash to buy its goods and keep the Chinese populace employed. Perhaps anticipating this, China has, over several years, been encouraging greater domestic demand (domestic demand growth was forecast to reach 15 per cent in China, and 10 per cent in both India and Brazil) and pushing its goods towards other (non-US) international buyers.

Of course America's reputation would take a knock, but for how long? A guess is that the financial markets would be willing to lend to the US again within six months, if Russia is anything to go by. After all, just three years after it defaulted on its internal debt in 1998, the international debt markets welcomed new bond issues from Russia – the City of Moscow issued a €400m (around US$600m) bond in November 2001.

Without a strategy of default, many fear America will remain locked in a stranglehold of debt and dependence from which it will be very difficult to credibly escape. Certainly, it can inflate the debt away as many countries are essentially now doing (a means of defaulting by stealth as inflation will erode the value of the debt anyway), but adopting this softly, softly approach will ultimately have the same consequences.

American Brinkmanship

If the playing field is not fair, and diplomacy has failed, then America has to fight back – fight fire with fire, and choose a different tack.

While playing a strategic game, the most astute players will role-play forward and determine who would hold the best/strongest position in the worst-case scenario, that is, were a complete breakdown in cooperation to occur. The result is, of course, that the player with the best hand under such a scenario is the one who has the upper hand, and is best able to ensure the other players' cooperation, today.

As in international politics, foreign policy, labour relations, military strategy and even in a game of poker, brinkmanship is the practice of pushing a dangerous situation to the verge of disaster in order to achieve the most advantageous outcome. Viewed through this lens America holds the best alternative to a negotiated agreement (BATNA) in the unlikely event of an economic nuclear option.

Consider for a moment what adopting an approach of economic brinkmanship could mean for America. Save for an outbreak of full-blown war, the worst-case scenario is one in which through the most aggressive protectionist policies, the key economic zones of the industrialized world each retreat into their respective corners. One could envisage that this would broadly yield roughly three economic power blocs.

First, there would be the American economic bloc (and, more likely than not, Canada would join as well). It's not just the nearly half a billion people (based on today's population statistics) with the highest purchasing powers based on per capita income that make a strong case for this region. North America could easily become self-sufficient. If massive barriers on trade and migration were erected, she could still feed her population, become energy self-sufficient (North America has been the leader in developing and producing shale gas, and increasingly it is becoming a more important source of natural gas in the US), and geographical considerations mean it would, in any case, be hard to invade.

Then there's Europe. Seen through a cold, hard economic lens, its prospects do not seem particularly rosy. The region continues to face structural decline, buttressed by policies that aim to achieve social cohesion, despite severe fiscal worries (as seen by the performance of Portugal, Ireland, Greece and Spain, collectively termed the PIGS for their economic performance and prospects). More generally, Europe, for better or for worse, can be characterized as lacking in capital preservation, and being short on labour determination and technological innovation, making its chances of long-term economic domination slim indeed.

Finally, there is China. True, it has a vast population and forecasts are that it could be the largest economy by 2017. But there is still a very long way to go before the average Chinese person on a per capita income basis rivals the American consumer. Beyond this, China's population of 1.3 billion have to make do with just 7 per cent of arable land. And while economically annexed natural-resource-rich regions of Africa and Latin America give China some reprieve, the nature of the Sino-Africa and Sino-LatAm relationships will always be laced with uncertainty; uncertainty an American economic bloc would not have.

So who then holds the stronger hand, and who the weaker? For whom is the protectionist brinkmanship worse? Certainly not the United States. In this game of poker, America still holds the cards, and the upper hand, but one would never guess.

If it came to it, American politicians could successfully advocate the merits of a closed-in America. Not so China. How would its leadership explain to the hundreds of millions of aspiring Chinese (out of 1.3 billion only around 300 million live at standards commensurate with average Western economic standards) that their chances of economic success would have to be managed substantially downwards?

Is it in the US interest to derail China's growth? After all, this is what an outright US default would most likely do – at least in the period immediately following the default. Faced with a burgeoning population that is simply globally uncompetitive and a forbidding step-down drop in living standards across the board, the plight of China's growth plans and their likely disruption will increasingly be of secondary importance.

Whatever the case, in a response to the question: 'How likely do you think it is, if at all, that your government will "default" in the next decade, i.e. be unable to pay back money it borrowed in the financial markets?', a May 2010 FT/Harris poll found that nearly 50 per cent of respondents answered 'likely'.

CONCLUSION

The past fifty years have been the longest period in the history of man without a major world conflict destroying plant, property and people. One of the great dividends of this peace has been the ability for the globe to accumulate wealth, leaving the world, in aggregate, wealthier today than it has ever been. And although the US, and other industrialized states, face greater economic uncertainty and widening income inequalities, the past several decades have seen more improvement in global living standards across the world than at any other time before. With the increase in income, living standards of the poorer countries have rapidly converged on those of the world's richest.

The value of this wealth needs to be channelled and stored somewhere, hence the near insatiable demand for financial products and all manner of assets over the last decade. The phenomenal ascendancy of China and many other parts of the emerging world added to this seemingly unstoppable rise in global prosperity. Over time the global economy became less industry-intensive, hoarding lower levels of inventory. All the money that would, in the past, have been tied up in plant, equipment and inventory was now available to purchase financial products, as were the vast sums of capital due to the high savings rates of the emerging Rest.

What is the blueprint for the West's survival? Before any practical solutions can be implemented, the West has to change its mindset. It can no longer afford to regard the up-and-comers as simply menacing gatecrashers. As we have shown, forging closer ties with the emerging economies and dismantling (rather than re-imposing) trade barriers will not work. However, overhauling their tax systems to encourage savings rather than ravenous consumption, and specifically addressing the three essential ingredients for growth (capital, labour and technology), would make it possible for the West to firmly get back in the race.

The odds are, however, the United States will be a *bona fide* socialist welfare state by the latter part of this century. Indeed, if nothing else changes it from its current path, it is almost certain that America will move from a fully fledged capitalist society of entrepreneurs to a socialist nation in just a few decades. The trouble is it won't be just any socialist welfare state (there is, after all, nothing inherently wrong with a socialist state *per se* if it's well engineered and designed and can finance itself).

While it is true that socialist-leaning states are clearly relatively well developed and engineered in Germany and across Scandinavia, well developed but perhaps badly designed in Greece and Italy, the trouble is that the US is on a path to creating the worst and most venal form of welfare state (poorly developed and designed) – one born of desperation from many years of flawed economic policies and a society that rapaciously feeds on itself.

America is already displaying the hallmarks of this fundamental shift. The pressure on the public purse is rising: the government's tax base is shrinking, but public expenditure is rapidly increasing (with healthcare, pension, unemployment and poverty spending all on the rise). This is set against the backdrop of a heavy debt burden, and with it the promise of sluggish economic growth for many years to come.

Looking at the link between different levels of debt and countries' economic growth over the last two centuries, the economists Carmen Reinhart and Kenneth Rogoff find that countries with a gross public debt exceeding about 90 per cent of annual economic output tend to grow significantly more slowly. In particular, in developed economies, above the 90 per cent threshold average annual growth was about two percentage points *lower* than for countries with public debt of less than 30 per cent of GDP. For the US (as well as the UK and other industrialized countries) this does not bode well.

Already, after the financial crisis debt levels in the US and other countries at the centre of the financial crisis are approaching the 90 per cent mark. In 2009 gross government debt in the US stood at 85 per cent of GDP and according to IMF projections will reach 108 per cent of GDP by 2014. Meanwhile, the UK's 2009 gross government debt stood at 69 per cent of GDP and is forecast to reach 98 per cent of GDP by 2013.

The problems with the misallocation of capital, labour and technology are not helped by the political imperatives (short political terms and decentralized power) that discourage American and indeed most Western policymakers from implementing the transformational policies that will set the industrialized economies back on the right economic path. Ultimately, it is on this point where state-led capitalist societies, like those of China, have the edge.

There are those who say that what the world witnessed in 2008 and the years ensuing was simply the failure of the West's experiment with a social welfare system. That now that the leaders of developed nations realize the folly of running large deficits and accumulating mounds of debt in order to finance social safety nets and big government, we will see the pendulum swing again towards more market-based economies; a re-emphasis on and re-engagement of the private sector and the entrepreneur by more deregulation and lower taxes to unleash the entrepreneurial spirit. This would and could all make sense as an economic strategy, except for one thing. Such a market-based philosophy is predicated on a skilled and highly productive labour force, which, given the labour data and education statistics of the up-and-coming generations, will be in woefully short supply.

If anything, a swing back towards more market-based economics, and away from social welfare, poses a risk of increased income inequality in developed countries. Indeed, it is almost certainly the case that the incomes of the relatively small share of educated innovators and entrepreneurs will be higher than the large base of the unskilled, undereducated population.

Across the West, everyone is culpable. As argued in this book, for example, over the last fifty years in the US, governments, corporations and private individuals have implemented catastrophic decisions that at the time looked cost-less, but in fact were extremely costly and detrimental to the core long-term sustainable operation of the economy.

Over multiple generations, and different US administrations both left and right, public policy has misallocated capital by urging housing access for all despite people's means, establishing a long-term unsustainable pension culture, underwriting R&D for the world at unrequited costs to itself, and bailing out whole industries with a pattern of buying high and selling low!

Western corporations have set up shop in the cost-competitive emerging world (helping vast swathes of the emerging world's labour markets), but the benefit, and in particular returns on capital, accrued only to a handful of shareholders. And of course the decision of millions of families across the West to pursue other, ostensibly better-paying careers at the expense of education is creating a fast-growing surplus of expensive, undereducated, unskilled and globally uncompetitive citizens.

Many questions remain. Will Westerners still be, more or less, living at their current standards of living and looking with envy at the economic successes of the Rest? Who will discover cold fusion? Or the next 'killer app' – that special something or nudge that makes you want to buy a product? Where will the jobs of the future be created? And in what sectors of the economy? Will they be temporary positions or permanent, for-life roles? In the public sector or in the private? Robotics and robot technology are already permeating the workforce. Japan's already includes over a quarter of a million robots. And even at the Cleveland Clinic in the US, for a fraction of human wages, robots travel about 1,800 kilometres (1,100 miles) and make 5,000 trips a day, moving everything from linens, surgical equipment, patient food, supplies and, yes, even trash. If, as Western politicians tend to proclaim today, the future of developed countries is in digital, low-carbon and pharmaceutical innovation, then richer countries certainly have their work cut out for them.

Of course, there are more political questions not dealt with here, such as who world citizens want to see as the global power? On the economics side, would the West be better off adopting a more insular stance and systematically reducing its economic and financial ties with the rising Rest? Though all parties are guilty of selectively applying the rules of fair trade, the West does garner benefits from trading with the Rest, and for some time yet the richer West will be appealing to the Rest. But the question is: are these economic benefits sizeable enough to warrant the mounting costs for the West of engaging with the Rest?

Contrastingly, the emerging Rest, by engaging with rapidly industrializing countries, will not only make strides in economic development, poverty reduction and technological sophistication but will advance economically in leaps and bounds.

But before this can take effect the West, and America in particular, must implement better policies and stop sowing the seeds of its own destruction. This is not sufficient to stem the economic tide, but it is certainly a necessary step. Changing trade patterns, financial destabilization of the world's most advanced economies, and the transition of economic opportunities to the emerging world are defining our world today, and will continue to shape the world we live in in the most dramatic ways.

This book has been about economics. While economics is one sort of warfare, one country seeking dominance over another, it's never just about the money. Other factors, political, social, even natural, shape and modify our world. Change is unsettling, unpredictable. But sometimes some things are clear; there is, if you like, a feeling in the air.

One suspects that when America's forefathers stepped off the *Mayflower* and took in the air, they knew, in their hearts, that a great adventure was being embarked upon, that this was the start of something big. In much the same way, although no one can say for sure what the outcome will be, in this, the beginning of the second decade of the twenty-first century, we all know that the world is standing on the lip of a global seismic change, where another country stands on the cusp of greatness. Though we have an inkling of how the land will lie when all is settled, what is also certain is that uncertainty and upheavals lie ahead.

To quote John Adams's world-famous 1987 opera *Nixon in China*: 'We live in an unsettled time. Who are our enemies? Who are our friends?' The good thing is, what history has taught us, is that while struggles, wars, disasters occur, the world survives and slowly, despite the setbacks, advances. Let us hope that is as true for the next hundred years as it was for the last.

Notes

PREFACE

1. This must not be construed as advocating asset protectionism; it is merely a statement highlighting a growing economic trend.
2. While it is true that fewer people around the world live under free, liberal democracies than do not, it is unquestionable that, led by the United States, the West's political doctrine and economic supremacy have characterized the last fifty years.
3. Economic growth (convergence) theory suggests that given how poor some countries are, they will tend to grow faster so that they may 'catch up' to the economic levels of more economically advanced countries. Because economic improvements in poorer countries are bound to contribute to global stability, it is in the interest of all countries (including richer states) that poorer ones achieve economic success.

INTRODUCTION

1. Of course, laissez-faire capitalism in its current form has arguably only existed since the era of the British prime minister Margaret Thatcher and the US president Ronald Reagan in the 1980s.
2. Many argue that, because of a political imperative (the fact that kleptocracies are more likely to fail), economic dominance is more likely to be in China, India, Brazil or non-Chinese Asia than, say, Russia or the Middle East.

1. ONCE UPON A TIME IN THE WEST

1. Of course, there have been challenges in the form of the Cold War and the threat from the rise of Japan's economic imperialism in the mid-1980s, but America's resolve has won out.

2. There is an extensive literature on some of the negative features of the New Deal, which arguably delayed the economic recovery.

3. For more on the Lend-Lease programme: http://en.wikipedia.org/wiki/Lend-Lease.

4. There was also Russia, which gained a lot of territory but lost many lives.

5. In economics, the Cobb–Douglas production function is a representation of the relationship of an output to inputs; growth to capital, labour and technology.

6. Details on the Apollo programme can be found at http://www.asi.org/adb/m/02/07/apollo-cost.html.

2. A CAPITAL STORY

1. Information on the Domesday Book: http://www.domesdaybook.co.uk/.

2. Domesday Book statistics: http://www.nationalarchives.gov.uk/education/focuson/domesday/take-a-closer-look/. Not strictly comparable, but in 2009 the Office of National Statistics estimated the total value of assets in Britain at just under £7tn, up from £4.2tn at the turn of the millennium.

3. Publications by Angus Maddison: http://www.ggdc.net/Maddison/content.shtml.

4. According to the Energy Information Administration, *Electric Power Annual Report* (published in January 2009), in 2007 net power generation in the US amounted to 4.156bn megawatt hours.

5. Two points are worth making regarding the *FT* rankings. First, relative to their GDP weights, the emerging market rankings are perhaps not that impressive, as there are only fifty-nine countries on the list. In fact, given their GDP rankings one would expect to see seventy-five to eighty companies from the BRIC world, and as such one could argue that these countries are under-represented in the rankings. A second point relates to foreign exchange movements, which naturally would affect the valuation of market capitalization of the different countries, yet this factor is not adequately reflected in the rankings.

6. Of course, another question relates to whether the West will remain geopolitically or militarily dominant – there are challenges as nuclear weapons continue to proliferate across many countries.

7. Where Russia is concerned there is an interesting debate on whether the country is exhibiting true economic growth, or whether its impressive growth rates simply reflect higher global commodity prices.

8. Barney Frank comment:

9. The stylized example presented assumes a one-period game. A multi-period game where a solvency test would preclude an insolvent enterprise (or one that has leveraged itself up to the hilt) from existing into future periods requires a more nuanced analysis; but the basic conclusion that an equity claimant is long volatility while a debt claimant is short volatility still holds.

10. Clearly, given that the expected value of the debt claim in both scenarios is less than US$50,000, it is unlikely that this business would ever be funded – nevertheless the point being stressed is that the equity claimant will always go for the higher variance on the enterprise value.

11. A put option is a financial contract between a seller and a buyer of the option. The buyer purchases the right, but not the obligation, to sell the underlying instrument at an agreed-upon price (the strike price). Broadly speaking the put buyer believes that the underlying asset's price will fall, whereas the put seller believes that the underlying security's price will rise.

12. This is just put–call parity.

13. There is arguably a strong and positive correlation between income volatility and asset price volatility – however, in the interest of keeping the analysis simple we abstract from that here.

14. Of course, this is true up to a point. If you expect things to go up anyway you don't want the volatility to dominate so much that it knocks out a perfectly good investment.

15. The issue with guaranteeing Fannie Mae and Freddie Mac is similar to the issue of ratings agencies (Moody's and Standard & Poor's), which are agencies encapsulated in the regulatory infrastructure but are themselves for-profit organizations.

16. Information on the Federal Deposit Insurance Corporation: http://www.fdic.gov/.

17. Information on the Securities Investor Protection Corporation: http://www.sipc.org/.

18. Information on the Municipal Bond Insurance Association: http://www.mbia.com/.

19. Of course, it is right to recognize the fact that many US banks did take the TARP bailout money and banking institutions around the world were able to raise cheaper money in the capital markets, and thus benefited from government intervention. Specifically, both banks did take advantage of the implicit government guarantee (which enabled them to access cheaper capital), both undoubtedly benefited from the programmes to get asset prices up, and both garnered benefits from government behaviour and investor reactions.

20. So too is whether the 'homeownership for all' policy happens to be the right policy but is just badly implemented.

21. George Bush ownership society: http://www.calculatedriskblog.com/2009/08/rentership-society.html.
22. Real estate investment trusts: Dambisa Moyo, 'Holding Housing's Head Above Water', *Barron's*, 27 November 2010, at http://online.barrons.com/article/SB50001424052970203676504575618580846900178.html?mod=BOL_twm_col.

3. THE HOUSE OF CARDS

1. Of course, depending on recourse and loan-to-value ratios and equity, home-owners do have delta (the ratio of the change in price of an option to the change in price of the underlying asset). Although many were house-poor; they had enormous homes financed by leverage but couldn't afford furniture.
2. Technically speaking, he has delta. Even if his mortgage is non-recourse, he still has 505 delta at zero equity.
3. A cashless society is actually quite helpful, especially if you want capital to flow, which is why debt is not in itself a bad thing. It is a perfectly reasonable (or desirable) thing to have some debt on a balance sheet; the issue is mispricing, misallocation and incorrect levels of leverage, but the correct level of debt is surely not zero.
4. British Bankers' Association, 'August 09 – Credit Card Statistics', at http://www.bba.org.uk/bba/jsp/polopoly.jsp?d=470&a=16656].
5. Lord Myners' comment: http://business.timesonline.co.uk/tol/business/industry_sectors/banking_and_finance/article6735905.ece.
6. Tulip mania: http://en.wikipedia.org/wiki/Tulip_mania.
7. The 2008 financial crisis was also financed by capital markets; it was just that the banks increased their leverage to own the paper assets more than they did in the late 1990s. The banks chose to behave differently because the cost of their own debt capital was so low, they had become very lightly regulated, and they got sucked into the same bubble. What is wrong now is the handling of the aftermath. Bailouts, forbearance and quasi-zombie banks rather than nationalization, privatization and functional banks.
8. Enron: *The Smartest Guys in the Room*, 2005 documentary film.
9. Of course, this was not so different from the junk bond market in terms of using diversification and tranching to lower spreads. None of this is in itself bad; it's just that people made bad decisions. Of course, the perennial question is why people made these bad decisions and what role, if any, government should have to stop them.
10. Committee on IMF Governance Reform, 4 September 2008: http://www.imf.org/external/np/sec/pr/2008/pr08200.htm.

11. Naturally, the velocity of money could have remained in control of the Fed, but the Fed leadership chose not to focus on velocity and money supply, or asset prices, instead focusing on money supply and core PCE.

12. 'Levittown: Documents of an Ideal American Suburb': http://tigger.uic.edu/~pbhales/Levittown/.

13. Housing and Urban Development Agency: http://www.huduser.org/Publications/PDF/gse.pdf.

14. Statement by Ron Paul: http://www.lewrockwell.com/paul/paul128.html.

15. The academic/economic commentator Nouriel Roubini and the hedge fund manager John Paulson, both of whom discussed the possibility of a credit collapse, are exceptions; however, more generally for market participants this collapse was clearly not the model scenario.

16. Statement by the US Federal Reserve Chairman, Ben Bernanke: http://www.federalreserve.gov/newsevents/testimony/bernanke20070328a.htm.

17. For information on first-lien sub-prime mortgages outstanding see comment by Ben Bernanke at http://www.federalreserve.gov/newsevents/speech/bernanke20070517a.htm.

4. LABOUR LOST

1. Alec Holden story: http://www.guardian.co.uk/uk/2007/apr/24/gambling.uknews4.

2. History of Detroit: http://www.historynow.org/03_2007/historian6.html.

3. Unless of course actual returns are sufficient – hence the controversy. Were pensions invested such that the return on capital was sufficient, then there would be no real problem. In the context of entire nations, this means in an environment of an increasing dependency ratio either there must be claims on foreign economies or domestic productivity must improve through accurate capital allocation to compensate – which is why 'forced' investment in government bonds is so unhelpful.

4. Lane, Clark & Peacock pensions survey report: http://www.lcp.uk.com/news/news.asp?ID=164.

5. California public employees retirement system and California teachers retirement system: http://www.altassets.net/private-equity-news/article/nz16323.html.

6. 'Chinese president urges to promote social security system', *Xinhua*, 23 May 2009, at http://english.sina.com/china/2009/0523/243392.html.

7. Deindustrialization of London: http://www.museumoflondon.org.uk/English/Collections/OnlineResources/X20L/Themes/1376/1127/.

8. Ratio of US lawyers to engineers: 'East versus West', *Forbes*, 11 May 2009, at http://www.forbes.com/forbes/2009/0511/024-opinions-science-psychology-ideas-opinions.html.

9. Poor performance of low-income and minority students in Washington, DC, and more generally: executive summary, 'The Role of Social Entrepreneurship in Transforming U.S.A. Public Education', 14 October 2008, at http://www.hbs.edu/centennial/businesssummit/business-society/the-role-of-social-entrepreneurship-in-transforming-usa-public-education-2.html].

10. Comments by the head of Tesco on the poor education standards in the UK: http://www.dailymail.co.uk/news/article-1220140/Tesco-chief-raps-woeful-education.html#ixzz0V9O4OQSs.

11. Comment by Kevin Green of the Recruitment and Employment Confederation: http://www.ft.com/cms/s/0/d687094e-918d-11de-879d-00144feabdco.html?catid=18&SID=google.

12. Nicholas Barberis story: http://www.businessweek.com/archives/1996/b3498010.arc.htm.

13. H1-B1 visa limits: US Department of State at http://travel.state.gov/visa/laws/telegrams/telegrams_1391.html.

14. Number of student visas issued in *Science*, 5 March 2004, p. 1453.

5. GIVING AWAY THE KEYS TO THE KINGDOM

1. Inventors: http://americanhistory.about.com/library/charts/blchartindrev.htm.

2. Chinese woman physicist: http://www.nwhm.org/Education/biography_cswu.html.

3. http://en.wikipedia.org/wiki/Christiaan_Barnard.

4. CNN, 'Lower costs lure U.S. patients abroad for treatment', at http://www.cnn.com/2009/HEALTH/03/27/india.medical.travel/index.html.

5. Stem cell research in Mexico: http://www.prlog.org/10109469-proven-stem-cell-treatment-available-in-mexico-now.html.

6. http://www.telegraph.co.uk/news/worldnews/asia/china/5071124/Chinas-global-cyber-espionage-network-GhostNet-penetrates-103-countries.html.

7. '850,000 Lawsuits in the Making', *Economist*, 10 April 2008, at http://www.economist.com/businessfinance/displaystory.cfm?story_id=E1_TTDNPNSD]

8. http://www.wipo.int/portal/index.html.en.

9. Hamilton Moses III et al., 'Financial Anatomy of Biomedical Research', *Journal of the American Medical Association*, 21 September 2005, at http://jama.ama-assn.org/cgi/content/full/294/11/1333.

10. US Joint Economic Committee, *The Benefits of Medical Research and the Role of the NIH* (2000).

11. http://www.guardian.co.uk/katine/2009/aug/12/katin-glaxosmithkline-andrew-witty-pharmaceuticals.

12. Krugman's piece in the *New York Times*: 'Hyper-efficient markets', at http://www.nytimes.com/2009/09/06/magazine/06Economic-t.html?ref=magazine.

13. Bank IT spending: http://searchfinancialsecurity.techtarget.com/news/article/0,289142,sid185_gci1345047,00.html.

6. A TOPSY-TURVY WORLD

1. Of course, this is now changing with more representation from the emerging world in global organizations.

2. China to lend Russian oil companies US$25bn: http://www.ft.com/cms/s/0/b29b499c-fd5d-11dd-a103-000077b07658.html?nclick_check=1.

3. China and Russia building a 4,000-kilometre (2,500-mile) pipeline from Russia's Far East Amur region to Daqing in north-eastern China: http://www.chathamhouse.org.uk/files/6619_russiachinamay06.pdf.

4. China lends US$10bn to Petrobras Brazil: http://www.pfie.com/china-makes-us$10bn-loan-to-brazil/413505.article.

5. Russia's purchase of all Libya's gas: http://www.ft.com/cms/s/d88035a6-4e16-11dd-820e-000077b07658,Authorised=false.html?_i_location=http%3A%2F%2Fwww.ft.com%2Fcms%2Fs%2F0%2Fd88035a6-4e16-11dd-820e-000077b07658.html&_i_referer=http%3A%2F%2Fsearch.ft.com%2Fsearch%3FqueryText%3Dft%2Brussia%2527s%2Bstate%2Bcontrolled%2Bgas%2Bcompany%2Bgazprom%2Bto%2Bbuy%2Ball%2Blibyas%2Bgas%26ftsearchType%3Dtype_news.

6. China's purchase of Peru's copper on Mount Toromocho: http://news.bbc.co.uk/1/hi/world/americas/7460364.stm.

7. China's lending to the United States: 'Major Foreign Holders of U.S. Treasury Securities', US Treasury Department (2009).

8. Russia loan to Iceland: http://www.telegraph.co.uk/finance/financetopics/financialcrisis/3151148/Financial-Crisis-Iceland-gets-4bn-Russian-loan-as-banks-collapse.html.

9. Brazil loan to the IMF: http://www.news.bbc.co.uk/1/hi/8094402.stm.

10. US and Europe launch co-ordinated action on China: http://www.ewactiv.com/en/trade/eu-us-act-china-raw-material-exports/article-183436

11. Wen Jiabao and Vladimir Putin, in Davos, Switzerland: http://www.finfacts.ie/irishfinancenews/International_4/article_1015803_printer.shtml.

12. Milton Friedman quotation: http://en.wikiquote.org/wiki/Economics.

13. Margaret Thatcher quotation: http://www.margaretthatcher.org/speeches/displaydocument.asp?docid=107195.

14. China's one-child policy: http://en.wikipedia.org/wiki/One-child_policy.

15. China's National Population and Family Planning Commission: http://www.npfpc.gov.cn/en/.

16. Singapore Social Development Unit: http://www.lovebyte.org.sg/web/SDU%20annual%20report%20FA.pdf.

17. Comment by Stephen Roach, Morgan Stanley's Chief Economist (2006): http://money.cnn.com/2006/03/03/news/international/chinasaving_fortune/.

18. Both China and the United States have been responsible for a misallocation of capital and undoubtedly both will have to pay a price.

19. Data on private investment: Bureau of Economic Analysis, 'Table 5.2.5 Gross and Net Domestic Investment by Major Type', http://www.bea.gov/national/nipaweb/TableView.asp?SelectedTable=139&ViewSeries=NO&Java=no&Request3Place=N&3Place=N&FromView=YES&Freq=Year&FirstYear=1997&LastYear=2008&3Place=N&Update=Update&JavaBox=no#Mid.

20. Of course, it can be argued that the investment was in (relatively unproductive) housing stock, rather than more productive PPE, but this is a second-order effect.

21. Henry Ford comment: see *My Life and Work: An Autobiography of Henry Ford*, NuVision Publications (2007).

22. The National Debt Clock and Seymour Durst: http://en.wikipedia.org/wiki/National_Debt_Clock.

23. Xiangqi Chinese chess: http://en.wikipedia.org/wiki/Xiangqi.

24. Chinese development plan: http://en.ndrc.gov.cn/hot/t20060529_71334.htm.

25. Barry Eichengreen, 'Sterling's Past, Dollar's Future' (April 2005), http://www.econ.berkeley.edu/~eichengr/research/tawney_lecture2apr29-05.pdf.

26. Song Hongbing and *Currency Wars*: http://en.wikipedia.org/wiki/Currency_Wars.

7. ALL IS NOT LOST

1. Homer, *The Odyssey*, Hackett Publishing Company (2000).

2. Rasmussen Report: http://www.rasmussenreports.com/public_content/politics/general_politics/august_2009/28_say_u_s_will_be_number_one_at_end_of_century_37_disagree; http://www.rasmussenreports.com/public_content/politics/mood_of_america/america_s_best_days.

3. The IEA's WEO-2008 projected a potential 7m bpd (barrels per day) gap between supply and demand by 2015. This gap represents 7.7 per cent of projected world demand of 91m bpd in 2015, and is equal to over 60 per cent of China's projected demand and 39 per cent of that of the USA.

4. India and forced sterilization: http://en.wikipedia.org/wiki/Compulsory_sterilization.

5. Rerouting the Brahmaputra River: http://haaretz.com/hasen/pages/ShArt StEngPE.jhtml?itemNo=1107596&contrassID=2&subContrassID =4&title='The%20Sino-Indian%20water%20divide%20'&dyn_server =172.20.5.5.

6. United Nations High Commissioner for Refugees, '2008 Global Trends: Refugees, Asylum-seekers, Returnees, Internally Displaced and Stateless Persons' (16 June 2009).

7. Wen Jiabao: China's economic stimulus plan paying off as of April 2009, according to Xinhua News, at http://news.xinhuanet.com/english/2009-04/ 18/content_11208884.htm.

8. 'China Announces Massive Stimulus Package', *Forbes*, 9 November 2008.

9. Gladstone quotation: http://en.wikipedia.org/wiki/Opium_Wars.

10. On steel tariffs: 'Behind the Steel-Tariff Curtain', *Business Week*, 8 March 2002.

11. European Common Agricultural Policy: http://europa.eu/pol/agr/index_ en.htm.

12. 1955 Fortune 500: http://money.cnn.com/magazines/fortune/fortune500_ archive/full/1955/.

13. Investing in the property market looked particularly attractive based on the confluence of three things (unlikely to be repeated): The 'Housing for All' policies that led the US government to push the asset class higher (Fannie Mae and Freddie Mac tax breaks etc.), an artificially and historically low interest-rate environment and baby-boomer demographics, which supported the buyers' market that ultimately became an asset price bubble.

14. One version of the US default scenario is to selective-default, essentially defaulting on anyone who holds US paper internationally, and offering 100 cents on the dollar on newly issued debt for anyone in the US (with a US passport). This would probably cause a devaluation of the US dollar, but this shouldn't be a worry for the US domestically in a closed economic world. And to counter any concerns that inflation would rise in the closed economic world, the government could simply issue inflation-linked debt.

Bibliography

Abbey Bank: 125 per cent: http://www.thisislondon.co.uk/news/article-23412907-abbey-branded-unwise-as-it-launches-a-125-mortgage.do

Alavi, Hamza, *Capitalism and Colonial Production*, Croom Helm (1982), pp. 62–3

Alzheimer's Association: http://www.alz.org

American Society of Civil Engineers, *Annual Infrastructure Report* (2009), at http://pubs.asce.org/magazines/ascenews/2009/Issue_02-09/article1.htm

Asymmetric Threats Contingency Alliance (ATCA), 'Is India a Poor Country? Black Money, World Aid and the Coming Sovereign Crack Down of Tax Havens' (2009)

Bank of International Settlements, Derivative Statistics: http://www.bis.org/statistics/derstats.htm

Bloomberg, Michael, Charles Schumer and McKinsey & Co., 'Sustaining New York's and the US's Global Financial Services Leadership', New York City Economic Development Corporation, January 2007

Bordo, Michael D., 'Is There a Good Case for a New Bretton Woods International Monetary System?', *The American Economic Review*, 85 (1995), 2, pp. 317–22, at http://links.jstor.org/sici?sici=00028282%28199505%2985%3A2%3C317%3AITAGCF%3E2.0.CO%3B2-A

Braithwaite, John and Peter Drahos, 'Bretton Woods: Birth and Breakdown', Global Policy Forum, April 2001, at http://www.globalpolicy.org/socecon/bwi-wto/2001/braithwa.htm

Bremmer, Ian, 'State Capitalism Comes of Age: The End of the Free Market?', *Foreign Affairs*, Council on Foreign Relations, May/June 2009

—, *The J Curve: A New Way to Understand Why Nations Rise and Fall*, Simon & Schuster, (2006; revised paperback, 2007)

British North-American Committee, 'The need for transparency in public sector pensions', June 2009, at http://www.bnac.org/files/BNAC%20Public%20sector%20pensions%20BN49%20-%208%20June%2009.pdf

Chorn, L. G., *A Forecast of Capital Requirements for the Oil and Gas Industry through 2030*, Platts Analytics

Compton, Robert A., *Two Million Minutes*, documentary, http://www.2mminutes.com/

Conference Board, The, *Are They Really Ready to Work? Employers' Perspectives on the Basic Knowledge and Applied Skills of New Entrants to the 21st Century U.S. Workforce*, October 2006

—, *Performance 2009: Productivity, Employment, and Growth in the World's Economies*, 22 January 2009

Dammasch, Sabine, 'The System of Bretton Woods: A Lesson from History', at http://www.ww.uni-magdeburg.de/fwwdeka/student/arbeiten/006.pdf

Economist, 'It's Wise to De-industrialise', 26 April 1997

—, 'A Slow Burning Fuse: A Special Report on Ageing Populations' 27 June 2009

—, 'China and the Dollar: Yuan Small Step', 9 July 2009

Edwards, Chris, 'Public Sector Unions and the Rising Costs of Employee Compensation', *Cato Journal*, Vol. 30, No. 1 (Winter 2010)

Eurasia Group: http://www.eurasiagroup.net/media-center; http://www.eurasiagroup.net/

Fernandez, D. G. and B. Eschweiler, *Sovereign Wealth Funds: A Bottom-up Primer*, JP Morgan Research, 22 May 2008

Financial Times, FT Global 500 (2008)

Finmeccanica's 5th Management Convention, 'A New Mindset', 30 November 2009

Food and Agriculture (FAO) Organization of the United Nations Statistics Division, Rome

Forbes, 'World's Most Dangerous Countries', 4 March 2009

Friedman, Thomas L., *The World is Flat: A Brief History of the Twenty-First Century*, Farrar, Straus and Giroux (2005)

Fukuyama, Francis, *The End of History and the Last Man*, Free Press (1992)

GaveKal Research, http://gavekal.com/

Goldman Sachs, *Dreaming with BRICs: The Path to 2050*, Global Economics Paper No. 99, October 2003

—, *The BRICs and Global Markets: Crude, Cars and Capital*, Global Economics Paper No. 118, 14 October 2004

—, 'The World and the BRICs Dream', 2006

—, *Immigration and the North American Economy*, Global Economics Paper No. 168, 27 May 2008

—, *A Small Price to Pay: Financing Africa's Infrastructure Bill*, Global Economics Paper No. 174, 14 October 2008

Gorman, Siobhan, 'Electricity Grid in U.S. Penetrated By Spies', *Wall Street*

Journal, 8 April 2009, at http://online.wsj.com/article/SB123914805204 099085.html

Government of Sweden, *Global Challenges – Our Responsibility: Communication on Sweden's Policy for Global Development*, Regeringskansliet, Government Offices of Sweden, 2008

Guardian, 'Let engineers make Britain great again', 8 February 2009

—, http://www.guardian.co.uk/football/2009/jun/11/cristiano-ronaldo-manchester-united-real-madrid1

—, 'Experts warned dispersal of Tamiflu would do more harm than good', 16 August 2009

Hackett, W. T. G., *Bretton Woods*, The Canadian Institute of International Affairs (BLPES pamphlet collection), 1945

Halberstam, David, *The Fifties*, Ballantine Books (1993)

Hockfield, Susan, 'Immigrant Scientists Create Jobs and Win Nobels', *Wall Street Journal*, 20 October 2009, at http://online.wsj.com/article/SB10001 4240527487043220045744777007615715 92.html

Huntington, Samuel P., 'Why International Primacy Matters', *International Security*, Vol. 17, No. 4 (Spring 1993), pp. 68–83

International Energy Agency: http://www.iea.org/weo/2006.asp

International Monetary Fund. Growth Forecasts

—, *International Financial Statistics*, various issues

Joffe, Josef, 'The Default Power: The False Prophecy of America's Decline', *Foreign Affairs*, Council on Foreign Relations, September/October 2009

Johnson, Wayne C., 'Declining Interest in Engineering Studies at a Time of Increased Business Need', Hewlett-Packard Company, 2008

Kanaya, Akihiro and David Woo, *The Japanese Banking Crisis of the 1990s: Sources and Lessons*, International Monetary Fund, Working Paper WP/00/7, January 2000

Kaplan, Robert D., 'The Coming Anarchy: How Scarcity, Crime, Overpopulation, Tribalism, and Disease are Rapidly Destroying the Social Fabric of Our Planet', *The Atlantic Monthly*, February 1994

Kohli, Atul, *State-Directed Development: Political Power and Industrialisation in the Global Periphery*, Cambridge University Press (2004)

Kotlikoff, Laurence, 'Is the United States Bankrupt?' *Federal Reserve Bank of St. Louis Review*, July/August 2006

Krugman, Paul, 'Rewarding bad actors', *New York Times*, 2 August 2009, at http://www.nytimes.com/2009/08/03/opinion/03krugman.html?_r=1& emc=eta1

Lane, Clark & Peacock, *LCP Accounting for Pensions*, 2009 report

Levitt, Steven D. and Stephen J. Dubner, *Freakonomics: A Rogue Economist Explores the Hidden Side of Everything*, Penguin Books (2005)

Lewis, William W., *The Power of Productivity: Wealth, Poverty, and the Threat to Global Stability*, University of Chicago Press (2004)

Mckinsey Global Institute, 'The Economic Impact of the Achievement Gap in America's Schools', April 2009; http://www.mckinsey.com/app_media/images/page_images/offices/socialsector/pdf.achievement_gap_report.pdf

Maddison, Angus: http://www.ggdc.net/Maddison/content.shtml

Marx, Karl, *Das Kapital*, Vol. I, Chapter 4 (1867)

Milward, Alan S., *War, Economy and Society, 1939–1945*, University of California Press (1979)

Moyo, Dambisa, 'Holding Housing's Head Above Water', *Barron's*, 27 November 2010; http://online.barrons.com/article/SB5000142405297 02036765045756185808469001 78.html?mod=BOL_twm_col.

Mylrea, Michael, 'The US Will Lose Its Battle in Cyberspace without a Leader at the Helm', *Foreign Policy*, 5 August 2009; http://www.foreignpolicy-journal.com/2009/08/05/the-us-will-lose-its-battle-in-cyberspace-without-a-leader-at-the-helm/

National Centre for Educational Statistics, *The Programme for International Student Assessment* (PISA), PISA scores; http://nces.ed.gov/surveys/pisa/

National Intelligence Council, *Global Trends 2025: A Transformed World*, November 2008, NIC 2008-003

National Science Board, *The 2004 Science and Engineering Indicators Report*; http://www.nsf.gov/statistics/seind04/

National Science Foundation, 'U.S. Business R&D Expenditures Increase in 2007; Small Companies Performed 19% of Nation's Business R&D', July 2009; http://www.nsf.gov/statistics/infbrief/nsf09316/

Pei, Minxin, 'Think Again: Asia's Rise', *Foreign Policy*, July/August 2009

Pritchett, Lant, *Let Their People Come: Breaking the Gridlock on Global Labor Mobility*, Center for Global Development, 2006

Rachman, Gideon, 'America is losing the free world', *Financial Times*, 5 January 2010

Reinhart, Carmen M. and Kenneth S. Rogoff, 'Growth in a Time of Debt', paper prepared for the January 2010 American Economic Review Papers and Proceedings, http://www.aeaweb.org/aea/conference/program/retrieve.php?pdfid=460

Roberts, Andrew, *A History of the English-Speaking Peoples since 1900*, Weidenfeld & Nicolson (2006)

Rohatyn, Felix, *Bold Endeavors: How Our Government Built America, and Why It Must Rebuild Now*, Simon & Schuster (2009)

Salmi, Jamil, *The Challenge of Establishing World-Class Universities*, The World Bank, 2009

—, 'What Makes a University Great?', *Forbes Magazine*, 10 August 2009

Saxenian, Annalee, et al., *America's New Immigrant Entrepreneurs*, Duke Science, Technology & Innovation Paper No. 23, January 2007

Simpfendorfer, Ben, *The New Silk Road: How a Rising Arab World is Turning Away from the West and Rediscovering China*, Palgrave Macmillan (2009)

Solow, Robert M., 'A Contribution to the Theory of Economic Growth', *Quarterly Journal of Economics*, Vol. 70 (1956), No. 1, pp. 65–94

Stiglitz, Joseph and Linda J. Bilmes, *The Three Trillion Dollar War: The True Cost of the Iraq Conflict*, W. W. Norton & Co. (2008)

Tassava, Christopher J., 'The American Economy during World War II', at http://eh.net/encyclopedia/article/tassava.WWII

Thornton, John, 'Long Time Coming: The Prospects for Democracy in China', *Foreign Affairs*, Council on Foreign Relations, January/February 2008

UNESCO Science Report, UNESCO Publishing, 2005: http://www.unesco.org/science/psd/publications/science_report2005.pdf.

United Nations Population Statistics: http://www.un.org/popin/

United States Department of Commerce, Bureau of Economic Analysis: www.BEA.gov

United States Patent and Trademark Office (USPTO): http://www.uspto.gov/

World Bank, *World Development Indicators 2008*, April 2008

Zarowin, Paul, New York University Stern Professor Presentation with data on the Enron debacle: http://pages.stern.nyu.edu/~pzarowin/Class%20Slides/SPEs.ppt

Acknowledgements

No book is a solo project. It involves the dedicated, meticulous and tenacioius work of agents, researchers, publishers, editors and friends. I have been so fortunate to work with an amazing array of people to take this project from a nascent idea to publication.

For me, this includes the gang at PFD, not least the indomitable Caroline Michel, and Tim Binding, without whom this book would never have been completed.

Charles Frentz provided thoughtful and detailed research in the most well-organized manner, and in the least amount of time, making my life a whole lot easier.

My publishers on both sides of the Atlantic have been nothing short of amazing: Will Goodlad, Richard Duguid and the team at Penguin in London have refined the art of hand-holding and provided advice, support and safe haven – going well beyond the call of duty. In New York, the folks at Farrar, Strauss, Giroux went from the pandemonium of *Dead Aid* to the production of *How the West Was Lost* without missing a beat. I thank Eric Chinski and Sarita Varma especially for exceptional publishing skills and for being my friends.

Later in the process, I have had the benefit of working with the Wylie Agency. Having Andrew Wylie and James Pullen on board has been transformational, and I look forward to our future projects together.

Geordie Young is as much a part of this book as I am. All views are my own, but without Geordie's comments, thoughts, and love for this project it would have remained simply an idea. Chris Rokos offered numerous scathing, and fortunately not-so-scathing, comments, which most certainly improved this book. I thank them ever so much for helping me stay on the straight and narrow – but again, all errors and misinterpretations are my own.

Everyone should have a best friend. For me it has been and remains Iris Chiseche Mwanza. As always, she has taken her role of 'friend' to be all encompassing – mentor, advisor, cheerleader and reprimander – and with enviable aplomb. Thank you, Nomsy.

Finally, my love and thanks have to go to my parents and family. Their degree of tolerance is super-human, and their blind belief that anything is possible is unparalleled – it is this that fuels me.

Index